Transforming
the
IVORY TOWER

ASIAN AND PACIFIC AMERICAN
TRANSCULTURAL STUDIES

Russell C. Leong
David K. Yoo
General Editors

Transforming
the
IVORY TOWER

Challenging Racism,
Sexism, and Homophobia
in the Academy

Edited by *Brett C. Stockdill*
and *Mary Yu Danico*

University of Hawai'i Press
Honolulu

In association with UCLA
Asian American Studies Center
UCLA

Library of Congress Cataloging-in-Publication Data

Transforming the ivory tower : challenging racism, sexism,
and homophobia in the academy / edited by Brett C. Stockdill
and Mary Yu Danico.

p. cm. — (Intersections)

Includes bibliographical references and index.

ISBN 978-0-8248-3526-2 (hardcover : alk. paper)

1. Discrimination in higher education—United States. 2. Racism
in higher education—United States. 3. Sexism in higher education—
United States. 4. Homophobia in higher education—United States.
I. Stockdill, Brett C. II. Danico, Mary Yu. III. Series: Intersections
(Honolulu, Hawaii)

LC212.42.T73 2012

378.1'982900973—dc23

2011036588

University of Hawai'i Press books are printed on
acid-free paper and meet the guidelines for permanence
and durability of the Council on Library Resources.

Designed by Janette Thompson (Jansom)

Printed by IBT Global, Inc.

For Hank, who came into my life at just the right time
and who keeps me true to myself and to the world.
For Joey, Darin, and Carla, who continue to support
me and remind me of the beautiful potential of life.

—Brett C. Stockdill

For Kaira and Soleil, who already understand
that standing up and speaking out for justice is a must.
For Bryce, whose friendship and love is treasured and
who remains my steadfast supporter and partner.

—Mary Yu Danico

CONTENTS

ACKNOWLEDGMENTS

I owe a debt of thanks to my family and friends for their wisdom and support during the course of this project. My coeditor, Mary Yu Danico, has consistently demonstrated both passion and vision for this project as well as a deep and enduring dedication to our friendship. Mike Armato and Martha Thompson, my incredibly giving and insightful writing group partners, read and commented on my chapter so many times they could be coauthors. They nurtured my writing skills and offered invaluable conceptual, organizational, and emotional feedback.

Hank Ruelas, *mi corazón*, helped me believe in not only this project, but also in myself, and he proved to be a copy editor par excellence. My friend, comrade, and lesbian boyfriend, Joey Mogul, supported me with great love and solidarity on our hundreds of "date nights," carefully read my chapter, and provided editorial suggestions that strengthened it immensely. My *querid@* Itzamna Arista, through his courage and actions, has inspired me and challenged me over the years to persevere and thrive. Newer friends Amanda Crawford and Mike Armato have quickly become steadfast allies in kvetching, consoling, and conspiring. I thank John Carney for helping me put away the ruler.

My mother, Joyce Pearson Stockdill, my first teacher, instilled in me a love of both learning and teaching and a deep respect for the potential of all students. My father, James W. Stockdill, through spirit and example, showed me that with privilege comes responsibility to speak out against injustice. My brother, Darin Stockdill, and *hermanita*, Flor de María Garay (aka Carla), have been at my side during my most painful and most joyful moments, comforting me and celebrating life with me. My sister Juli MacKenzie and brother-in-law Mack MacKenzie made time to help me relax and recuperate. My niece and nephews, Kelsey and Devin MacKenzie and Andres and Emiliano Stockdill Garay, have been a source of inspiration and laughter.

I have been extremely fortunate to have a wonderful network of friends and colleagues whose insight and camaraderie has contributed to the completion of this anthology: Sergio Antoniuk, Shelley Bannister, Arlene Benzinger, Renee Sherman Bracey, Tori Booker Fuentes, Ann Botz, Cassandra Cantú, Bryce Danico, Jeff Edwards, Juan Ibarra Flores, Laurie Fuller, Christina Gómez, Debbie Gould, Vida Hernandez, Robin Matthies, David Maurrasse, Erica Meiners, Carole Mitnick, Saa Meroe, Aldon Morris, Anne Mothkovich, Wamucii Njogu, Johnnie Owens, Jorge Ortiz, Freddy Pacheco, Lisa Sun-Hee Park, David Naguib Pellow, Chris Poulos, Lui Sanchez, Laurie Shrage, Emery Smith, Susan Stall, Michael Tajchman, Nora Turgeon, Michelle VanNatta, Linda Trinh Võ, and Dorothy (DD) Wills.

My political horizons have been expanded by the members of numerous activist groups over the years, including Free South Africa Coordinating Committee, United Coalition Against Racism, Task Force Against Police Violence, ACT UP/Chicago, Cal Poly Pomona Faculty/ Staff Pride Alliance, Student/Staff/Faculty Coalition in Support of CPP Janitors, Queer to the Left, Union Professionals of Illinois 4100, and Asociación Hogar Nuevos Horizontes. I have derived great inspiration from student activists at Cal Poly Pomona: MEChA (Movimiento Estudiantil Chicano/a de Aztlan), Red Nations, and the LGBTQ Pride Center; and at Northeastern Illinois University: GLBTA (Gay, Lesbian, Bisexual, Transgender Alliance), MCLA (Movimiento Cultural Latinoamericano), the Sociology Club, SAW (Students Against War), and CUFFS (Coalition United for Free Speech).

—Brett C. Stockdill

This project has come a long way since we began voicing our observations about our respective experiences in the ivory tower. From workshop participation and panel presentations I gained invaluable support from colleagues and strangers. This project, however, is what it is largely due to my comrade and friend Brett Stockdill. His passion for justice is contagious and his desire to act up and name inequalities is what really helped shaped this anthology. Our relationship started out as colleagues, but it has become much more than that through our shared struggles.

I know I would not really be here today if not for my high school teacher Mr. Roland Christensen, aka Mr. C. While I have failed to stay connected with him, his thirst for knowledge, love of teaching, and modeling of advocacy on behalf of underrepresented students planted the seed in a Korean American high schooler. My interest in and passion for teaching started with watching Mr. C.'s dynamic pedagogical style.

I am also thankful to have amazing students who inspire me to be better every day. Jessica Kizer and Phi Su remind me that when we as faculty members, advisors, and mentors invest wholeheartedly in students, the payback is priceless. Their commitment and dedication challenged me every day to be a better professor and reminded me why I chose this profession to begin with. I am also fortunate to work with a group of students that gives back by serving as peer mentors for our department. For the past four years, I have worked with amazing students who helped me develop a program that institutionalizes advocacy, mentorship, advisement, and outreach for close to 1,300 majors.

My friends and colleagues have continued to show unyielding support for me as a person and scholar. Sergio Antoniuk, Ibrahim Aoude, Rick Bonus, Jose Calderon, Shilpa Davé, Arif Dirlik, Auguste Espiritu, Yen Le Espiritu, Anna Gonzalez, Shirley Hune, Kate Kendell, Karen Joe Laidler, Masako Ikeda, Hagen Koo, Saul Landau, John Lie, Martin Manalansan, Franklin Ng, Gail Nomura, Dave Odo, Franklin Odo, Jonathan Okamura, Michael Omi, Jonnie Owens, Sheila Palomo, Mike Palomo, Edward Park, Hye-Jung Park, Rakhi Patel, Wayne Patterson, Carlos Perez-Mesa, Jessica Perez-Mesa, Laurie Roades, Donna Ryu, Ned Schutz, Smitty Smith, Alvin So, Steve Sumida, Agnes Suzuki, Bob Suzuki, Amy Tam, Rosemary Thomas, Linda Trinh Võ, Ling-chi Wang, Barbara Way, and David Yoo.

There are several associations that have shaped my professional identity, but the Association for Asian American Studies has nurtured and helped me grow in a way that no other association has. I thank the Ethnic Studies Department at the University of Hawai'i at Mānoa for introducing me to an inclusive and social justice–oriented organization. I am also thankful to the Asia/Asian America section of the American Sociological Association, who sponsored one of our first panels on academic inequalities.

The most influential people in my lives, my mommy Ann Kyoung Ja Yu and daddy James Jingseung Yu, have faced multiple hurdles in their lifetimes. Through them, I learned that fighting for what is just and working to make it right is what keeps us going. I adopted my mom's spirit, gregariousness, assertiveness, and activism in everyday interactions. My dad's practical and pragmatic nature inspired me to not jump but to observe and respond in a proactive manner. The generous time, love, support, and energy of my other parents, Edward and Cynthia Danico, is something I am so thankful for. Finally, my partner Bryceton and daughters Kaira and Soleil. They are the core of my happiness and my muses. Their unconditional love and appreciation touches my being.

—Mary Yu Danico

We give our heartfelt thanks to the diverse constellation of individuals and groups who have touched this anthology and helped us bring it to fruition. Michael Armato and Martha Thompson generously read the introduction multiple times and provided both invaluable editorial feedback and vital encouragement. Jessica Kizer was especially helpful in the literature review and proofreading of the chapters. Phi Su skillfully proofread all the chapters, provided helpful feedback, and assisted in formatting the references and endnotes. Renee Bracey Sherman provided eagle-eyed proofreading for the introduction and the references. Darin Stockdill shared insightful perspectives on the history of education in the United States that strengthened the introduction, and he provided editorial advice on two of the chapters.

We are thankful to our editor at the University of Hawai'i Press, Masako Ikeda, who shared our vision for a book that would make waves. She committed herself to this anthology and shepherded us through the publishing process with patience, insight, and political acumen. We are also appreciative of the two external reviewers who offered thoughtful, constructive, and supportive reviews of this book that were pivotal in its publication. Their keen understanding of the issues raised in the chapters and their incisive suggestions propelled us to refine the manuscript. Our managing editor at UH Press, Ann Ludeman, and our copy editor, Drew Bryan, provided superb assistance in the final stages of the project.

The contributing authors crafted compelling and provocative analyses of their multifaceted resistance to inequality as teachers and activist-scholars. Their chapters are testimony to their courage to take risks to defy narrow, elitist, and self-serving norms of the academy and speak truth to power in teaching, mentoring, research, writing, and activism. Collectively, their chapters demonstrate that while the path to social equality and justice is difficult, when we work in solidarity with colleagues and comrades inside and outside the academy, our struggles bear fruit.

—Brett C. Stockdill and Mary Yu Danico

CHAPTER ONE

The Ivory Tower Paradox

Higher Education as a Site of Oppression and Resistance

BRETT C. STOCKDILL AND MARY YU DANICO

> Our solidarity must be affirmed by shared belief in a
> spirit of intellectual openness that celebrates diversity,
> welcomes dissent, and rejoices in collective dedication
> to truth.
>
> —bell hooks (1994: 33)

The academy is often imagined as an idyllic place, neutral and untarnished by the ugly inequalities that mar the "outside world." Yet the "ivory tower" is a part of the world and, like other institutions, is a site of oppression, resistance, and transformation. As educators and scholars, we have a profound opportunity and a responsibility to speak out and to take action against social injustice both outside and inside the academy. The contributors to *Transforming the Ivory Tower* thoughtfully critique academic inequalities and provocatively challenge us to collectively remake the academy. We ground our vision of higher education in justice, activism, equality, and hope. In this introduction, we identify paradoxical dynamics in higher education to contextualize the chapters that follow, all of which provide theoretical and strategic models for igniting social change in the academy.

Heterosexist, affluent, White males have historically dominated universities and colleges in the United States. Marginalized groups have fought for access and equality in educational settings and have made significant progress toward these goals. In contrast to notions of ivory tower neutrality and openness, the costs of entrance for oppressed groups have been high. Academics from both privileged and oppressed groups are professionalized to conform to dominant norms that reinforce social inequality, and those who disrupt the status quo typically face negative sanctions, including harassment, stigmatization, and discrimination in retention, tenure, and promotion. All too often, the expectation of working-class people, people of color, women, and lesbian, gay, bisexual, transgender, and queer[1] (LGBTQ) people in academe has been that they will assume the politics, values, and ideals of their upper-middle-class, White, male, heterosexual peers (Dews and Law 1995; Ladner 1998; Latina Feminist Group 2001; Mintz and Rothblum 1997; Stanley 2006).

While conventional teaching pedagogies, research, and theories have historically perpetuated racial, class, gender, and sexual inequalities, there is also a rich legacy of utilizing education in the pursuit of liberation. When we look, there is a dissident tradition in virtually all disciplines, from physics to economics to sociology (Anzaldúa and Moraga 1983; Ayers, Miller, and Quinn 1998; Feagin and Vera 2008; Freire 2000; Lengermann and Niebrugge-Brantley 1998; Mihesuah and Wilson 2004).[2] Because our privileges as faculty members rest upon this historical legacy as well as on broader movements for change, we have an obligation to do more than passively occupy the spaces created. Our goal for *Transforming the Ivory Tower* is to build upon this living history of thoughtful critique and collective struggles of women, LGBTQ, racial/ethnic minority, progressive, and leftist faculty in the United States. Such an intellectual project is crucial because academic inequalities are interconnected with inequalities in other spheres of the social world. Grounded in lived experiences shaped by a matrix of oppressions and privileges, the authors dissect the complex mechanisms of bias and inequality in the ivory tower as well as strategies to make it more inclusive and democratic. Along with our contributors, we offer this anthology—a collection of testimonies of survival, cultural and institutional critiques, and alternative approaches to research, teaching, and service—to illuminate ongoing efforts to transform the ivory tower into an inclusive, egalitarian community grounded in social justice.

Origins in Solidarity

This project began in 1998 when, as newly hired assistant professors at a state university in Southern California, we grappled with the contradictions that reflect, in the words of bell hooks (1994: 4), "the difference between education as the practice of freedom and education that merely strives to reinforce domination." Discovering a colleague who shared similar views about education, scholarship, and advocacy was energizing and supporting. Interestingly, our personal biographies do not mirror each other, but are in fact quite different: Mary is a straight, 1.5 generation[3] Korean American woman who immigrated to the United States from South Korea as a child. Brett is a gay White man born in the United States. Mary attended a public school—the University of Hawai'i—for graduate school, while Brett attended a private school—Northwestern University. Politically, Mary might best be described as a liberal and Brett as a queer leftist. Though our shared middle-class background is no doubt significant, one might expect that we would have little in common based on narrow notions of identity politics. But we immediately bonded as junior faculty members because we both valued struggles for social equality and we believed passionately in social justice and the power of teaching and mentoring students. Building on our previous activist experiences in antiracism, immigrant rights, decolonization, feminism, and HIV/AIDS, we endeavored to place social change and social justice at the core of our teaching, research, and professional activities. While we were not strangers to bias and discrimination in academia, having endured our respective undergraduate and graduate programs, we grew increasingly troubled by systemic attempts to dismiss our concerns about inequalities on campus and quash our individual and collective defiance of these inequalities.

We experienced quite viscerally a central paradox of the academy: Critical thinking was promoted only to the extent that it did not call into question biases and bigotry *within* the department, the classroom, or the university. Within the university, there is an inherent expectation of loyalty and unquestioned conformity from faculty. Yet institutions themselves are often not loyal to faculty, students, or staff. Multiple inequalities linked to hierarchical, undemocratic decision-making processes make higher education an alienating place for many students and staff and faculty members. When we questioned institutional contradictions and bigotry, some staff, faculty, and administrators viewed us as "troublemakers."

While we certainly faced the generic biases that commonly target, in Mary's case, immigrants, Asian Americans, and women, and in Brett's case openly LGBTQ people, our deliberate decisions to speak out against classism, racism, sexism, and homophobia within our department and university provoked much deeper antagonism and reprimands. We possessed less institutional power than did tenured faculty and administrators, but our recognition of our privileges compelled us to confront both subtle and overt inequities. We recognized that the inequalities we both experienced in our respective lives were interconnected and that we could not fight one form of social injustice without fighting others. For five years, we watched each other's back, provided mutual support, and helped each other navigate the peaks and valleys of the academic terrain. It would have been difficult to emotionally survive our early career had we not had each other to articulate our shared consciousness of being targeted and in some cases ostracized for not going with the flow. We viewed our resistance as a continuation of our earlier activism and as a contribution to broader political struggles. In a sense, our camaraderie and teamwork[4] represent a microcosm of key themes in this book: While teachers and scholars who work for social justice face negative reprisals, we can effect change by strategically and defiantly working together, in particular by building alliances between different groups and communities.

We have sometimes been met with looks of bewilderment and shock when we share our stories about racism, sexism, and homophobia with friends outside the academy. Many people believe that members of the academy are somehow more enlightened and open-minded than other people: "You would think people in higher education would know better!" Yet denial is a common response to charges of racism, sexism, and homophobia. Many university staff, faculty, and administrators, particularly those from privileged groups, minimize or do not recognize the inequalities they condone or enact in departmental meetings; retention, tenure, and promotion proceedings; administrative policies and practices; or as teachers, advisors, and mentors to students. This lack of recognition is frequently exacerbated by the self-righteous belief that possessing a PhD exempts one from complicity in systems of oppression, particularly among social scientists who perceive themselves as "experts" in their fields. When we identified bias, we were accused of "being too sensitive," "not being able to let go and move on," or simply being "the problem."

While we faced barriers within our department and university, our shared experiences reminded us that we did not have to remain silent or invisible, but rather we had to be proactively outspoken, visible, and engaged in the university. Although we were junior faculty (without tenure), we felt compelled to expose the language and politics of exclusion and marginalization and to offer alternative ways of thinking and acting within the ivory tower. In particular, we saw tremendous opportunities to educate, mentor, and advocate for our students in ways we had never experienced.

Our experiences were not and are not unique. When we participated in and organized conference panels that addressed inequalities in higher education, attendees commonly expressed surprise, solidarity, appreciation, and encouragement. They were not surprised by the experiences described, but rather that we were willing to name in public forums the inequalities within our own departments and institutions. There were audible sighs of relief from those who realized they were not alone, but instead part of a collective who shared experiences of being tokenized, alienated, and exploited. In formal and informal discussions, we talked about the root causes of such prejudice and discrimination—some that were clear-cut and others that were murky or even bizarre. We met many other scholars committed to pushing for an inclusive curriculum, equitable practices and policies in departments and universities, and working in solidarity with student and community activists.

Many people told us that publishing analyses of the often hidden dynamics of oppression and resistance in the academy would be invaluable to graduate students, new faculty, administrators, and especially those in various fields who defy the status quo to work for social justice. We realized then that we had to seek out scholars who not only had endured alienating doctoral programs, divisive department and university politics, or the grueling retention/promotion/tenure process, but who were also willing to share their perspectives publicly.

Our invitation for submissions was received with great enthusiasm, and professors from across the United States sent us both their insightful critiques and their strategies to fight for social change in the ivory tower and beyond. The contributors speak from different social spaces and individual biographies, but they share a commitment to using their privileged roles as professors to examine the legacy of oppression that permeates higher education, to mentor students, and to give back to their communities. They reflect on different facets of higher education including teaching, mentoring, research, academic culture and practices, university-community partnerships, and campus activism. Each chapter is guided by a commitment to praxis—the idea that theoretical understandings of inequality must be applied to concrete strategies for change. The chapters build on the historical struggles to open up colleges and universities to oppressed groups and to dissenting voices.

Social Change and the Academy within the United States

Contrary to notions of ivory tower intellectual and political neutrality, universities have been crucial sites of social conflict and change around the world for centuries (Boren 2001; Lipset 1993). Here we provide a brief historical backdrop of key patterns in higher education in the United States. A focus on the United States is important because the educational system, particularly the theoretical knowledge produced therein, has played a key role in promoting Western colonialism and contemporary neoliberal domination of less industrialized countries (Connell 1997). In turn, anticolonial and antiglobalization movements have been interconnected with antiracist and anti-imperialist activism on United States campuses (Wei 1993; Welton and Wolf 2001; Zinn 2003).

On the one hand, United States universities have contributed to systems of oppression—racism, sexism, homophobia, classism, and imperialism. Mainstream scholars—from a vast array of disciplines in the humanities, social sciences, and natural sciences—have portrayed people of color as violent, lazy, stupid, and conniving and in general inferior to Whites (Goldberg 1993; Gould 1996); women as irrational, physically and mentally weak, and necessarily subordinate to men (Fausto-Sterling 1985; Russett 1989); and lesbians and gay men as diseased, perverted, and a threat to (straight) families (Chauncey 1994; Fone 2001). Such depictions have been used to justify patterns of exploitation, abuse, and violence too numerous to even summarize here, but we provide a few examples. The "science" of eugenics laid the groundwork for the coerced sterilization of hundreds of thousand of immigrant women, poor women, and women of color (Davis 1983); physics, chemistry, and math have been harnessed to make more accurate and deadly weapons of mass destruction such as the atomic bomb, napalm, and white phosphorous (Langford 2004); and neoliberal economic theories have facilitated the atrocities of free trade—environmental destruction, sweatshop labor, poverty, genocide, and ethnocide (Danaher 2001; Gedicks 2001).

On the other hand, dissident academics have cultivated oppositional ideologies including myriad forms of Marxism, feminism, critical race theory, and queer theory that provide theoretical frameworks for dismantling inequalities (Freire 2000; Mihesuah and Wilson 2004; Pellow, this volume; Vargas 2002). Campus activists across the country have nurtured protests against slavery, militarism, segregation, and disenfranchisement. Radical students in particular have time and again been the midwives of social movements including the students of the Student Nonviolent Coordinating Committee who galvanized the civil rights movement (Carson 1996) and Students for a Democratic Society who ignited the antiwar (Vietnam) movement (DeBenedetti 1990; Pekar, Buhle, and Dumm 2009).

Such revolutionary thought and action have often been intertwined with demands for full equality in education for women, people of color, lesbians and gay men, and poor and working-class people. Until the 1970s, the vast majority of students, faculty, and administrators were affluent White males—publicly heterosexuals. In the face of exclusion and discrimination, oppressed groups have struggled to attain equal rights to formal education.

While White boys and girls across the socioeconomic spectrum were provided with public primary schools beginning in the mid-1800s, their schooling was stratified by class, and few poor and working-class students went to high school until after World War I. In turn, few poor and working-class people—men or women—met the necessary admissions requirements for colleges and universities until well into the twentieth century, and costs for tuition and room and board effectively barred many from entry. After World War II, several interrelated factors including activism, the GI Bill, economic trends, and political developments such as the Cold War led to the expansion of city and state university and college systems, allowing a greater number of poor and working-class people to pursue higher education (Thelin 2004). Class inequalities at colleges and universities include economic obstacles (e.g., high tuition and other costs), lack of support services for low-income students, and middle-class biases in teaching and research. In the post–World War II era, academics of working-class origin have challenged such inequalities as well as the related pressure to assimilate to the constrictive, upper-middle-class values and ideals that are often at odds with their communities of origin (Dews and Law 1995; Ryan and Sackrey 1984). Classism often works in concert with racism and sexism, and working-class people of color and working-class women experience—and resist—the effects of multiple, interlocking forms of bias and discrimination.

Throughout the nineteenth and twentieth centuries, communities of color organized to gain access to primary, secondary, and higher education. Pioneers, such as African American scholar and activist W. E. B. DuBois, endured racial bigotry at White institutions, blazing paths for future generations (Marable 1986). Communities of color also acted collectively to challenge inequities in higher education. For example, a significant number of African Americans, largely from the middle class, attended historically Black colleges and universities established primarily during the Jim Crow era (Bennett 1993; Roebuck and Murty 1993).

The exclusion and underrepresentation of students and faculty of color in the academy have frequently been framed within a Black-White paradigm. The racialized discourse has often rendered invisible the experiences of Asian Americans, Native Americans, Chican@s and Latin@s,[5] and other ethnic minorities in higher education. Native Americans, of course, lived in what is now the United States for millennia. Many Latin@ and Asian communities predate United States colonial expansion into what is now the southwestern and western United States as well as the Caribbean. Falsely portrayed as newcomers and habitually ignored, these diverse communities have waged battles for equal access to education that have often been erased from public discussions and academic research (Calderon, this volume; Champagne and Stauss 2002; Mirandé 1989; Takaki 1987).

Social movements in the post–World War II period such as the civil rights movement, the Chican@ movement, and the Third World Liberation Front tackled racial and class exclusion and marginalization. These movements commonly focused on the integration of schools on all levels, leading to increases in the number of students of color in United States colleges and universities in the 1960s and 1970s and catalyzing more multicultural approaches to education (Muñoz 2007; Wallenstein 2009; Wei 1993).

Beyond primary (and later secondary) school, the majority of women did not attend college until the 1970s due to gender inequalities. Some upper-class White women attended finishing schools to prepare them for marriage, and a significant number of young women attended "normal schools" to become teachers. Women such as Jane Addams[6] attended women's colleges created by middle- and upper-class White women in the 1800s. These colleges were central sites of organizing for women's suffrage and other first-wave feminist campaigns. Other women, such as African American Anna Julia Cooper,[7] attended predominantly male (and White) schools. Women fought for and gained greater access to higher education after World War II, a movement that escalated with the emergence of second-wave feminism—the women's movement of the 1960s and 1970s—and contributed to increased opportunities in higher education for women (Solomon 1986). In 2007–2008 women earned 57 percent of all bachelor's degrees in the United States (U.S. Department of Education 2010).

Social movements won integration as well as affirmative action policies that resulted in more people of color and women entering graduate school in the 1960s and 1970s and joining the ranks of faculty in the 1970s and 1980s. However, changes in the composition of the faculties of colleges and universities have been much slower than changes in the student population. In 1941, the Julius Rosenwald Fund surveyed predominantly White colleges and universities and found only two Black faculty members in the United States (Wilson 1995). The numbers of Black and other faculty of color were miniscule until the 1970s and remain alarmingly low today. Though they make up approximately one-third of the U.S. population, racial minorities make up only 17 percent of full-time professors and only 13 percent of full professors (the highest professorial rank). Latin@s, African Americans, and Native Americans, who respectively make up about 15, 12, and 1 percent of the United States population, account for only 2, 3, and 0.3 percent of full professors. White men make up approximately 32 percent of the total population, but 63 percent of full professors (*Chronicle of Higher Education* 2009).

By 1940, women held 25 percent of tenure track positions in the United States, a percentage that declined after World War II to 23 percent in the 1950s and 22 percent in the 1960s (Chamberlain 1988). While women account for slightly more than half the total population, they make up 42 percent of full-time faculty and only 26 percent of full professors (*Chronicle of Higher Education* 2009).

Systemic sexism and racism (e.g., androcentric/Eurocentric curriculum, pedagogy, and research; gender/racial stereotypes; bias in performance evaluations and promotion and tenure decisions; harassment and violence) shape the experiences of women and people of color on college campuses today. Both female faculty and faculty of color earn lower salaries than their White male counterparts and are disproportionately concentrated in the lower ranks of faculty (e.g., nontenure track) and in less prestigious universities and disciplines (American Association of University Professors 2008; Barbezat and Hughes 2005; Bernal and Villalpando 2002; Toutkoushian 1998). The interactive effects of racism and sexism compound the structural barriers facing women of color who make up only a small percentage of tenure track and tenured faculty (Myers 2007; Thomas and Hollenshead 2001; Vargas 2002).

Lesbian, gay, bisexual, and transgender people have historically faced systemic harassment and discrimination in the ivory tower, and homophobia has forced many students, faculty, and administrators to live double lives or risk expulsion or dismissal. Fueled by other movements of the 1960s, the gay liberation movement encompassed gay male and lesbian student demands for the right to education free from prejudice, harassment, and discrimination. In recent decades an ever-increasing number of students, and a smaller portion of faculty, have been "out" on college campuses, but homophobia continues to pervade higher education, creating barriers for both LGBTQ students and faculty members. The pervasive hostility toward LGBTQ communities in broader society spills over onto campuses. Systemic heterosexism and homophobia—often interacting with class, race, and gender—create a hostile cultural climate in the classroom, in meetings, at campus events, and within the performance evaluation of staff and faculty for those who challenge heteronormative ideals and norms (American Sociological Association 2002, 2009; McNaron 1996; Mintz and Rothblum 1997; Stockdill, this volume).

The entrance of larger numbers of women, working-class folks, and people of color as well as the increased visibility of LGBTQ people in classrooms, departments, and disciplines has provoked challenges to heteropatriarchal, racist, and elitist teaching pedagogies, research methodologies, theoretical frameworks, and professionalization practices. Beginning in the late 1960s, student-led movements forced universities to create minors, majors, programs, and departments in Ethnic Studies (including Black/African American, Native American, Latin@ and Chican@, Asian American, and Arab American Studies) and Gender/Women's Studies (Butler 2001; Butler and Walter 1991; Champagne and Stauss 2002; Lim and Herrera-Sobek 2000; Mihesuah and Wilson, 2004; Võ, this volume). Students and faculty organized Gay and Lesbian/LGBT/Queer Studies courses in the 1970s and 1980s with the first programs created in the 1990s. Students also demanded and gained various cultural or student centers organized to provide resources, support services, and safe spaces for students of color, women, LGBTQ people, and other oppressed groups.

In the wake of the social movements of the 1960s, other marginalized groups have also organized for access to (and better quality of) higher education, including differently abled people. In recent decades there has been an increase in the number of "nontraditional" students (students over the age of twenty-five and/or students working full-time who are not recipients of the GI Bill) and undocumented immigrant students on U.S. campuses as well.

As the wave of affirmative action, Ethnic Studies, Women's Studies, and related programs and services surged, conservatives mounted attacks against such initiatives beginning in the 1970s (Butler 2001). The leaders of the backlash focused on dismantling affirmative action policies and stating a need for "color-blind" curriculum, admissions, and hiring policies. Opponents argued that affirmative action constituted "reverse racism," discriminatory racial preferences benefiting people of color and hurting Whites (Connerly 2000). Detractors framed the existence of Ethnic Studies, Women's Studies, and support services for students of color and women as "proof" of special treatment and as evidence that racism and sexism were no longer institutionalized. Conservative people of color such as Thomas Sowell, Ward Connerly, and Dinesh D'Souza joined conservative Whites in assaulting affirmative action and asserting that institutionalized racism against people of color no longer existed. Since the 1980s, many universities have moved away from directly addressing racism and other inequalities. Within the context of the dismantling of affirmative action and related policies, racial minorities have experienced significant bias and discrimination in purportedly color-blind settings (Dovidio and Gaertner 1996; Gómez, this volume; Plaut, Thomas, and Goren 2009).

The dialectical forces of oppression and resistance continue in the twenty-first century. Collective action, including the development of coalitions between oppressed groups, regularly shakes the ivory tower and holds the doors open to marginalized groups. Women, people of color, LGBTQ people, and other oppressed groups such as undocumented immigrants continue to struggle against systemic inequalities on campuses throughout the United States. To both the public and insiders, the university is still commonly viewed as a neutral or benevolent institution where all who enter its halls are evaluated and treated equally; in reality, myriad types of bias and discrimination persist. While blatant inequalities continue, as Eduardo Bonilla-Silva (2006) argues in the aptly titled *Racism without Racists*, in the post–civil rights movement era, more subtle forms of "color-blind racism" have emerged that complicate the inequalities targeting people of color (see also Bonus, this volume; Brown, Lomax, and Bartee 2007).[8] The paradigm of color-blindness has been applied to gender and sexuality as well, and more covert types of sexism and homophobia have emerged that target women and LGBTQ people. The specious contention that systemic oppressions have been virtually erased adds another layer of complexity to the interlocking forms of oppression that undergird the ivory tower in the twenty-first century (Vargas 2002).

While some members of marginalized groups have blended into the mainstream by assimilating to the dominant norms of the academy, others have used their own privileges as teachers, researchers, and activists to not only study inequality but also to challenge it. Feminist, queer, and antiracist faculty, including male, straight, and White allies (Armato, this volume), have increasingly forged a shared political consciousness that guides multifaceted campaigns for social justice on and off campus (Banks 1996; Brown-Glaude 2008). The chapters in *Transforming the Ivory Tower* shed light on such efforts to build alternative approaches to higher education.

Transformative Voices, Transformative Actions

Just as the contributors to *Transforming the Ivory Tower* derive inspiration and courage from past struggles, one central purpose of presenting our perspectives is to offer strategic solidarity to members of marginalized groups and their allies. A related goal is to educate those in the academy from all backgrounds on ways to better understand social inequalities and work toward social justice. While interconnected inequalities pervade the everyday practices of the university, critical analyses of resistance to these inequalities expand the horizons of the transformative power of higher education.

Following in the Black feminist tradition of *testifying* (Collins 1990),[9] the contributors share their testimonies of the many faces that oppression and resistance take in the ivory tower. Telling such stories pierces the silence that masks the very real costs and pains of bias, harassment, and discrimination that permeate the academy. Dominant academic culture inculcates myths of race, class, gender, and sexual(ity) neutrality as well as norms of docility and complicity with domination into faculty and administrators. We must unmask these myths and breach these norms to reinvent a university, one that is not only diverse, but also just.

The chapters by no means represent the totality of the forms of academic inequality or the types of faculty dissent. Most of the authors focus primarily on the impact of racism on faculty of color and efforts to confront the racisms of the academy. This emphasis reflects the strong representation of Ethnic Studies scholars and should not be read as prioritizing racism over other forms of oppression. The activism and scholarship of feminists of color and lesbian feminists (overlapping groups) reveal that White supremacy, patriarchy, homophobia, and economic exploitation interlock and often operate simultaneously. In turn, an intersectional approach is essential to battle crisscrossing inequalities (Anzaldúa 1987; Cohen 1999; Smith 2006). Collectively, the chapters exemplify ways to build alliances not only between communities of color, but across race, class, gender, and sexual lines. Such a coalitional approach is essential to combating the overarching oppressions that impact all people, in both oppressed and oppressor groups. In turn, this requires recognition of not only relative oppressions but also relative privileges that landscape the halls of academia.

By grounding their analyses in personal experiences and observations, each contributor illuminates how her or his experiences with inequalities have been shaped by both oppression and privilege. The narratives presented here represent the complicated interplay between personal biographies and social forces that characterize life in the academy and beyond. Such critical analyses are crucial in challenging inequalities inside and outside the ivory tower. Though the anthology is only a partial exploration of social inequality and social justice in the academy, it addresses many of the inequities that confront women, LGBTQ people, and people of color navigating the academy, as well as resistance to these inequities.

While oppressed groups have made inroads in the academy, underrepresentation is still a problem today. Poor and working-class students and students of color are not proportionately represented at the most elite schools. These students are more likely to attend community/junior or city colleges and/or lower-tier public institutions that have fewer resources. What is also clear is that from junior colleges to Ivy League schools, conventional approaches to teaching and mentoring regularly fail students in oppressed groups because they do not take into account the many ways in which inequalities shape the educational experiences of working-class students, students of color, women, and LGBTQ students.

This problem is intimately connected to the even greater racial, gender, sexual, and class disparities among faculty and administrators. As faculty, we work in a system that has not yet caught up with the student population. Increasing numbers of women, people of color, openly LGBTQ students, first-generation students from low-income backgrounds, and immigrant students have changed the face of college campuses, yet a disproportionately high number of tenured faculty and top-level administrators are White men operating within a heteronormative framework. Multiple studies demonstrate that White men receive more mentoring than women and people of color and that this disparate socialization of graduate students and junior faculty provides more cultural capital and accompanying advantages for White males than for others (Margolis and Romero 1998; Tierney and Bensimon 1996; Turner and Thompson 1993). LGBTQ graduate students and junior faculty are also faced with inadequate mentoring and often do not receive other forms of social and academic support (American Sociological Association 2002, 2009; McNaron 1996; Mintz and Rothblum 1997).

Sensitive to the obstacles posed by institutionalized sexism, racism, and homophobia, female faculty, faculty of color, and openly LGBTQ faculty typically spend considerable time and energy working with students in marginalized groups. Women and faculty of color are often beleaguered with enormous teaching, mentoring, and service responsibilities that reinforce their vulnerability with respect to tenure and promotion (Fogg 2003; Turner 2002).

In "Transforming the Place That Rewards and Oppresses Us," Rick Bonus explores how he responds to these and other dynamics related to inequality. His analysis reveals how academic racisms shape the teaching, research, and service of faculty of color as well as how faculty can utilize their privileges and resources to combat endemic racism that isolates and alienates students of color. Within the context of the ongoing backlash against affirmative action, Bonus argues for the need to expand educational opportunities in higher education, in his words, "to convince those who think that this quest is reserved for the few elite or those who are White, and that it is only they who can lay claim to such a pursuit." He describes how Pacific Islander Partnerships in Education (PIPE), a university-wide mentoring program he founded, simultaneously promotes cultural empowerment among Pacific Islander students and provides them with the tools to excel academically. The success of PIPE led to the creation of allied mentoring programs for Chican@ and Latin@, African American and African diasporic, and Native American students at his university.

Bonus also dissects the double binds experienced by many faculty of color. In academia, decisions on the retention, tenure, and promotion of faculty are typically based on evaluation of three areas: teaching, research, and service. Mentoring students of color, which frequently encompasses all three of these areas, is often seen as the responsibility of faculty of color, but such mentoring is repeatedly devalued in retention, tenure, and promotion evaluations. In the face of this reality, he emphasizes faculty support of students' well-being as one path to transform schools.

This investment may come at the cost of producing scholarly research that is deemed of sufficient quality by the gatekeepers of academic work. Bonus analyzes how senior scholars have often deemed his research on Filipino Americans as unworthy of inquiry—another form of academic racism. On a broader level, he explains how Ethnic Studies as a whole is underprivileged and undervalued, both in terms of resources and legitimacy (a topic taken up in Linda Trinh Võ's chapter as well). Here again, he argues that struggling—both internally within Ethnic Studies and in the larger world of the academy—is necessary to transform universities. These struggles necessitate moving beyond "nonthreatening" approaches to diversity (for example, merely counting the number of faculty of color) to approaches that challenge institutional barriers to oppressed groups and center social justice as a goal on and off campus. Despite the challenges, Bonus finds pleasure in developing community-based, antiracist teaching and mentoring as well as conducting research that critiques Eurocentric conventions and centers the lives of people of color. As other chapters also demonstrate, supporting, inspiring, and giving hope to students produces rewards that keep many faculty members motivated to stand against the many obstacles within the ivory tower.

The bodies of LGBTQ people, women, and people of color are not the sole indicators of transformation in the university. Representation of oppressed groups has increased among faculty members, and some forms of blatant inequality have diminished, but both old and new forms of the "isms" have marked the post–civil rights movement era. The more subtle forms of homophobia, sexism, and racism are sometimes difficult for people to identify and comprehend, particularly for straight people, men, and Whites. When faculty from oppressed groups speak out against systemic institutional and cultural factors that negatively impact their productivity, many faculty and administrators view them at best as noncollegial and at worst as the sources of conflict. Instead of assessing historical and contemporary practices that create hostile work environments, other faculty and administrators, whether consciously or unconsciously, blame the victims and in many cases directly or indirectly push such faculty out of academia (Stanley 2006). Decoding the different manifestations of inequality that operate in the academy is therefore imperative in order to retain faculty committed to diversity and social justice.

It is critical that progressive and leftist faculty understand and name the "new" racisms and other inequalities encoded into (sometimes) subtle language and practices. Only when faculty members speak out and testify about the inequalities that shape their lives in the classroom, in faculty meetings, and as they move through retention, tenure, and promotion can we collectively move toward meaningful change in university policies and culture. Because many straight, male, and White academics (including administrators) are oblivious to their roles in perpetuating inequalities in the workplace, the individual and collective voices of dissident faculty play a critical role in educating their colleagues.

In her chapter "Telling Our Stories, Naming Ourselves: The Lost María in the Academy," Christina Gómez identifies incidents of racial and gender discrimination she has endured in higher education. As is often the case, even as her research and teaching deconstruct and critique institutionalized racism and sexism, she faces both blatant and subtle discrimination from colleagues and students. She writes, "With overt forms of bigotry, one learns very quickly whom to stay away from, whom to be aware of, and whom to trust. But the covert forms of racism that now permeate our society create perilous ambiguity." Gómez uncloaks this ambiguity by naming particular instances of bias and discrimination.

On multiple occasions, White male faculty advisors and colleagues have misnamed Christina as "Maria," Gómez as "Gonzalez." Gómez writes that in contrast to students of color, who typically address her as professor or *doctora*, many White students and faculty refer to her by her first name (see also Turner 2002). Such incidents are emblematic of the common sexist and racist customs that impede women of color in the academy, customs commonly unacknowledged, but enacted, by male faculty and White faculty. They reflect the monolithic gendered and racialized perceptions of Latinas and women of color in general.

The prisms of race and gender distort individual characteristics and qualifications. The demonization of affirmative action policies provokes the questioning of the professional worth of women and faculty of color by their peers. Like other women and faculty of color, Gómez reports being automatically seen as a beneficiary of affirmative action. In turn, such dynamics often make faculty of color and women feel that they have to prove that they deserve their position (Chilly Collective 1995). As Gómez writes, one by-product of this is the pressure on faculty of color to take on an excessive amount of service commitments (see also Brayboy 2003; Turner and Myers 2000). Faculty of color and other marginalized groups face a double bind in the area of service. Many faculty of color want to contribute to efforts to increase the representation of students and faculty of color, but in the process, administrators and White colleagues exploit their labor and commodify faculty of color as representations of racial and ethnic diversity (Tierney and Bensimon 1996), diversity that is typically very thin. Women of color, like Gómez, face being tokenized doubly as symbols of both gender and racial diversity.

Gómez explores the tensions in being not only a woman of color, a Latina, whose scholarship focuses on race and ethnicity, particularly Latin@ communities. On the one hand, her research and writing on Latin@ experiences is sometimes devalued, while on the other hand, she is often expected to conduct research only on "Latino" issues. For many women of color, race- and gender-based research is seen as "self-serving" by many White and male colleagues (Wright 2006: 86).

Echoing other scholars (Chilly Collective 1995; Stanley 2006; Turner and Myers 2000; Myers 2007), Gómez describes the isolation and emotional pain that result from such abusive patterns at a primarily

White institution. Creating community with other faculty of color to share experiences and provide mutual support has helped Gómez to survive the ordeals of the ivory tower. Faculty of color who have support systems and diverse social networks are more likely to be retained and promoted (Cooper 2006; Rockquemore and Laszloffy 2008; Wright 2006). These communities of resistance—as chronicled in this volume—are crucial in nurturing the collective voices, visibility, and activism of queer, feminist, and antiracist faculty.

Gómez's writing is her weapon in fighting for inclusion and justice. Writing about her own experiences and using ethnography to chronicle the experiences of Latin@ communities, she presents perspectives commonly absent in scholarly discourse. Like Bonus, Gómez proclaims that her privilege as a professor comes with a responsibility to challenge the barriers of the ivory tower. She visualizes her research as a vital tool to understand inequality and to cultivate new opportunities for oppressed groups.

Recognizing the responsibility that accompanies privilege is particularly important for straight faculty, male faculty, and White faculty who are committed to struggling against homophobia, sexism, and racism. Michael Armato, in his chapter "Striving to Be Queer: Challenging Inequality from Positions of Privilege," embodies a call to action against the everyday "mundane, ordinary practices" that reproduce privilege and inequality in the academy and beyond. In this case, Armato analyzes how as a graduate student, he challenged a prominent leftist male professor who, in a letter published in *The New York Times*, argued that men "should be able to obtain an injunction against the abortion of the fetus he helped create."

His careful examination of a specific incident of academic sexism exposes the common dynamic of "progressive" faculty whose unwillingness to reflect on their own privilege is part and parcel of their participation in oppression. In turn, Armato critiques another pattern: people who disagree with bigotry remaining silent. Though there were many feminist graduate students and faculty members (including tenured professors), few spoke out publicly against the patently sexist ideas in the writings of the prestigious White male scholar. In the face of this knowledge without action, Armato reminds us that there is never "a good time" to challenge sexism and other inequalities, "because doing so disrupts the everyday goings-on that constitute academic (and other institutional) life." Armato vividly illustrates how allies can (and must) interrogate straight, male, and White privileges to contribute to the transformation of the ivory tower. He writes about the legitimacy accorded White heterosexual men who speak publicly about inequality and the tendency for men to enact their privilege by acting in "chivalrous defense of women." He describes pivotal life events that led him to question his own privileges, including his immersion in feminist theory and men's studies, which led him to speak out publicly against sexism, racism, homophobia, and classism in his department and the ivory tower in general.

Armato points out that privilege obligates people to *consciously* struggle to take action against sexism and other forms of oppression because their silence is complicity (see also Stockdill, this volume). His analysis is relevant not only to White heterosexual men, but to all people who occupy any position of privilege. Straight academics should "strive to be queer" by undermining heteronormative ideas and confronting homophobia in their teaching, research, and activism. Whites must combat racism, and men must battle sexism. For Armato, "striving to be queer" is about recognizing privilege while simultaneously undermining the categories and assumptions that buttress privilege and oppression. More than an identity, it is taking action against injustice when others turn away from it.

Social justice work has not historically been highly valued by elites in the ivory tower. Activism often falls into the category of service—one of three traditional criteria used to evaluate professors for retention, tenure, and promotion. Service is frequently a paradoxical area for members of marginalized groups. As mentioned above, women, people of color, and LGBTQ faculty are often called upon to participate in service activities related to "diversity." Such diversity initiatives include promoting diversity in the composition of students and faculty as well as improving the campus climate and support services for marginalized groups on campus. Members of oppressed groups are also more likely to be sought out by students to advise clubs, direct student research projects, and provide mentoring than are men, Whites, and straight faculty. In turn, because of their own experiences with oppression, they are likely to actually want to engage in these types of service, including campus and community activism. But in United States colleges and universities, service is less valued than research or teaching (Baez 2000). Thus, as Padilla (1994: 26) writes, faculty from oppressed groups often experience "cultural taxation":

> the obligation to show good citizenship toward the institution by serving its needs for ethnic representation on committees, or to demonstrate knowledge and commitment to a cultural group which may even bring accolades to the institution but which is not usually rewarded by the institution on whose behalf the service was performed.

One way for progressive and leftist faculty to navigate such paradoxical hurdles is to integrate activism (one form of service) into both teaching and research. In his article "One Activist Intellectual's Experience in Surviving and Transforming the Academy," Jose Guillermo Zapata Calderon chronicles his four decades as a public sociologist.[10] Calderon's commitment to using sociology in the pursuit of social justice was inspired by the sacrifices of his parents, who were Mexican immigrant farm workers, and the courageous organizing of Cesar Chavez and the United Farm Workers Union. Along with Calderon's own experiences with racism and anti-immigrant prejudice, these examples of struggle propelled him to participate in antiracist and antiwar activism in the late 1960s and early 1970s. While some faculty of color feel burdened to address "minority issues" (Baez 2000), Calderon views antiracist activism on and off campus as his vocation. Calderon states that "public sociology has particular salience for historically excluded individuals from diverse racial, class, gender, and sexuality backgrounds, for whom the educational experience can be both an alienating and empowering experience." He outlines a wide array of community-based teaching and community-based research projects that encapsulate his role as a public sociologist and social change agent.

Calderon vividly describes his challenges to academic sociology in graduate school. Frustrated with the failure among many graduate students and professors to discuss theory's relevance to peoples' lives, he has dedicated himself to applying both theory and research methodology to promoting social change in various communities. Rejecting traditional research approaches, Calderon's doctoral research was grounded in participant observation as a resident and community organizer. He used this methodology to analyze social conflict stemming from changing racial and class dynamics among long-time Latin@ residents and new Asian Pacific immigrants in Monterey Park, California, and to work with community members from both groups to bring about change. Calderon has utilized this type of community-based research to reduce racial tension in Alhambra, California, high schools and to document and support the struggles of farm workers and day laborers.

Following the path of Paulo Freire, Calderon also infuses social justice into the classroom, teaching students not only theories and concepts, but also how to apply them to effect change. In one of his classes, students learn about community-based organizing theories in class, and during an "alternative spring break" they learn directly from farm worker union activists. Students then participate in service projects that support the goals of the union. This and other similar initiatives provide insight into how teaching can be utilized to galvanize awareness and collective action.

Like other anthology contributors, Calderon has survived and thrived in the ivory tower by actively seeking out and building communities of like-minded scholars and activists. He demonstrates the transformative power of creating alternative spaces in which scholars link teaching, learning, and research to catalyze social justice. These "democratic spaces" provide critical ideas, support, and resources for developing the types of alternative approaches to teaching, mentoring, research, and service/activism featured throughout this book. In contrast to hegemonic teaching pedagogies, research methodologies, and theoretical frameworks that fuel oppression, Freirean educational models (Freire 2000; hooks 1994), Participatory Action Research (PAR; see Feagin and Vera 2008), and other community-based research strategies, as well as various *critical* theories—feminist, queer, critical race theories, etc. (Collins 1990; Smith 2006)—promote empowerment, liberation, and self-determination. The creation of alternative approaches to teaching and research are essential to transforming higher education.

David Naguib Pellow's chapter, "Activist-Scholar Alliances for Social Change: The Transformative Power of University-Community Collaborations," demonstrates the social change potential of two alternative projects that bridge the gap between campus and community. Because, as Pellow states, education has been "consciously and deliberately used as a tool of control and social reproduction by political, cultural, and economic elites," the academy is often like a bubble in which students, faculty, and administrators are separated from the experiences, ideas, and desires of other communities. Pellow proposes bursting the bubble and fundamentally changing how universities relate to activists and oppressed communities. In contrast to traditional paradigms in which universities operate in a top-down, hierarchical fashion to provide resources and expertise, Pellow argues for a framework in which universities are transformed by communities as much as the reverse. University-community collaborations produce new knowledge that is essential in catalyzing change within and beyond the ivory tower.

Pellow helped create the Transatlantic Initiative on Environmental Justice (TIEJ), a network that links universities, legal support centers, and community organizations in the United States and central and eastern Europe. TIEJ produces knowledge and applies it to advance struggles for social change for disenfranchised communities in the United States and Europe. For example, an international letter-writing campaign led to the relocation of a Roma community from a toxic waste site in Kosovo. Pellow created a website where activists share case studies of community campaigns against environmental injustice. TIEJ illustrates the capability of universities to support community activist initiatives, in particular by using resources to document and combat human rights abuses related to environmental racism.

Pellow also analyzes the collective efforts of faculty, students, and community activists to create the Activist/Scholars Dialogue (ASD). ASD established a nonhierarchical forum for dialogue that nourishes the social justice campaigns of community organizations and enhances learning at the University of California, San Diego. During the week, ASD faculty and students dialogue with community activists working around a vast array of issues affecting communities of color including sweatshop labor, HIV/AIDS, war, economic exploitation, environmental injustice, domestic violence, immigrant and refugee rights, indigenous rights, and prisoner rights.

ASD has had an extremely positive impact both on and off campus. Community organizations have gained student volunteers, faculty participation, equipment, and other resources. As students have learned about local social movements, they have become more engaged politically both on and off campus. The political consciousness they have developed has led them to demand changes in university curriculum and internship offerings. Collaborative efforts, such as ASD, help break down common deep-seated divisions between universities and marginalized communities and can potentially spark radical collective action on and off campus. Both TIEJ and ASD provide models for what universities can and should do to nurture democracy locally and globally.

There is an intimate connection between student and community protest and the increased diversity of student populations as well as diversity within university curriculum. Campus social movements have forced universities to establish different interdisciplinary programs including Women's/Gender Studies, LGBTQ Studies, and Ethnic Studies (Asian American, African American, Chican@ and Latin@, Native American, and Arab American Studies). Such disciplines have faced a great deal of sexist, homophobic, and racist critique from some members of more established fields that deem them illegitimate. Departments and programs in these disciplines have historically been underfunded and often face the threat of budgetary cuts or elimination. Though internal conflict and division have emerged in most of these disciplines (and individual programs) over time, they frequently embody the most inclusive, democratic consciousnesses and practices on United States campuses (Butler 2001; Espiritu 2003).

Linda Trinh Võ, in her chapter "Transformative Disjunctures in the Academy: Asian American Studies as Praxis," reflects on these issues within the context of Asian American Studies. She explores how both her personal biography as a Vietnamese American and the field of Asian American Studies are products of United States colonialism, writing that "were it not for western imperialism in all its forms, we would have never left our homelands for America nor infiltrated academic institutions where we critique U.S. empire building." Võ underscores the obstacles faced by Asian American Studies in its history, obstacles that continue to make it difficult for the discipline to secure legitimacy and security in an often hostile institution.

As Võ weaves together her personal experiences and the path of Asian American Studies, she examines specific forms of racial and gender inequalities in higher education and suggests strategies for making the academy more supportive of people of color and women. These inequalities include racist and elitist views of scholarship, deficient mentoring for women and people of color, tokenism, and a work environment unaccommodating to women faculty with children. Võ describes how these assaults thwart productivity and damage mental health, and she stresses the importance of building community as a key form of resistance, including survival strategies shared among women of color to balance career and family.

Võ also highlights political struggles that gave birth to Asian American Studies and analyzes the tensions—both internal and external—that have shaped its development since. Faculty and administrators in mainstream disciplines working within Eurocentric theoretical frameworks often devalue Ethnic Studies scholarship, particularly because of its interdisciplinary character and commitment to centering the experiences of people of color. As Võ explains, this translates into the lack of institutional support for Asian American Studies and Ethnic Studies departments in general that leaves such programs vulnerable to budget cuts. While the number of Asian American Studies programs has increased in recent decades, inadequate university support fosters challenges in balancing academic, community, and political missions (Lee 2007).

In the face of elitist and Eurocentric notions of scholarship, Võ refreshingly refuses to restrict her research on race, ethnicity, and immigration to one narrow, compartmentalized discipline even as she acknowledges that "shortsighted faculty" continue to penalize graduate students and other faculty who work outside disciplinary borders. Her commitment to interdisciplinarity is twined with a responsibility to produce scholarship that catalyzes social change. Võ reminds other Asian Americanists of the roots of the discipline in community- and student-led protest, warning against assimilationist intellectual and social projects. She advocates for research on the social problems facing Asian

American communities that challenges many aspects of the model minority myth (Wu 2002) and lays out the importance of community-based research and the engagement of students—in both research and activism—as crucial ingredients in charting a transformative path for Asian American Studies.

Võ thoughtfully links the trials and tribulations of Asian Americans to other communities of color and is attentive to the intersections of race, class, gender, and sexuality. Võ's chapter holds provocative lessons for not only fellow Asian Americanists, but for all academics invested in teaching, researching, and advocating for social justice.

The devaluation of Asian American Studies, Ethnic Studies, Women's/Gender Studies, and LGBTQ Studies parallels the bias and discrimination facing faculty of color, female faculty, and LGBTQ faculty. Racial, gender, and sexual inequalities are rooted in institutional policies, practices, and culture that deny marginalized group members adequate mentoring, resources, and support. University relationships with these communities—on and off campus—have historically been antagonistic. Over the past two decades many colleges and universities have instituted cosmetic diversity initiatives that do little to change entrenched structural inequalities (Bonus, this volume). Cosmetic workshops on multicultural issues and various heritage/history months—Black, Latin@, Asian American, Women's, LGBT, etc.—in many cases contain rather than expand social change. The hiring of women and faculty of color is crucial, but it is insufficient if not part of larger efforts to address inequalities entrenched in interpersonal interactions, faculty evaluation criteria, program funding disparities, retention of both students and faculty from oppressed groups, and the undemocratic decision-making processes that govern university functioning.

One of the challenges in the twenty-first century is to expose the fundamental flaws in such approaches to diversity. Diversity without equality and justice is worthless. It is critical therefore to identify the particular manifestations of contemporary color-blind racism, gender-blind sexism, and sexuality-blind homophobia. While students, staff, and faculty who challenge racist, sexist, and homophobic practices of marginalization are often met with stigma and negative sanctions, the chapters in this anthology exemplify how collective struggles have chipped away at inequities in the ivory tower and carved out more spaces marked by critical thinking and equality. Sustaining these struggles today still requires defying the status quo in a multiplicity of ways.

Brett Stockdill speaks to the need for disrupting business as usual in the academy in his chapter "Queering the Ivory Tower: Tales of a Troublemaking Homosexual." Inspired by Black feminists and other feminists of color, he argues that strategic disruption must be collective and intersectional. Stockdill asserts that "a queer politic traverses both private and public situations, unmasking and defying the power differentials in the heterosexist, racist, sexist, and classist social order that shapes all of our lives." Queer activism is grounded in a commitment to consciously and actively resist inequalities on a daily basis.

Reflecting patterns in social movements in general, collective action in the academy has commonly been focused on one form of inequality rather than taking aim at multiple, interlocking inequalities. This is often seen in diversity initiatives that specify the need to make changes with respect to race and ethnicity, but give minimal attention to gender, sexuality, immigration status, etc. Stockdill examines the ways in which blatant homophobia continues to be more acceptable than other blatant forms of inequality and highlights strategies for challenging heterosexism and homophobia in the areas of teaching, research, professionalization, and hiring.

While stressing the importance of resisting heterosexist oppression, Stockdill consistently argues that homophobia must be analyzed within the context of other crisscrossing oppressions including sexism, racism, and classism. "Queering the ivory tower" requires recognition of both the distinctions and the connections between different oppressive systems, including both their attendant privileges and injustices. Stockdill explores how these systems of domination warp teaching pedagogies, scholarship, and the evaluation of faculty performance.

In turn, he examines the negative sanctions that target activists struggling for social justice in the academy. Though there are definite costs of dissent, there are also tremendous gains to be made. Stockdill outlines concrete strategies to assist academic "troublemakers" to survive and to integrate activism into teaching, research, and service. Central to these strategies is the need to build alliances between different social groups on and off campus. In particular, Stockdill urges faculty to both nurture and follow the leadership of progressive and leftist student activists who are continually at the forefront of struggles for social justice. Stockdill concludes by exploring how critical approaches to teaching that challenge dominant ideology and center the experiences of oppressed peoples can plant the seeds of student empowerment and social change.

* * *

Transforming the Ivory Tower centers the analyses of antiracist, feminist, and queer teachers and scholars to catalyze social change. While equal representation of marginalized groups is still a key issue, the contributors focus primarily on what happens once "we"—and our allies—are in the professoriate. The costs of entrance often include isolation, alienation, harassment, and discrimination, particularly for those who agitate for institutional changes. Whites, men, and heterosexuals throughout the university hierarchy are commonly ignorant of their privileges and insensitive to the realities of racism, sexism, and homophobia. In turn, while having more faculty and administrators who are women, people of color, and openly LGBT people signifies progress, tokenizing individual figures deflects attention away from ongoing, systematic inequalities that continue to haunt higher education and society in general. Because more assimilated, conservative faculty members of underrepresented groups are more likely to be selected for high-level administrative positions, their positioning can at times be more of an obstacle rather than a harbinger of broader growth and change.

The paradox of token diversity is intrinsically connected to the failure of universities to change organizationally since the 1970s—despite increased numbers of women and people of color as well as increased visibility of LGBTQ people. The analyses in this anthology explode the myth that prevailing color-blind, gender-blind, and sexuality-blind policies and practices are equitable. They expose the absolute necessity of race-, gender-, and sexuality-conscious understandings and actions to promote diversity *with equality and justice.* A proactive approach encompassing both institutional and cultural changes is crucial to ensure that all faculty—and all members of the campus community—are valued and respected. In particular, the evaluation for retention, tenure, and promotion must take into account the crucial importance of antiracist, feminist, and antiheterosexist teaching, mentoring, research, and service.

In critiquing various forms of oppression in the academy, professors and others run the risk of being labeled "political" by detractors, but mainstream policies, practices, teaching strategies, and scholarship are riddled with political content. A central goal of this anthology is to shine light on often hidden forms of bias and discrimination. This requires examining personal and collective struggles that are frequently painful. Expressing such pain transgresses academic norms of "objectivity" that include an aversion to emotions. Yet social justice work is grounded in emotions: pain, anger, frustration, compassion, joy, and hope. The voices of struggle presented here are both analytical and emotional. Collectively they provide critical perspectives that embody the potential of an ivory tower that is diverse, but also collaborative, just, and democratic.

Notes

1   The term "queer" was historically used as both a term of self-identification by gay men and lesbians as well as a pejorative epithet targeting them. In recent decades many LGBT people have reclaimed the term, and it has been used to be more inclusive of the different groups outside the boundaries of heteronormativity (not only gay men and lesbians, but bisexuals, transgender people, and other groups). For many, being queer means celebrating sexual difference, destabilizing dominant sexual and gender (and other) categories, and challenging multiple forms of inequality. See chapters by Stockdill and Armato in this volume for discussions of queer identities and politics.

2   Because our backgrounds are in sociology and Ethnic Studies, the references in this chapter are largely from these and related disciplines.

3   1.5 generation are those who immigrated during their formative years and are also bilingual and bicultural. See Danico 2004.

4   Some colleagues derisively labeled us "the Siamese Twins."

5   We use the nonsexist terms Chican@s and Latin@s to include multiple genders often collapsed into "Chicanos" and "Latinos."

6   See Brown 2007.

7   See May 2007.

8   During a jury trial involving a Black Muslim male professor from the Sudan who was denied tenure at California State University, Hayward, David Wellman (Texeira 2001: 1) presented his criteria for "decoding" racism and successfully argued that academia, like society at large, has discarded "in-your-face" racism for "the subtle, easily disguised sort."

9   Lengermann and Niebrugge-Brantley (1998: 161) write that African American activist-scholars Anna Julia Cooper and Ida B. Wells-Barnett "create sociology from the standpoint of the oppressed; for them, the project of social analysis is justice and the method appropriate to the project is cross-examination. . . . Standing in the situation of the oppressed, they use social analysis to *witness* to what is happening, as a means of empowering the African American community, exposing the oppressors, and appealing to the conscience of potentially supportive publics."

10   See Burawoy (2004) for a discussion of public sociology.

CHAPTER TWO

Transforming the Place
That Rewards and Oppresses Us

RICK BONUS

Whenever anyone asks me about what I find most troubling in my experiences as a professor of color, my usual response is the observation that I almost never get "mistaken" for a professor. That is, many people who do not know me, especially even on my campus, oftentimes assume that I am this or that. But they rarely guess that I could possibly be a professor. I mention this not so much to air a gripe about the persistence of a particular kind of racial/gender/class stereotyping that places people like myself outside of a usually imagined category of affluent, White, male "professor," but to call upon just one aspect among a vast array of experiences that collectively make critical differences in the ways professors of color are perceived and treated. Experiences of this sort have been narrated and dealt with in many places before, but I venture that in the contemporary period of anti–affirmative action, anti-intellectualism, and the defanging of "diversity," professors of color now face challenges that are much more insidious, complex, and contradictory (Howell and Tuitt 2003; Lim and Hererra-Sobek 2000; Stanley 2006; Turner and Myers 2000; TuSmith and Reddy 2002). In this chapter, my intention is to offer a set of claims that connects the specificities of these struggles with racism as a historical formation and with its intersecting forms of oppression in society in general, on campus, and within the academic professions.

I would like to offer my experiences as well as the experiences of others like myself to elucidate conditions and practices that expose such racisms, to examine the multiple consequences of racism especially to professors' careers, and to offer different ways to combat these racisms. This is not to say that race is a stand-alone category of power and privilege. Even though I emphasize race in this chapter, I am mindful that ideas and practices of diversity and inequality also encompass class, gender, sexuality, and other social categories that intersect with race.

Many professors of color choose academic careers because of the rewards they offer: participation in knowledge production and transformation, opportunities for enhanced and enriching pedagogy, stature, and security of tenure. At the same time, professors of color also choose to wage battles against institutional practices that present themselves as color-blind, well-meaning, and fair. They find themselves working in environments that devalue their culture over others. And for those whose scholarship is on people of color, they are usually perceived as unsophisticated and out of place (Aguirre 2000; Benjamin 1997; Center for Advancement of Racial and Ethnic Equity 2004; Cooper and Stevens 2002; Exum and Menges 1983; Hune 1998; Turner and Myers 2000). Despite these, many professors of color devise strategies to make meaning out of their careers, to enable themselves and others to persist in the struggle, and to transform the very place that simultaneously rewards and oppresses them (hooks 1994).

While it is true that struggles of this sort can be found in every work setting, campus environments provide significant and unique places for understanding and combating oppression because they can be assumed to exist outside of the corporate milieu, where freedom of expression and critique may be stifled. At the same time, university settings may also be seen as an inseparable, though distinct, part of society in general where hierarchies of power are mirrored and reproduced. The myth of campuses as ivory towers separated or shielded from state and societal intrusion is one that cannot be sustained, given the governance of public research and teaching universities such as the one I belong to by state bureaucracies and the increasing dependence of such universities on corporate support. So, on many levels, universities are but one among many institutions that have direct, multiple, and complex connections with those who are regarded to be outside of them. Simultaneously, they are in themselves unique communities with their own sets of rules, protocols, and cultures that permit a narrow sense of autonomy and distance from outsiders.

Just like many academics, even for the above-mentioned reasons, I have come to regard the university as a "safe" space in which particular kinds of intellectual and advocacy work can be nurtured. Indeed, I enjoy the privilege of developing academic projects that interest me, teaching the courses that I prefer, and choosing the service work I am inclined to do, all with little or sometimes virtually no intrusion from a demanding boss. In turn, my mother has always chided me for choosing a profession that is "cushy," one that can be comfortably conducted outside of the nine-to-five and forty-hour week work regimen, one that does not have to engage with life-or-death situations, and one that pays well. While these hold some measure of truth in them, I have also learned to challenge my mother if people who agree with her can easily quantify the exchange value of intellectual work or find the trust in acknowledging the work of scholars who do not necessarily save lives or "cure" people of their illnesses on a daily basis, no matter how long their work hours are. Add to these the hidden pressures and punishments of what could turn out as a demanding and overwhelming "publish or perish" career that such so-called intellectuals have to endure. This business of producing knowledge, of educating and mentoring students, and of performing many varieties of community service is one that is as desired as it is quite misunderstood and oftentimes devalued.

I write these not to ask for mercy or for an apology, for the real injustice to me lies not at the devaluing of the academic profession per se, but in the ways in which the quest for justice both by those within and beyond the profession is imagined, defined, and practiced. I do believe that I have chosen a profession precisely because it is where this quest for justice can be clarified, articulated, and changed. And it is in continuing to believe this that I have persisted and flourished in my work, almost always disregarding whether people outside of academia have found me useful or not. To me, the more difficult challenge is to convince those who think that this quest is reserved for the few elite or those who are White, and that it is only they who can lay claim to such a pursuit. Although my mother and others like her will not say it openly, the professoriate continues to be regarded by many as a career for people who are above the rest and that people of color have no place in it.

Such has been the "theme" of my struggles as a university professor. It is rendered legible by the surprising looks I get when I say I'm a professor, as much as it has taken a prominent and persistent place in my memory from the time I first thought of becoming an academic when I was in college, continuing through all my years in graduate school, to becoming an assistant professor and eventually a tenured professor in a research university. Of course, this theme does not stand on its own. It intersects with the larger contexts and long histories of racism in American society along with their implications in schools and schooling practices, the persistent critique of American higher education, and the entry of professors of color in academia as one expression of that critique. Indeed, current debates surrounding academic disciplinary and professional standards are not coincidentally linked to such an entry of minority professors in the fields. But we should also acknowledge the ongoing resistances and transformative advocacy that professors of color and their allies have mounted to improve and change the university. It is beyond the scope of this chapter to plunge deeply into all of these aspects of struggle; rather, my goal in writing this chapter is to provide a reasonably substantive account of the multiple terrains of racism as they are experienced mainly by professors of color. In effect, I wish to identify and explain the conjunctures of racial histories that professors of color find themselves in, their experiences and the consequences of racism's presence on their careers, and the opportunities for thinking and practicing resistance that can be integrated into, or actually be generated from, their struggles. My contention is that the daily struggles against racial oppression faced by those who look and think differently can themselves be transformed as tools and opportunities for a rewarding individual career only if they are understood as parts of larger histories of racial resistance, regarded as meaningful activities and practices experienced by collectives, and imagined as sites that are generative of possibilities without limit despite the risks and because of the potential rewards.

Institutional Racisms and the Contradictions of Diversity

Schooling in the United States has had a long history of elitism and segregation. Even though higher education, in particular, has often been perceived as a tool for social mobility, that tradition is tainted by an earlier emphasis on exclusive schooling for elite members of society, for upper-class White males whose education amounted to the maintenance and enhancement of their social status. It was only in much more recent times, what Ryan and Sackrey would refer to as the "golden period of American higher education," when higher education became accessible to wider sectors of society (Ryan and Sackrey 1984; also see Simpson 2003; Thelin 2004). Even then, much of the original structural elite-centric and hierarchical formations of university education have remained in place, if not exacerbated (Brown, Lomax, and Bartee 2007; Leonardo 2005). We have research institutions versus teaching institutions, community and junior colleges versus trade schools, all understood as having distinct locations in the hierarchy of most valued (and therefore expensive and more difficult to get into) to less prized. And corresponding with such locations are the differential mission statements, funding and grant allocations, disciplinary arrangements or instructional practices, and perceived quality of faculty, staff, and student bodies by which each institution is defined. This is a history and contemporary reality that is all too familiar to many of us.

Yet many forget that even though universities have remained structurally the same over the years (or at least have been altered at a glacial pace), their population of faculty, staff, students, and other stakeholders has changed or is changing considerably. We need only to be reminded that at the center of the demands of race-based advocacy groups that arose in the wake of the civil rights movement, particularly in the 1960s and 1970s, were revolutionary calls for schools to make themselves more accessible to minority students, offer curricula that are relevant to the histories and lives of minority populations, and hire appropriate faculty, staff, and administrators who can participate inclusively in scholarship, teaching, and decision making. To a certain degree, these calls have been translated into action and have thus radically altered the makeup of many institutions of higher learning (Lesage et al. 2002; Orfield, Marin and Horn 2005; Sill 1993; Smith, Altbach, and Lomotey 1992). On my campus, the struggles of student protesters brought about the creation of a Black Studies program, and it is now subsumed under a Department of American Ethnic Studies, with major tracks in African American Studies, Chicano Studies, and Asian American and Pacific Islander Studies. Our campus has had its share of growth of minority faculty, students, staff, and administrators, though still minimal according to many (American Association of University Professors 2006).

This history of progress is relatively recent, but thirty years later, it is already mired in a set of attitudes and arguments regarding both the wisdom of allowing "strangers" to come into the university and the terms of their power and presence on a campus such as mine. Such a backlash must most definitely be understood as part and parcel of American society's regressive attitudes toward race relations emblematized by anti-affirmative action, anti-immigration, and anti–bilingual education stances at present (Giroux 2005). Of course, these attitudes are not expressed out loud in department office hallways, but are rather demonstrated through professional evaluations that devalue the work of minority faculty, through their marginalization and intentional isolation, and simply through the lack of support and care they experience. For many underrepresented faculty, these have amounted to a range of consequences, from difficulties in and denials of tenure, to overwhelming pressure and oftentimes immobilization, exasperation, and loneliness (Aguirre 2000; Turner and Myers 2000).

These experiences are difficult to document, much less act upon, not only because oppressions of this kind happen subtly and indirectly, but also because of the vulnerability of minority faculty, most of whom are just starting their careers, to quick and hidden punishments such as nonpromotion, negative performance reviews, heavier or riskier workloads, and further isolation once they complain. As one minority faculty member once told me, "[i]t's like walking on eggshells. I can't even trust my own colleagues and I don't know why they hired me in the first place. They are always worried about my work but they don't do anything to help me." In a case such as this, it is easy to remind oneself that a campus can be so hostile or uncaring probably because it is set up for certain people to succeed and for others to fail. And I am tempted to believe so not because those who are in power do not know how to make others succeed (as is often said) but because they probably do not want them to succeed.

So why bother? With confidence, I know that many faculty of color would say they were hired as decoration, to fulfill some kind of diversity requirement, or to be able to show evidence that a department tried to do good. Diversity is such a buzzword these days, but I will also venture that many are confused or unsure about it, much less know how to practice it. Diversity, to me, is about transformation, change, and inclusiveness. It is when many different people are called to the table to participate and contribute equally, to share in decision making, and to constantly ask questions. I have heard diversity talked and written about as something that promotes the sharing of points of view, or something that promotes good business practices, or one that moves toward equality. But I contend that diversity should be more than these nonthreatening, obligatory, and compliant activities. Diversity should be about power and difference, a way to act upon social injustice and inequity, privilege, and disadvantage. No wonder then that many faculty and administrators are fearful of it and so would rather support its less risky versions, one of which is the simple addition of a "presence" in the list of minority faculty hired (Hale 2004).

In effect, most minority faculty get hired and are made to "represent" diversity as a number in the school's statistical data and as a body for display. Diversity then, in many schools, appears as a contradiction, for it is brought into practice as a site for transformation, yet its very nominal and defanged practice is the one that impedes the transformative work it is supposed to fulfill. Such work might include meaningful participation of minority faculty in decision making, the decentering of dominant cultures in curriculum design, and the valuing of nonmainstream scholarship and service records in professional reviews. Institutions that are opposed to substantive change use a nominal form of diversity to appear as if real change is taking place. Hence, the faculty of color gets mired in a wide range of diversity-related business (after all, that's the reason they were hired), from appearances in important events to chairing committees charged with "enhancing" campus diversity, to mentoring students who also count as "diverse," and representing the university in off-campus community festivals. Incidentally, almost all these activities do not count during tenure review!

These institutional practices of conservative, tolerant, and ornamental diversity are matched by attitudes and practices by colleagues who themselves are often clueless about or disengaged from the experiences of their non-White counterparts. When I was newly hired as an assistant professor, I attended a set of presentations and workshops offered by my university to familiarize newcomers on various aspects of the campus and our corresponding work on it. I went to a presentation on "diversity" and noticed that there was just a small number of us in the room, all persons of color. When I stepped out of the room after the presentation, I asked several other new professors, all White, where they went and why they did not attend the one I did. "Oh," said one, "that's the diversity workshop. Isn't that for you guys?" I was shocked and infuriated. Since when was the work of diversity reserved only for non-Whites?

True enough, most of the business of working on and through diversity on my campus has been led by faculty of color in the trenches and organized as collectives. There are many individuals who take on the struggle quietly, who pursue their work diligently without much disruption, and who are therefore rewarded handsomely. They are rewarded because they do not rock the boat, they get the work done, and they make the institution look good. But the more remarkable instances of advocacy I have seen have been the activities that were initiated by a critical mass of underrepresented faculty and their allies, with loud and sometimes angry voices, and in terms that brought out into the open the unsupportive and damaging climate of pervasive institutional racism on our campus. The rewards have been reaped not only by individual faculty members, but they have permeated into campus-wide advantages for many. Because of minority faculty demands, for example, our university now has an associate vice provost for faculty advancement, someone who is principally charged to ensure that we hire, promote, and retain a diverse faculty. On regular days, this is a person who underrepresented faculty can turn to for advocacy in higher administration—someone we, as a group of concerned faculty, fought to have so that our concerns are heard and acted upon right at the top of the administrative hierarchy. I also co-led a set of closed-door workshops for underrepresented faculty modestly funded by our president's office prior to the creation of this new position and after it, so that conversations about meeting the challenges of being a minority professor and sustaining networks of support for those who feel isolated are now close to becoming regularized (Bonus and Simpson 2005).

Initiatives of this kind have been small and big steps, and it is not as if all of our troubles have been removed. The nature and rules of the game in the professoriate have remained essentially the same, but I do believe that the conditions for playing the game have been altered as more of us continue to engage the university's structures of power by way of collective action and as more of us enter into positions of power and work with administrators who understand and support our needs. On my campus, opportunities for advancement and support of the work of minority scholars are not as abundant as in other private campuses and are oftentimes thought of as unfairly exclusive. But we have many pockets of potential sources of support, both individual and institutional, that keep the interests of underrepresented faculty in mind in their projects and funding allocations so long as our critical mass remains vigilant. This vigilance includes being alert to administrators of color, including tenured faculty of color, who are part of the diversity charade and serve to weaken genuine support for faculty, staff, and students of color.

The challenge of being both a representation of diversity and a scholar of color in places that continue to be strongholds of institutional White male domination is something that will haunt many of us in our careers. In such a context, the battles are multiple and intersecting, so much so that it is not surprising to hear about a colleague's burnout. In graduate school, I don't remember anybody preparing me for this. And now, as a professor, my colleagues and I grapple with untested or risky strategies, unanticipated reactions, and truly exasperating conditions. But the worst ones are when we hear about one of us undercutting our own collective efforts, dismissing our claims, and usually ending up defending White privilege. And, of course, the worst cases are when we see these people rewarded. In these cases, promoting acquiescent liberal and conservative personnel of color comes out as a very effective strategy in deflecting attention away from institutionalized racism.

Working with Students

By far and so far, my most rewarding and inspiring experiences as an educator have been my interactions with students. True, I have had my share of derisive and disrespectful comments from some of them who mostly question my authority (e.g., "Are you really a teacher?" "Are you really the teacher of this class?" "Where did you get your degree?") and expertise (e.g., "You're not so smart." "You did not prepare for class today, did you?" "Are you sure you read the book?"). I am sure that these students would not have asked me so directly and abrasively had I been a White professor, and I am positive that they were expecting higher and different standards for me. But the vast majority of students I have taught have shown me respect, empathy with my struggles, and appreciation for my work with them. Equally, I have been so motivated by them to do my job better, and every time they succeed, I have felt immense pleasure.

Minority students' experiences in college have been amply documented, but minority professors' experiences insofar as they relate to teaching specifically minority students have not (Howell and Tuitt 2003; TuSmith and Reddy 2002). I suspect there are many success stories out there in this regard, but I also don't want to ignore the less favorable experiences of faculty of color, especially women, in dealing with student disrespect and harassment on campus coming from all kinds of students. The power and authority that we as faculty of color hold (at least symbolically) are things that can both shield and render us vulnerable to doubt, higher expectation, or abuse. Oftentimes, we anticipate our minority students to be allies with us as most of them tend to be, but I have had a few brushes with such students who treated me as if I were their servant or who expected me to provide them with special favors because I am presumed to be "down" with them. Some of these incidents even find their way as complaints in our student evaluations. These are experiences that are not uncommon.

My primary strategy in enabling what could be a most meaningful experience with students of all kinds—and in particular of students who are acutely underrepresented on campus, which for many of us constitute the most important targets of our efforts as educators—is to remain conscious of the larger political contexts within which these students can be understood. Numerous scholarly studies and personal experiences of faculty and students demonstrate that the inability or failure of certain students to succeed in school cannot be appropriately and justifiably explained solely by students' lack of intelligence or drive to do well. Rather, it is the schools that have continued to devalue, set aside, or even completely ignore the needs and interests of these students that would have allowed them to succeed in the first place (Aragon 2000; Hale 2004; Sanders 2000; Valenzuela 1999; Watson et al. 2002). Just like the case with minority faculty, many unfairly expect students to do well in an environment that is set up to make them *not* do well (Rodriguez et al. forthcoming).[1]

So, as an example, several Pacific Islander American students on my campus and I advocated for the establishment of a retention program built around the creation of a politically and culturally meaningful set of practices of schooling with an appreciation of both the limitations and possibilities within a large university setting. Calling it the Pacific Islander Partnerships in Education mentorship project (or PIPE), we set up a community of care and student support to make the experience of university schooling much more intimate and nurturing. We organized sets of conversations for students to understand better what we call "the politics of schooling" so that participants became more conscious of the operations of power on their campus and the potentials of subverting this power by being pro-active about their needs and interests as university students. We argued for culture, or the practice of indigenous-inspired forms of collectivity, to be appropriately integrated or, if possible, centered into their academic and campus advocacy work. One of its founding student members said, "In this school of about 35,000 students, only a handful know we exist or care about us. We are here to learn just like everybody else, but people also need to learn from us. We should be part of the curriculum, and this is where we start, by making our culture be valued and practiced as part of school." PIPE eventually became, to borrow from Angela Valenzuela's (1999: 20–32) work, a "place" in school where Pacific Islander culture is valued rather than subtracted, where culture is a source of empowerment rather than merely a site of extracurricular activity.[2]

PIPE's work, begun only in 2002, has earned the distinction of receiving regular funding (mainly through UW's Office of Minority Affairs and Diversity, a nonacademic unit), has resulted in the creation of allied mentorship programs (*Adelante*, a Chicana/o Latina/o mentorship program; *Yehawali* Native American mentorship program, and *Ubuntu* African American and African Diasporic mentorship program), and has garnered for me an internal grant to develop a book project with it as its focus. It is easy to dismiss something like this as not quite disruptive in the ways our institution has accommodated the demands of students in PIPE. But even though PIPE has not revolutionized the dominant structure of power at UW, it has nevertheless dramatically altered many students' ways of thinking about their school and has transformed many students' practices of being people who matter, whether or not they end up at the top of their class.

All these we have accomplished through intensive and regular mentor-mentee get-togethers, collective study sessions, workshops on effective studying and career planning, collaborative writing and class project assistance, field trips, and socials. From time to time, students would invite staff and faculty members, especially the newly hired ones, to meet with them as a group. Graduate students would also be asked to help in mentoring. They would oftentimes assist in planning for graduate study. Every year, students would take up a project they would work on across the school's terms, from proposing curricula to organizing teach-ins and retreats. Undergirding all such work are conscious efforts at making the students' social/cultural backgrounds the center of all their activities in the program and the source of their abilities, capacities, and potentials. We balance an appreciation of individual struggle with a collective commitment to succeed together.

Working with students in these programs as their teacher, advisor, and mentor has energized and brought meaning and pleasure to my work. Early on in my career, I vowed to keep it as a central aspect of my work. Yet doing a lot of it has also meant paying the price of doing less of what is principally expected of me: make myself strongly visible in scholarly publication. For many years now, colleagues from within and outside of my campus have chided me for engaging with students too much, for allowing them to take significant roles in my life and career, and for nurturing them over and beyond my ascribed duties as a professor. I have ignored them whenever I can, and from what I have heard repeatedly, there are many of us out there who nevertheless persist in the struggle to balance the demands of a growing number of minority students who need our guidance (for oftentimes we are the only one they could find to guide them) with taking care of our own careers and personal lives. There are many who cannot simply say no to students in need despite our already heavy involvement in serving our communities, both on and off campus, in other ways. Many faculty in these situations endure the double whammy of receiving warnings when they take in too many students while bearing the onus of being the only one in their unit who is pressured into mentoring that unit's minority students (Moody 2004).[3] To top it all, in many research universities, these are the kinds of student mentoring and advising work that do not find their prominence and value in career evaluations.

For these reasons, many faculty of color face the dilemma of prioritizing what may be called ethical obligations to the communities we come from along with career expectations in the places that employ us in which these obligations do not count so much. Put another way, we can and do find ourselves frequently doing activities that are meaningful to us, while entertaining the nagging thought that these very activities might cost us our promotion or our job itself. I am not suggesting that faculty of color precisely emulate what I do because it is far from ideal and too costly to endure for some. Yet I want to strongly encourage those of us who are committed to intervening in the transformation of our schools to keep student well-being and support as a prominent focus of our work, appropriate to our capabilities and resources. I usually tell my most promising mentees that I mentor them so they can join me in the struggle in academia at some point in our future. And I always emphasize the collaborative spirit and nature of our mentor/mentee partnerships as an index of our participation in the struggle, in that we do not need to be in the struggle all by ourselves. I help them navigate the paths I have taken already, teach them strategies I myself have tested, and patiently model for them a set of practices in the profession I deem respectful and compassionate. For minority faculty, there is no need to imagine these practices as inflexible directives or burdensome additions to one's full plate, because in my experience, as I know also from many colleagues, work of this sort, especially if performed within a collaborative context, can have the capacity to seep through our daily lives almost effortlessly, without much fanfare, and with rewards that accrue holistically in all aspects of our lives.

Academic Racisms

While racism and other forms of oppression are pervasive in campuses both to the degree that minority faculty are subjected to their various forms within their own institutions and through their interactions with students, deeper and more intense battles are waged within the larger contexts of academic disciplines and fields. In these battles, the arenas for contestation are wider and participants are not likely to confront one another face to face, hence it is difficult to perform intervention work. As a quick example, each discipline has its own gatekeepers—senior scholars who determine what kinds of work are approved, legitimated, and eventually published. It is these scholars institutions turn to for external reviews of their faculty, these arbiters who are situated elsewhere and those whose imprimatur almost always forms the sole basis for whether or not to tenure or promote the individual faculty member. Therefore, if one's work is not regarded as adequate or appropriate enough by such disciplinary evaluators, the chances of surviving such a process are slim.

It takes a perceptive historical consciousness to be able to grasp the nature and gravity of the politics of intellectual production that drive the direction of specific disciplines. Even though some people believe that only one's individual intelligence can independently secure a safe and venerable spot in their discipline regardless of the politics of that discipline, I would instead claim that survivability (and eventually honor) in the disciplines depends almost entirely on one's networking skills and creative maneuverings. This is something that, I am sure, many academics will either vehemently disagree with or staunchly keep silent about.

But to me, it is not a secret at all that many professors are able to advance in their fields because they say the right things that will not threaten the power of the dominant gatekeepers, they know and hang with the right people, and they have access to the right places, the right venues for publication, and the right positions in academic associations. Of course, I myself am implicated in this game, for I have played it to some degree and because I have been rewarded also to some degree. But I also think that the system is not right and that many of us who have privileged access to that system are engaged in the struggle to transform it.

There is a fine line between trying to achieve success by adhering to the rules of an oppressive system and working within that system to change it, especially because one needs to be successful in that system to have one's advocacy be heard in it. This is a similar situation that I described above with my students. Such a line gets obscured and complicated not only because I believe there is no such thing as "pure" activism with neither the strings of rewards and privileges attached to it nor the vacuum-sealed environment in which it takes place, but because I also believe that activism is a practice of negotiation. It is defined in relation to the dynamics of particular times and locations as it is practiced in relation to the communities and collectives that constitute it. Its participants grapple with the risks and benefits that will result from their work, and it is never a clean, safe, or sure process with a determined final outcome.

In my own field, Ethnic Studies, our principal struggle with activism—whether as academics engaged in scholarly production, teachers, or community service workers—is defined by our very location in the university, a location that was once a site for our founders to critique society and schooling, as it is now increasingly becoming the site for a full-fledged critique of our field's incorporation into the university. Add to this the gross misunderstanding and hence persistent disagreement regarding the value of our scholarly field, expertise, and teaching as well as service to the university. In this struggle, no one's hands are clean. Many of us can be said to have reaped the benefits of university legitimation and incorporation through secure jobs and prestige, and many of us have been accused of distancing ourselves from the communities we are supposed to serve, of forgetting our activist roots by focusing more on intellectual activity, and of compliantly acceding to the conservative interests of dominant groups or defending our worthiness too often at the expense of more important things to be done. But a whole lot of us in the field also have an acute and deeply personal investment in reflecting on, tracking, and changing these very conditions that are at once disappointing and energizing. Compared to other fields, Ethnic Studies has had a long tradition of critique, self-reflection, and transformation, with both senior and emerging scholars devoting intellectual activist energies toward the pursuit of alternative ways of thinking about race and ethnicity in intersectional, interdisciplinary, and global or transnational angles (Butler 2001).

Yet, the professoriate in Ethnic Studies is also multigenerational, multidisciplinary, and battle-scarred. Different generations of scholars have different and sometimes competing research interests and scholarly expectations. Different scholars trained in different disciplines offer very particular and sometimes conflicting accounts and analyses of similar objects of study. Different professors also come to work with different levels of energy and commitment to the field, nurtured precisely on one hand by the devaluing of their work and worth by their own institutions and by the larger, more powerful disciplines, and on the other hand by their different capabilities and choices of strategy in combating these forces. Within Ethnic Studies also comes a variety of differential positions of power, identities, and experience that are oftentimes ignored and therefore result in the perpetuation of elitism, sexism, and homophobia. Some have accused the field of having an overwhelming focus on race that has been detrimental to the interests of others, such as women of color and sexual minorities of color whose racial identities ostensibly intersect with other categories of difference. These internal fissures oftentimes effectively weaken an already frail and vulnerable academic unit, and it is usually easy for many people to accuse Ethnic Studies of causing its own illnesses while forgetting the historical disadvantages that continue to undermine its well-being. I once helped my department in arguing for a seemingly trivial issue regarding the potential loss of an office room that an administrator of university space told us that another (larger) department desperately needed. "We just want to be fair to every department in this building," the administrator said, "and we want everyone to contribute their share in losing one or several rooms that other departments with new hires need." My department vehemently opposed this, claiming that the loss of space for a small and weak department such as ours should not be seen as equal to the loss of space for a larger, wealthier, and more powerful department. We won our case eventually, but only after convincing our higher administration, in the spirit of affirmative action, that pursuing fairness should not mean similar treatment for every department. People forget that even though a unit such as Ethnic Studies has its own internal conflicts and divisions just like other units, it hovers at the bottom of the hierarchy of power and privilege compared to other units.

As both a department and a multidisciplinary field of study, Ethnic Studies always has to clarify and convince others of its worth. Scholars in it usually find themselves explaining the value of their work both to the disciplines where they got their training and to the field where they are academically located. In particular disciplines like sociology and English, for example, it is not rare to hear about Ethnic Studies scholars being subjected to the most severe evaluation of their work, especially when the assigned disciplinary evaluators do not comprehend the field or have a low regard for it even while they pretend to be "professional" about their evaluation. I myself was warned early on that at the most basic level of objects of study, of which my preference was to study social networks of Filipino American immigrants in the field of communication, my chances of landing a book contract and eventual career advancement were low to none. Gatekeeping scholars clearly thought Filipino Americans as objects of study were not interesting enough. And even though I was able to defiantly oppose this and have my book published eventually, I still have a hard time to this day convincing editors and many scholars of the "publication worthiness" of any study about this group. I have a strong feeling as well that this chapter, focused on professors of color and potentially in an anthology of essays about minority professors, will not secure an easy promotion for me!

It is not as if the field of Ethnic Studies is devoid of such gatekeeping politics, and while it is disappointing to me that it exists in our own backyard, the very fact of the field's history of defiance and struggle against institutional forms of oppression that is simultaneously the context that is used to regulate and maintain its underprivilege makes me appreciate even more its value as a rich and meaningful contested academic space. This location has enabled many scholars like me to imagine our roles as academics in ways that do not disconnect us from our lives away from school, from the histories that we inherit and continue to live through, and from the many communities that provide us with reason for our work. In this field, we have vibrant debates about the populations that we ourselves minoritize or forget, those groups that we privilege and normatize, those communities that travel to or stay in places outside of the United States, and those "others" who defy or are in excess of the traditional categorizations provided to us by our theories and methods. For example, many scholars in Asian American Studies devote significant parts of their work to exposing the limitations of the category "Asian American" itself in accounting for the heterogeneity of its populations, including its immigrant and transnational groups, and in registering its historical connections to and modes of intervention against U.S. imperialism and colonialism in Asia as well as in the context of globalization and beyond what a typical analysis of immigration and settlement patterns would do (Chuh and Shimakawa 2001; Lowe 2001). To wit, scholars in Filipino American Studies have been at the forefront of claims regarding the incommensurabilities of global Filipino labor migration histories with U.S.-centric assimilation narratives ascribed to many other groups, histories that consequently require a different narration and a wider scope than that captured by the usual triumphant stories of the American dream (Tiongson, Gutierrez, and Gutierrez 2006). Contrary to what many of its detractors believe, Ethnic Studies scholars, while located in places that restrict and devalue them, are engaged in work that is vibrant and transformative.

Strategies for Transformation

I have heard it said many times before that professors of color are unfairly saddled with the expectation that they serve their communities, that unlike "regular" professors who are simply in the university to write and teach, these professors are supposed to write and teach *and* take care of "the community." My assumption is that this is said mainly because we owe gratitude to those from "the community" who initially advocated for our inclusion into the university. I agree. But oftentimes, I also wonder whether people have a particular definition of "the community" that includes only those situated outside the university, or if "the community" can also be imagined as inclusive of those who are also in the university, those who are located outside of the United States, and those who do not literally have access to our work. I ponder upon these questions of exclusion and inclusion in relation to our work as scholars and teachers to remind ourselves how easy it is, in this profession, to lose our bearings and keep in mind what we think is important. We live through the daily forms of oppression we find ourselves in and the resistances and challenges we mount in their wake, we preoccupy ourselves with survival strategies for career promotion, and we represent, mentor, and advocate. So what is this all for?

For this, I turn to the wisdom provided by our histories and experience, the power that collective thinking and action can provide, and ultimately the pursuit of and pleasure that can be derived from transformative practice. First, I think we need to remain knowledgeable and alert about our histories. The constant injunction to "never forget where you came from" can sound hackneyed only if its application does not move beyond telling ourselves that we owe it to our ancestors to narrate over and over our tales of exclusion and injustice. In order to move forward from this potentially unproductive and actually inadequate practice that does not do real justice to those who struggled before us, we not only need to be mindful of how certain histories are lost or forgotten or told from dominant perspectives, we also must require ourselves to renarrate these histories with an eye toward alternative interpretations, outside-of-the-box perspectives, and with dynamic connections to the present. We need, for example, a much more nuanced understanding of our history in the contemporary university so that we have a view of our profession that does not forget the conditions of our inclusion into the university under the context of a transformative collective politics. Against the urgings of a color-blind anti–affirmative action ethos, we must not strive to negate this history of differential exclusion in order to prove our worth and as a condition of our advancement. Oftentimes we are encouraged to look away from this history because we are made to believe that our own achievements are ours alone. Instead of being mired in this individualistic progression toward stature, visibility, and otherwise false notions of excellence, we ought to build upon a history as one that has actually been collectively productive in our quest for social justice, embracing and alternative in its scope as far as the objects, lenses, and audiences of our study can include, and feeding into the present as we balance our roles as activists and radical intellectuals beyond the limits imposed upon us by mainstream requirements of our profession. These, I think, are the kinds of historical vectors and contours that we need to keep alive.

Second, I believe that combating pervasive forms of oppression and injustice necessitates building pervasive collective forms of resistance and struggle mounted against them. Of course, I am not saying anything new here, for we have myriad examples from history that have taught us valuable lessons of collective struggle in its diverse forms, whether organized through singular or horizontal sets of identities, positions, and locations. Here it is instructive to convince ourselves that our struggles as minority academics must be considered not from the purview of us as individuals engaged alone in our own particular conditions, but rather should reference, to borrow and extend from Grace Kyungwon Hong (2001), a subject position that marks the various registers of our multiple identities and connects them with multiple collectivities.[4] In such a referencing, we not only acknowledge the reality that our presence in the university is intimately tied to and dependent upon power differentiation by groups in general and that we are not alone in this circumstance in particular, we also obtain the benefit of realizing how these seemingly discrete circumstances are connected and defined by hierarchical group treatment, as much as they are productive of differential consequences and opportunities by group experience. Here I am thinking of advocacies that simultaneously constitute, for example, multiracial people of color working with White allies, gender and sexual minorities working with straight men, and U.S.-identified workers in the struggle with immigrant and non-U.S.-based laborers. As we learn from the politics of collective action underscoring diversified group efforts against injustice that have been waged within and outside the university, when these connections are strengthened, they become fertile grounds for mobilization, alternative and inclusive practice, and transformation. They also serve to remind us of possibilities, prospects, and potential alliances that cut across multiple identities in which we may find connection and compassion with those whose experiences may not be similar or familiar to ours.

Finally, I argue that the work of transforming the university and academia as a whole is too difficult a task for it to depend solely on the fulfillment of duty in our profession or to certain people and communities, or obligation as required by law. This is like an academic institution having a compliance officer to make sure "diversity" hires and promotions take place. Not to say that this is not good practice (for indeed, we need the law to ensure that diversity gets practiced), but diversity, to me, is not meaningful and productive unless we are genuinely committed to it and unless our commitment to it is bound to issues of power and difference, precisely the registers within which diversity operates and ought to change. Whenever I am invited to present a lecture or workshop on "diversity in the classroom," for example, my first order of business is to ask participants if they are in attendance because they are required to be or if they desire to transform their classroom in ways that will address social injustice. I ask this because I want to make clear that nothing substantive will come of any practice of diversity if we don't ask ourselves first if we *want* any transformation in relationships of power to happen. Then, and only after then, can we proceed to talk about why and how we want it to happen, what its risks and rewards might be, and how we might want to continue the practice of transformation as an ongoing process.

Undergirding the transformative processes entailed in working in a place that both oppresses and rewards us is the sheer pleasure that I find very few academics talk about but that many experience. This, to me, is quite strange, yet understandable in that pleasure on the job has been interpreted as being nonserious, nonsmart, or simply unprofessorial. Pleasure, in my case, has been my most treasured ammunition for convincing myself to stay on in this profession when the going gets rough as much as it has been my constant source of energy and reason to write, teach, mentor, and serve the communities I care about, both within and outside of the academy. I do my job because it gives me pleasure, and I say this not out of a sense of narcissism or shallowness, but with a great deal of pride in the ways people in the collectives I am a part of have vigorously and vigilantly, as well as with much pleasure, committed to try to change the places that impede opportunities for us to live better lives and to transform the conditions of our existence so that they are more just. More than these, they have charted alternative maps and brought us new ways of thinking and doing even in the face of high risk but inspired by the unlimited prospects of greater rewards for many. I hope that many others join us in our struggles.

Notes

1   The connection across student retention, campus climate, and faculty diversity is briefly touched upon in Rodriguez et al. (forthcoming: 11), in which the authors state that "the fact that students of color perceive the campus as more negative than White students is not altogether surprising. At the University of Washington, and many other campuses across the country, the vast majority of faculty members are White and while most are interested and committed to campus diversity, this is not uniformly the case."

2   Also see a parallel argument on the significance of racial identity formation for youth in school in Pizarro 2005. For more general treatments of the importance of "culture" in curriculum and pedagogy, see Banks 1996, Gay 2000, and Nieto 1999.

3   For a general overview of the dimensions of mentorship, see the essays in Allen and Eby 2007.

4   Hong's (2001: 123) original reference, as discussed in her book review of *Orientations: Mapping Studies in the Asian Diaspora* (Chuh and Shimakawa 2001), is her citation of Lisa Lowe's (2001: 274) Asian immigrant subject as one who "is not reducible to individuals but, rather, references a subject position: a variety of social subjectivities and historical conditions that demonstrates . . . the 'impossibility of a single Asian formation.'" Another way to think about multiple subject positions is to consider the intersectionalities of our politics and identities with other groups (see Dill and Zambrana 2008).

CHAPTER THREE

Telling Our Stories, Naming Ourselves

The Lost María in the Academy

CHRISTINA GÓMEZ

(Mis)Naming

To name is to identify. It is to make real; to give a name is to recognize. When no name is given, or a name is forgotten or confused with another, then there is no existence. One is rendered invisible—insignificant, unworthy.

Naming brings order, allows us to put things into categories, opens a space, and allows for a relation to develop with other named objects or people. We name children when they are born; we name each other upon introduction. "Why then," do I ask myself, "has my name been forgotten, or confused? Why have I been called *María* so often?" Is it that I, and other people of color in the academy, bring chaos to the order? Do we not fit into the pre-existing structure that has been put in place? Are we not yet recognized as individuals but as groups, and thereby as interchangeable (i.e., we can all be *María* at the same time, since we are all the same)?

I came to the academy because I wanted to tell stories; I wanted to tell stories about the experiences of people who are usually not heard from, whose views have been marginalized or completely ignored.

I wanted to ask questions that I felt were not being asked, consider variables that appeared unnoticed, and select samples that previously were unspecified.

What I didn't realize is that in the process of trying to become a writer of other people's stories, I was also a character in a plot. And as a character in real time, I was not in control of the endings, or at least not totally. Events occurred while I completed my doctoral work and while I was a faculty member that were out of my imagining; new protagonists were taking over, and twists in the story lines confounded me. Dissertation committees, chairs of my department, and colleagues became central players in shaping my life and thoughts. But still they are my stories, and I take ownership of them. I write these stories in the hope that they will help others and will perhaps make the journey easier for others who choose this path. I also write because my stories help me; they help me better understand and navigate my own past and future and they help me rest and give meaning to the present.

I never imagined myself as part of the academy, and neither did anyone else, I guess. Over the years during my climb up the academic ladder I have been shocked by the tokenism, stereotyping, and outright discrimination I have seen displayed toward faculty of color, myself included. Some remarks or actions have been described to me as accidental or unintentional, while others appeared deliberate and even antagonistic. I find it easier to deal with the latter, the overt racism; in a strange way I feel safer when intentions are clear, when hostility is up front and unabashed. But on the occasions in which the underlying intentions are unclear, where the incidents might be construed as "something else," these are the situations that make me appear paranoid, overvigilant, and too sensitive—I am left feeling uneasy and on guard. These incidents build slowly and secretively inside me, and then one day their weight overwhelms me, and again I am left feeling as though this is *my* problem. And over the years I have come to the conclusion that for the moment it is my problem, since the "problem" is not being fixed and in many cases the issues are rarely discussed, or even acknowledged.

I will illustrate just three experiences of (mis)naming that have happened to me in my brief academic career that have caused me to feel marginalized, isolated, and unrecognized. They are situations where I have been forgotten, confused for someone else, or made invisible. While these stories are personal, they are emblematic of stories my colleagues of color have shared with me over the years and represent a collective voice of frustration, anger, disappointment, and disillusionment. These moments, pages from the story of my academic career, remain confusing, shocking, and painful, and they leave me uncertain about my place in the academy. They make me feel like I want out. I question myself, and my fears of not being "good enough" or "smart enough" resurface. I feel as though I have no place—no space where people like me belong. I am a poor Latina from the barrio (or at least I once was). How can I be a writer, a scholar? Why should my words matter? Who will be my audience?

Yet I also have moments when I feel good about my work and teaching, when I know I am doing the right thing, when I believe I have found my calling. I have moments when I am writing or teaching and "magic" happens; ideas become exciting, teaching becomes transformative and I am forever changed. I cherish these moments; they energize me and push me forward. My stories are stories about my life, the people I know, the Latinos and Latinas whose voices have been rendered silent.

Case #1—The *West Side Story* Syndrome

I am the daughter of Mexican immigrants. My father first arrived in the United States as an undocumented farmworker in the 1950s, was caught by *la migra*, and returned to Mexico. Years later, and with papers in hand, he settled with my mother in the predominantly Mexican area of Chicago. Like so many immigrants, our plan was to return to Mexico one day, but one day never came.

After almost failing first grade (partly because I had not yet learned English), I excelled in school and found refuge in the classroom. I was a chameleon of sorts and as long as I knew what the rules were, I was able to follow and behave accordingly. But ironically it was also not knowing that caused me to succeed. My total lack of cultural and social capital in my early years permitted me to embark on projects or programs that I otherwise would not have. I didn't know what was not possible, and

I didn't even know that I should ask. Naively I joined in assuming the best, not yet knowing how structural realities of American race and class relations can undermine dreams and hopes. There was so much I didn't know and so much that was never told to me.

While in college the idea of obtaining a PhD had never occurred to me, and oddly no one had ever mentioned it. For many first-generation collegegoers, attending college means majoring in something that will get you a good job. My father desperately wanted me to become an engineer or accountant; instead I had majored in romance languages and literature. So after a few years of working in the "real world," I found myself applying to graduate school; I was aggressively recruited and entered a top-tier PhD program sure of myself, knowing exactly what I wanted to study. During my first week in the department I made sure that I introduced myself to faculty members, was active in the classroom, and talked about my research intentions. I wanted to be the model graduate student.

Then one sunny afternoon not more than a few weeks later I found myself outside the main office of the department, when a senior faculty member, who later would become chair, started a conversation with me. He referred to me as María Gonzales. Given that I was the only Chicana in the department, and at that point the only Latina, I was a bit surprised. "Do I correct him?" I thought to myself. Why did he call me María? There was no other María in the program, so it wasn't a case of mistaken identity. I chatted with him for a few minutes and said nothing. I played the role of the eager graduate student, intending to please, and remained silent.

María—I am María Gonzales—my long lost alter ego. Was this just an inadvertent mistake he made, or was it about something else? In his eyes were we all the same—interchangeable brown women who merely represent a token diversity quota? Had he watched *West Side Story* one too many times? I had watched *West Side Story* one too many times, and frankly I wanted to be Anita. Had he called me Anita, I would have felt better. Anita is sassy, assertive, and smart; she speaks out. María wears a white communion dress and plays the role of the virginal, submissive, all-too-accommodating Latina (although she too has a major conversion at the end of the script, but only after Tony and her brother, Bernardo, are killed). Had I become María in trying to please everyone and succeed in school? Were we, Latinas, merely interchangeable? I had the sudden urge to speak with my Speedy Gonzales accent and outsmart the gringo cats. But I didn't. It would take years before I would learn to speak up. The power differentials of the academy were well entrenched in me—and I remained silent.

Was I being too sensitive? Was I being the hysterical minority woman? So he confused my name—what does it matter? According to anthropologist Renato Rosaldo (1984: 13), "[n]aming people not only designates unique individuals and discriminates social categories, but also shapes the quality of social interactions and reflects the dynamics of interpersonal histories." Thus, without names interactions break down, histories are lost. And with no history, futures are unimaginable.

It did matter. Here I was María, and if I was going to embody her I was embodying all the Marías who never had the chance to attend universities or to have a voice. I would become *María Cristina, María Dolores, María Socorro,* and the millions of other *Marías* who go unnoticed as nannies, housecleaners, and service workers. I would tell their stories, study their lives, and write about them.

Case #2—It's the Real Thing

As I neared the completion of my dissertation, I went on the job market, understanding that the first time would be a warm-up. I would write my cover letter, gather letters of reference in my file, collect my writings, and, if I was lucky, I would be called for a job talk.

My dissertation was about Latino/a racial identity. I was interested in the racial diversity we as Latinos/as encompass: Are we White? Black? Indian? All of the above? How are Latinos/as racially understood in the United States and how do we understand ourselves? Most identify with a national origin group, such as Mexican or Puerto Rican. But in the United States we are often asked to describe ourselves in terms of race; for many this is confusing and makes no sense. Government forms put us into categories such as white Hispanics or black Hispanics, and generally this is decided based on our physical characteristics such as skin color or hair type. Racial ideology in the United States is different from the racial ideology of Latin American countries—history matters. So where to situate Latinos/as in the racial rubric of the United States that rests on a racist foundation has been a quagmire.

As fate would have it, I landed two job talks with elite private liberal arts colleges. What was curious to me was that even though I was applying for a sociology position with a joint appointment in Latino Studies, I felt that I was being quizzed on how "ethnic" I really was. My Spanish language ability was tested, even though neither job listed fluency in Spanish as a requirement. My "Latino pedigree" was questioned; there seemed to be an underlying question as to whether I was *really* Latina, whatever that meant. Fortunately, I passed with flying colors—I had grown up in a poor barrio, my father was an undocumented migrant farmworker, and I "looked" Latina. I was the "real thing," or at least I fulfilled all the stereotypes that they might have had.

Oddly, my research was little discussed during my interviews, which puzzled me, and in some cases I wondered if my file had been thoroughly reviewed. Was this normal? If I were not a minority woman, would the interview be any different? Was I being recruited for my research and what I could bring as a scholar, or was I recruited because I was Latina? The one question that caused me the greatest concern was asked by a senior scholar: "I notice your name is spelled with an 'h'? Why is that?"

In Spanish, my first name is not spelled with an "h." However when my mother gave birth to me in a U.S. hospital, the Anglo nurse warned her about giving her newly born daughter too many names, a reference to the often multiple names Latinos/as carry. My mother, who spoke very little English, took the advice to heart, giving me not only no middle name and no double last name, but also spelling my name in the English-language fashion. She wanted life to be easy for her children in this new country. So instead of being named María Cristina Gómez Camorlinga, I simply became Christina Gómez—a name I have kept over the years.

But why would a scholar who is evaluating my research care whether my name has an "h" or not? Does this matter? Was this mere curiosity? Or was it a questioning of my Latinoness?

As a writer/researcher, I have often felt constrained by my "Latinoness" because of the expectations that others (particularly non-Latinos/as) have of me as a "minority scholar." I am often expected to write about Latino/a topics and nothing else. My other identities and expertise are vanished from the page. I become one-dimensional. I am allowed to be only a *Latina* scholar, not a scholar who is Latina. Yet it is because I am Latina that I write. My ability to empathize, to see things others might not, to experience life in a particular way, and to theorize are channeled through my Latinoness. My identity as a female scholar who is Latina widens, not narrows, my abilities to be a scholar.

Case #3—The Substitution Effect

In economics, the substitution effect is the rate at which consumers transfer spending to or from a commodity when its relative price changes but the total utility for consumers remains constant. The substitution effect predicts how much consumers would switch their spending away from or toward an item whose price had changed. The substitution effect is always negative: consumers always switch spending away from items whose prices rise as they attempt to shield their living standards from the impact. For example, if the price of butter rises by 20 percent, the consumer who can switch to margarine incurs no great loss (Bannock, Baxter, and Davis 1999). Although each good is unique, it has substitutes—other goods that will serve almost as well. This, too, is the case with scholars of color—one is substituted for the other.

After teaching for several years at an elite liberal arts college, I had gotten the unfortunate reputation of being a good lecturer. The truth is I love teaching and do it well, a kiss of death for many faculty, since this means students flock to your classes, visit you during office hours, and ask you to serve on committees for independent research projects and theses. For faculty of color, this is an added burden to the many committees on which we are already asked to serve. Research has shown that women and minorities in academe are seen as more approachable and have a harder time saying no. In addition, they have to do more to prove themselves and consequently take on too many service commitments, hindering their chances for tenure (Turner 2002). As one of the few scholars who did research on Latino/a issues, I had been asked by my colleagues to guest lecture in their classes. I was a "green card" holder; I would be brought in when issues of diversity, ethnicity, race, or gender were being considered (even if it wasn't in my field of research) for one week during the term.

After feeling exploited, I decided to pull back and stop providing this service. However, a visiting (White) professor teaching an education class had already heard of me. He e-mailed me three times and left two messages on my voice mail. My efforts at avoiding him during my research term failed. Finally, I gave in and agreed to guest lecture for his course.

On the day of the lecture I arrived early at the auditorium. Approximately eighty students were eagerly awaiting my lecture on educational issues concerning Latinos/as in the United States. He began the class by taking care of some logistics, and started to introduce me. He began, "Today I am happy to introduce Professor, uh . . ." There was a pause. Suddenly, I realized he had forgotten my name. I was horrified. I have no doubt my face turned red. I hope not too noticeably, given my olive complexion, and for a split second I considered leaving the lecture. But having "been here" before, my automatic pilot kicked in. "Professor Gómez," I finished the sentence for him as he stammered. He then continued to say, "Professor Gándara, Professor Gómez, I get them confused." He was making reference to a professor I had invited to give a public lecture a few days earlier on bilingual education. She had received an honorarium.

I was left speechless. Could this really be happening to me? Was he just so forgetful? Was I losing my mind? I was lost, but I managed to keep it together and give a passionate lecture on the critical issues confronting Latinos/as in schools, covering topics such as immigration, bilingual education, dropout rates, and discrimination. How appropriate, I thought. After I concluded, the students applauded. He then stood up, and went on to say, "I would like to thank Professor Gonzales for coming to visit us today."

Was I in a time warp? There were no words to explain how I felt. I stood frozen at the front of the class and before many students who knew me. At this point he understood his mistake, and saw my dismay. As he approached to offer what seemed like an apology (or maybe this was wishful thinking on my part), I interrupted and said, "I think it is better if you don't speak to me at this moment. You have no idea how angry I am." And I left for my office and cried.

I was anonymous. I was *María* all over again. I was a substitution of myself. My anger simmered for a very long time. As I recounted the story to colleagues, some thought I was misinterpreting the situation; others thought I was taking it too seriously. Fortunately, many of my colleagues who were Latino/a or African American understood. And instead of just staying mad, I got even and wrote about it. I was now a character in my own stories, and I could write my own ending.

Learning to Name

We learn to name at the point of learning language. A ball is shown to a child and the adult states the word "ball." After a series of repetitions the child will learn that the word ball refers to a round object that has been held for her to see, touch, or play with. And often after the child says the word ball, her naming is reinforced, "yes, it is a ball." This process is called echoing (Horne and Lowe 1996). Perhaps I should have echoed my name to my various colleagues. I should have given them positive reinforcement when they named me correctly. Maybe I needed to do a better job at reminding my colleagues just exactly who I am.

But actually we learn to name before language is even possible; first the child learns to listen, in what is called listener behavior. Names are repeated and the child learns to discriminate the speech sounds within their native language. When my son was two years old, he learned the word "ball," but soon after also learned to differentiate between different balls. He quickly learned the difference between soccer balls, basketballs, baseballs—and he names them as such. He knows they are not all the same. Why then do my colleagues seem to have difficulty differentiating between faculty of color? Maybe my colleagues weren't listening to me? Maybe our languages weren't the same? Perhaps my accent made it difficult for them to understand me or maybe I was speaking too quickly?

Naming is a powerful tool. It can be used as an instrument of domination and oppression. The use of certain names (i.e., think of racist or sexist language) as well as the failure to name constitutes a form of power; individuals who have greater linguistic facility can persuade, influence, control, or set the terms or agenda for how we think about certain issues or persons. Included is not only what is said (what or who is named) but also how it said (Brittan and Maynard 1984).

Within some circles of scholars of color, the title "doctor" and "professor" is used carefully and frequently. I often refer to my colleagues of color as professor or doctor (and I always use their title when speaking of them in public). This is not only a matter of respect; I believe we do this because we all know too well the painful reality of being marginalized or of being denied our titles. Many of my African American and Latino/a students refer to me as Doctor Gómez or as *Profesora*. I have to confess it makes me feel good. I worked hard to earn my degree and there are few of us in the academy. Moreover, the chances are good that others, students and faculty alike, will deny me this honor, assuming an intimacy with me that does not exist and referring to me by my first name because I am a woman and/or faculty of color.

Many years ago when I first started working in universities, an African American female colleague of mine told me I should always wear a suit jacket at work or keep one in my office. "Why?" I asked, since not all the women dressed so formally. Her response was, "If you don't, they will assume you are the secretary." She was right.

¿Andas Perdida?

Some years ago a doctoral student came to the college where I was teaching; he had been awarded a fellowship that would enable him to finish his dissertation. He, too, was Chicano and, to my surprise, had grown up a few blocks away from where I lived as a child. In a funny way, he was the male version of me, and this made me uneasy. Was there enough room for both of us?

Although we hadn't known each other as children, I irrationally feared he would know about me, that if he knew what I was once like (*pobre*/poor, *greñuda*/uncombed, and *maleducada*/uneducated) and he told, I would be revealed for the impostor that I am. I was merely pretending to be an assistant professor at an elite college wearing suit jackets with neatly trimmed hair. He could name me for what I really was. But what was I? And who am I?

There is this constant tension within me; there is a binary. My past and my present do not seem to fit so neatly inside these ivy-covered walls. Issues of race, class, and gender circle around me, defining and undefining who I am and what I can be. At times, I am unrecognizable even to myself. In the words of *Profesora* Montoya (1995: 531):

> For stigmatized groups, such as persons of color, the poor, women, gays, lesbians, assuming a mask is comparable to being "on stage." Being "on stage" is frequently experienced as being aware of one's words, affect, tone of voice, movements and gestures because they seem out of sync with what one is feeling and thinking. At unexpected moments, we fear that we will be discovered to be someone or something other than we pretend to be. Lurking just behind our carefully constructed disguises and lodged within us is the child whom no one would have mistaken for anything other than what she was. Her masking was yet imperfect, still in rehearsal, and at times unnecessary.

As it turns out, this doctoral candidate from the "barrio" and I became good friends and colleagues. We shared stories about our neighborhood and our various experiences. But after almost a year of being at the college I invited him to a lecture and informed him of the building and room where it would be held. He never arrived. Later I saw him and asked what happened. He responded, "I got lost." I found it very funny and almost impossible that this could be true. The campus is tiny by most standards and the building is prominent. I joked with him—"*andas perdido*"—in Spanish this can simply mean to be lost, but it also has the connotation of being misguided or having strayed. Its double meaning was appropriate to our situation. We had strayed; we were in new territory with no maps to guide us. Neither of our families understood our work, our positions, or our turmoil, nor did the institutions where we now held precarious membership. Our class backgrounds do not give us the support to negotiate our new situations. We do not have networks easily in place to call upon. In many cases we are the first to have finished college in our families, much less receive a doctorate.

The fact is that I often feel *perdida* in the academy. I lose myself and I grow weary. My writing has no manual that tells me where to turn, but it does keep me always moving. I let myself wander and explore new areas. As a writer/scholar, I reinvent myself and my life over and over again. I set the plot, create characters, and tell the stories I need to hear.

In my research, I try to tell the stories that have not been told—issues of discrimination, inequality, and marginalization that have not been understood or have been misunderstood. I recognize the privilege that I now have and consequently the responsibility that comes with it. My hopes are that my research, my stories, will open new pathways for those who have been shut out and new ways to understand for those who are already in. It is powerful and empowering.

La Búsqueda: Strategies for the Return

Several years ago I was asked to facilitate a discussion after a screening of a documentary that dealt with Proposition 187. The documentary was *Fear and Learning at Hoover Elementary* (Simon 1997). It is the story of the effects that California's Proposition 187 (a ballot initiative denying public education and health care to all undocumented immigrants) had on children in the state. Prior to that evening, I had never seen the film. But as I watched, I wept throughout the entire film. It wasn't a soft weeping with occasional tears rolling down my cheeks, but one of those uncontrollable sobbing moments that we occasionally allow ourselves. By the time I had to lead the discussion I felt completely overwhelmed.

But something magical happened—the discussion, which lasted more than three hours, became a conversation mostly of faculty and administrators of color about our concerns, our fears, and our experiences in the academy (the students had left early in the evening). We shared our stories, and it was clear we needed a forum for this exchange. We needed a space to gather and to talk among ourselves. And so some members organized, found a meeting space, and called us all together. We share food, stories, information, and community.

What has been amazing is how free-flowing and easy our conversations are. We debate, argue, laugh, and are often just plain silly. Conversation is spontaneous. The gathering has provided a space for me to be myself, to find myself. It is a space where I do not have to perform—a space where I do not wear a mask. I can be myself, whoever that might be, on any given night. We talk, we eat, we laugh, and sometimes we cry. I leave these gatherings feeling empowered to teach and do research; I feel stronger and know that I am not alone in this journey. There are others with me and we support each other.

I share this story because I believe one of the greatest resources I have is this community of friends. In sharing our stories with each other weekly, we have created a history for ourselves, and we understand it as a shared history. In this space I have a name. And because I have a name, I can write.

CHAPTER FOUR

Striving to Be Queer

Challenging Inequality from Positions of Privilege

Michael Armato

I should begin by acknowledging that I am White, heterosexual, and male. Given the privileged categories that have structured my life, I appear, at least on the surface, among the least likely of contributors to a volume on challenging privileges in the ivory tower. Nevertheless, I have come to realize that it is precisely my occupation of these privileged categories that places a responsibility on me to challenge those very privileges and work toward social justice. I've also come to realize that those of us who are privileged have plenty of opportunity to challenge inequalities—if we open our eyes and choose to see them. A rigorously critical understanding of how inequalities operate illuminates how mundane, ordinary institutional practices are riddled with privileges of race, class, gender, and sexuality, privileges that get normalized precisely through mundane, ordinary practices in institutional settings.

Challenging these inequalities is never easy. It is never "a good time" to speak up about racism, sexism, classism, or homophobia because doing so disrupts the everyday goings-on that constitute academic (and other institutional) life. Putting Seidman's (1995: 118) notion that "queer politics mobilizes against all normalized hierarchies" into action is at the heart of what striving to be queer means to me, and academic life provides innumerable opportunities to take queer action. I use *striving to be queer* rather than simply *being queer* to underscore that action is required rather than my having an identity as a queer person. As I will discuss below, a politics organized around identity often undermines a queer politics and reinforces the status quo.

Questioning My World, Finding Sociology

I am one of four children born to working-class parents in Chicago, a factor that would eventually help shape my current political orientation. This is not to say that my parents or other extended family members were involved in working-class (or any other) politics in any sense. I have no memory of my parents ever talking about politics. They were not members of a union. To my knowledge, they did not even vote. I suspect that if I were to speak with my estranged father or magically be able to have a conversation with my deceased mother, there would be little we would agree on politically. Nevertheless, my working-class background helped yield my political orientation in an entirely different way. Having no one in my family who had a bachelor's degree, much less a graduate degree, afforded me the potential to resist taking academia and myself as an academic too seriously. I, of course, care about and take seriously my academic work in all of its manifestations, but not enough so that I view it as separate from politics and give it primacy over all else.

I eventually found my way into a PhD program in sociology due to two crises of my early adult life that caused me to question all that I held true about my world. Prior to these crises, I had attained a number of goals common to boys and young men my age. In addition to getting good grades, I was a popular high school athlete, affording me status among my peers, including getting voted a member of homecoming court in my junior and senior years and getting voted "most popular" in my senior year. As someone so entrenched in the upper echelons of the heterosexual high school popularity power structure, I would seem perhaps the person least likely to get a PhD in sociology with a focus on undermining White heterosexual masculine privilege.

Nevertheless, in September of my senior year of high school, I discovered that my father was a pedophile, and I was the one who turned him into the police. I had long idolized my father. He was not typical of the fathers my friends had. He was generally affectionate and relatively engaged in what was happening in my life, something I had attributed to his coming from a large Italian family. Learning of his pedophilia shook the foundations of my existence and made my concerns with high school status seem silly and juvenile. To top off that extremely difficult school year, my mother, having suffered various health issues over the preceding year, was diagnosed with pancreatic cancer within a week of my high school graduation. She died five days later.

These two horrible events caused me to re-evaluate what I had previously taken for granted about the world and my place in it. To outside observers, my struggle was probably invisible, yet the decade following my graduation from high school was marked by a painful process of personal exploration, a process where I felt generally unmoored in my life. This unmooring proved useful in allowing me to make choices that were atypical for lower-middle-class heterosexual White men like me. My lack of mooring also had an elective affinity with understanding and taking queer actions later in life.

I am the only one in my family to get an advanced degree, but I had not initially planned on continuing with my education beyond my undergraduate degree in marketing. After graduating I got a sales-support job with a small company that sold playground equipment. Selling playground equipment seems like a job far removed from political issues, but I was constantly uncomfortable with the racism and sexism of the workplace. For example, on a road trip to visit a supplier's factory with two White men who were field sales representatives, we drove through Gainesville, Florida, the location of the University of Florida. It must have been sorority pledge week because there were hundreds of young women dressed in virtually identical black cocktail dresses walking around town in large groups. At the sight of the women, one sales representative commented on "all the pussy in this town." Sitting alone in the back seat, I felt extremely uncomfortable with how these two men were talking about the women, yet I felt that as a member of the office staff who was younger than they and who had only recently joined the company, I was not in a position to say anything. I was made uncomfortable again later in the day when, upon seeing what looked to be a freshly painted bright orange car, one of the sales reps commented to the other,

"What do you call that color? Metallic nigger!" They both laughed at the comment, and I felt claustrophobic in the back seat.

Of course, I could have said something, but I was intimidated by the idea of speaking up. I was also frustrated with myself for not saying anything, for allowing them to believe that I shared their views toward women and African Americans. Over time, I grew to hate my job, and I found myself becoming almost obsessed with thinking about how gender and race structured the workplace and the world around me. I mentioned my ideas to my roommate at the time, and he said he thought that sociology was the field that dealt with those issues. Soon after, I returned to my alma mater's library to find books on sociology. The first book I opened was a reader in sociology. The first two essays dealt with race and gender, respectively, and I felt as if the essays were addressing exactly what I had been thinking about. I gravitated to sociology because it provided the best explanations of how the world worked.

I decided to quit my job and return to school to get a master's degree in sociology, with no idea of what I was going to do with it. I simply wanted to think and read about social issues. Soon after beginning graduate school, I learned that if I got a PhD I could teach sociology courses and get paid for it. I had found my calling. I feel lucky that I enrolled at the University of Florida because it allowed me to cross paths with Joe Feagin, a prominent scholar on White racism and a good example of an academic who is an ally to students of color and a proponent of challenging the power structure of higher education. At the time, I did not fully understand the example Feagin, as a heterosexual White man, set for me. I completed my master's degree at the University of Florida and moved to New York City to be with my partner. I got accepted into a local sociology graduate program.

Although switching schools delayed my completing my PhD, studying sociology in two departments taught me that there are different ways to do sociology, different ways to be an academic. Different departments have a different "feel" to them, focus on different sets of research questions, and enjoy different levels of prestige in the field. Despite these differences, switching programs allowed me to see that different types of sociology were viable in the field. In the aggregate, my experiences in graduate school presented me with a paradox that is central to academia.

I learned to develop critical insights into how and why inequalities play out in the social world. I also learned that many academics are quite removed from the politics that relate to the topics they study and teach. And even those who are politically engaged often find that their political activities are treated more like a hobby than serious academic work. Academic sociology and related fields prepare graduate students to develop critical insights while socializing us to be professional academics. This paradox caused me to question how people who know so much about the world and its inequalities could turn around and reproduce those inequalities. This paradox has always troubled me and made me feel naive.

My naiveté often takes the form of thinking that other people with PhDs in sociology should know what I know. Yet they often act in ways that reflect the status quo, reproducing the racism, classism, sexism, and homophobia that they purport to challenge in their research and teaching. Below, I recount and critically interrogate an experience I had in my final year of graduate school. I view this experience as important for a number of reasons. First, it captures how "progressive" faculty often lose themselves in their reputations, promoting ideas that are politically problematic. At the heart of this situation, I believe, is an unwillingness to be reflexive, to take the insights of the sociology and related fields and apply them to our own experiences and actions. The way the events played out in my department shed considerable insight into how we, as academics, are often complicit in the production of inequalities.

The situation I describe below is important for a second reason. It was the first time in my academic career that I spoke out against a fellow academic and, in so doing, felt I had found (and used) my voice to challenge a faculty member in my department and the ivory tower more generally. This experience, though unnerving initially, was also one of the most exhilarating experiences I have had so far in my professional life, tantamount to finding my calling, my place in the field. The final reason why the example below is important is because it highlights how being a White heterosexual male speaking out against injustices automatically brings along with it a unique combination of privileges and challenges that dominant group members should be aware of if we truly want to strive toward queerness.

Challenging Sexism in the Academe

In December 2005, one of the faculty members in my department, Professor Carius Shubri,[1] published a controversial op-ed piece in *The New York Times*. Let me be clear: Shubri was no run-of-the-mill professor. This was not the first time he had gained access to the pages of the *Times*. He was and remains well known as a New York public intellectual. He has been acknowledged as a top-notch scholar by a number of academic and scientific institutions, including the National Science Foundation. When he wrote the piece in the *Times*, he was still only in his mid-thirties, and there was much buzz about him in the department and among the elite in the field of sociology. At the time of his publication, he was in many ways the Golden Boy of sociology. His publication of the op-ed piece in the *Times* is important not only because his career was on a skyrocketing upward trajectory, but also because he was a leftist thinker and an excellent example of an academician as public intellectual. This made his op-ed piece all the more surprising and disappointing to me, prompting me and other graduate students to ask among ourselves, "How could he do this?" In his exceptionality, Professor Shubri embodies the best and worst of academia.

In his op-ed essay, Shubri argued for the expansion of fatherhood rights:

> The bottom line is that if we want to make fathers relevant, they need rights, too. If a father is willing to legally commit to raising a child with no help from the mother he should be able to obtain an injunction against the abortion of the fetus he helped create.

What was troubling about the piece—in addition to its dangerous thesis above—was that it was riddled with sexism. Women as agents were largely absent in his essay, except when they made choices that went against Shubri's understanding of men's interests. For example, Shubri explained that he had once been in a relationship and his girlfriend at the time had gotten pregnant and decided to get an abortion against his wishes. This relationship ended, but his "desire for fatherhood was eventually fulfilled by two wonderful children," phrasing that makes the woman who carried and birthed those children invisible. He also downplayed the significant risks and labor involved with pregnancy, offsetting them with fathers' lifetime commitment to their children:

> But how many times have we heard that fatherhood is not about a moment, it is about being there for the lifetime of a child? If we extend that logic, those 40 weeks of pregnancy—as intense as they may be—are merely a small fraction of a lifetime commitment to that child.

He also employed the oft-cited but misguided metaphor of the male seed: "Pro-choice advocates argue that the debate is really about a woman's control over her body. Hence my lack of rights to have any say in whether my seed comes to fruition."

When Shubri's essay was published by the *Times*, I was immersed in evaluating the data I had collected for my dissertation research, converting my findings into dissertation chapters, and applying for jobs in the academic job market. In short, I was very, very busy. I had what seemed like a thousand things to do before responding to Shubri's piece in the *Times*. Yet my initial outrage at the tone and content of the essay remained alive. For the first time in my academic career, it was clear that I knew considerably more than a faculty member about a topic. You see, despite his prominence in the field, Professor Shubri was not a gender scholar. By contrast, I had spent my graduate education focusing on gender, including lots of reading in feminist theory and men's studies. I even served as the graduate student organizer for our department's monthly "gender workshop," a forum in which faculty and students presented their research and received feedback.

My decision to respond was also informed by the general lack of a public response from faculty members in the department, especially tenured full professors. As the saying goes, their silence was deafening. The only public responses to the essay within the department came from female graduate students who were not as far along in the program as me, but these responses were generally brief, too brief to fully articulate the problems with what Shubri had proposed. There just seemed to be so many things that were not being said within the department.[2] There

seemed a gaping void where there should have been critical public discussion. I could not help but think that the void in public discussion was
a tacit approval of Shubri's ideas. I was particularly concerned with what
this meant for the female graduate students whose dissertation research
was being overseen by the professor. More generally, I was troubled by
the message the collective silence sent to all members of the department, women and men. For all these reasons, I decided to publicly speak
out against Shubri's essay.

My response took the form of an open letter that I e-mailed to
everyone in the department in which I took issue with the central premise of the essay:

> The logic is one in which once a woman gives any
> consent at all (and oftentimes it's not clear she gave
> it), she loses the ability to change her mind, retract
> her consent, and, heaven forbid, actually keep control
> of her body. [Carius'] hope is that, with the pregnancy
> situation he describes, once a woman consents to
> having sex with a man, all bets are off. He wants her to
> forgo future claims to her body.

I also criticized his sexist tone and examples that characterized the piece,
pointing out the biological and political problems with using the notion
of "his seed":

> The seed metaphor, though common, is inaccurate.
> Seeds need nutrients from the soil, but they are
> complete in terms of their DNA. [Carius'] sperm (or
> any other man's) is not. But by using the metaphor
> of a seed, he employs a rhetorical sleight of hand that
> reduces women to a vessel, merely something that helps
> the baby grow. . . . Women provide half the genetic
> material (and all the work) needed to produce a healthy
> newborn. Also, the seed metaphor, especially when
> phrased as "my seed," smuggles in not only the notion
> that the fetus is separate from the woman, but another
> common notion: the fetus as actually belonging to the
> man, despite the fact that it's "housed" in and intimately

connected with a woman's body. So, biological language
aside, it's clear that the seed metaphor has very real
political significance.

I concluded with a call to Professor Shubri and all men to rethink
our complicity in gender politics: "I would urge [Carius], and all men,
to rethink our personal sense of entitlement to women's bodies. After
all, the personal is political for us as well." I purposely used the feminist-
inspired phrase to make visible how men's lives are intimately connected
with gender politics.

I sent my response to the entire sociology department as well as to
the editors of *The New York Times*. I was pretty sure the *Times* would not
publish my response since it was considerably longer than their publication criteria for responses to op-ed pieces. The *Times* did publish a couple
of responses to the essay, but, predictably, the editors chose to reinforce
a "gender-wars" approach to the topic, publishing the views of a woman
who was critical of Professor Shubri and the views of a man who was
supportive. By gender-wars approach, I mean that the framing of the
issue served to reinforce the sense of men and women as monolithic
and mutually exclusive categories with fundamentally different and dia-
metrically opposed interests.

In contrast to the gender-wars framing of the *Times*, I felt it was my
responsibility as a man to respond given my knowledge of the subject
matter and that I found Shubri's ideas repugnant. My gender was important because, as had happened in the *Times'* framing of the issue, I feared
the issue would devolve into a gender-wars approach, with women being
the only ones speaking out critically. By speaking out *as a man* who
found his ideas problematic, I was destabilizing the general pattern of
gender debates, a practice that gets at how I view queerness. I can strategically deploy my privileged status as a White heterosexual man to work
toward gender and other forms of social justice. I thought the men and
the women in the department needed to hear a man speak out against
the unjust ideas.

Speaking out as a heterosexual White man comes with a caveat:
we heterosexual White guys get to speak as experts on all sorts of issues
(even when we are not experts, as evidenced by Carius Shubri's actions),

and one way our privilege is sustained is through our chivalrous defense of women. I want to underscore that the women in the department did not need my protection. They were well equipped to defend themselves against Professor Shubri's sexism. I was aware at the time of the tension between disrupting the typical gender-wars pattern of debate around gender issues and reinstating heteropatriarchal White privilege through those same actions. This tension cannot easily be overcome; it is part and parcel of any challenges posed by those on the privileged side of power relationships. Despite this tension, it is important that dominant group members challenge the status quo.

In response to Shubri's piece in the *Times*, those of us active in the department's "Gender and Inequality Workshop," a space in which faculty and students typically met monthly to discuss and get feedback on their writing projects, decided to convene a special meeting of the gender workshop to discuss the essay. Professor Shubri was invited, and he accepted our invitation. The format of the meeting was for Shubri to give an opening statement and then two female faculty members and two female graduate students would provide feedback and criticism on his essay. Professor Shubri then responded to the comments, and a broader discussion ensued among all the workshop participants. One aspect of the meeting that struck most of us as odd was that Professor Shubri's nonsociologist wife attended the meeting, as if to signify to the other women in the room that they need not worry, she was representing women's interest in the relationship. To make matters even weirder, she explained that her husband had received so much hate mail that she was contemplating setting up a bot, a computer program that would search for keywords in the e-mails and generate an auto-response based on the keywords, to handle all the e-mails. Both she and Professor Shubri failed to see the irony that he had been able to exploit his masculine privilege and express his personal experiences for the readers in the *Times*, while the women who contacted him with their experiences with abortion would be handled by an automated system. She jokingly referred to the "bot" as "wifebot," only contributing to our collective ire.

The faculty members provided good criticisms. As senior faculty members, they scolded him for his irresponsible actions, especially sign-ing off on his op-ed piece as a professor of sociology when gender was not one of his areas of specialty. It seemed to me that these faculty members, both established feminist scholars, were disappointed by Shubri's actions. They also seemed somewhat angry at his actions, but they remained quite calm; perhaps their many years in academia had provided them with many similar experiences and they had hardened to such sexism.

As a graduate student, I was particularly impressed with my fellow graduate students' well-thought-out criticisms of Shubri's essay and its intellectual and political implications. As they launched their insightful criticisms of the gender, racial, and class-based implications of the essay, I got the sense that they had channeled all their shock and outrage at the professor into preparing for the workshop. The erudition of their feedback seemed outside of Shubri's understanding. It was not that he could not understand what they were pointing out, but that he seemed dismissive of them and indeed all critics of his position, indicating that he had read some of those criticisms but that he wasn't convinced by them. The arrogance of his responses, perhaps an outgrowth of feeling ganged up on by those of us in the workshop, only fueled the discontent among those of us in the room.

Shubri also had a tendency to come up with hypothetical situations that he thought supported his position that men should have a legal say in abortion decisions. One such example included the hypothetical "case" of a woman who had consensual sex with a man and the man used a condom. "What if," he inquired, "after he leaves, she pulls the condom out of the trash can and inseminates herself with his semen or pokes a hole in the condom before they use it?" Each of his hypothetical situations offered portrayals of manipulative women, femme fatales that were out to trap men by getting pregnant. They were situations much more likely to be found in fictitious films or dramatic television shows than in the real world. The likelihood that they happened in the real world at all was slim, especially when compared with the prominence of, say, men abandoning women with whom they have produced children. Members of the gender workshop tried to explain to Shubri that the examples he was giving were largely fictional and that we were all better served by discussing empirical data that are more likely to capture the implications of his policy suggestions. But when it comes to sexism and misogyny, it seems that it is easy to lose track of empirical evidence in favor of rehashing cultural stereotypes of women out to get their claws into men.

At some point during the meeting, it became clear to me that Professor Shubri was not listening to the comments by those of us in the workshop and that workshop members were remaining professional in their approach to the issues. I knew from conversations with a number of the women prior to the meeting that they were outraged by what he had written and interpreted his suggestion that men have legal rights in abortion situations as a personal attack on their bodily integrity. Yet this outrage was not allowed to emerge in the discussion because of the norms of academic debate and engagement. Yet the professor was permitted to be arrogant, flippantly dismissing the well-thought-out criticisms of the women in the room. It was not that he had to agree with the women; it was that he was totally dismissive of them. It was clear to me that a number of them were becoming visibly agitated with him, not unlike how women often become visibly agitated or uncomfortable with men who sexually harass them but their discontent does not seem to register with the men harassing them. As I watched this play out, I recognized that if the women should express their outrage in any way other than reserved and academic, they ran the risk of falling into the stereotype of emotional women. The norms of academic decorum favored his sexism over their outrage.

My observation of these processes playing out made me angry, and I decided to disrupt the flow of the discussion by expressing my anger. My emotions were legitimate, but my decision to express them in an "unprofessional" way was strategic. When I had the opportunity to speak, I pointed out to Shubri that, as men, we need to recognize the effects of what we say and do on women in our lives, trying to point out that many women in the room had expressed discontent almost uniformly against what he had written in the op-ed piece and then said during the discussion. I purposely then advised that he spend more time listening to women rather than merely defending himself.

At this point, he took offense to my comments, presumably because they came across as condescending. He interrupted me by pointing out that I had called his wife a vessel for his kids in my written response to his essay, to which I responded, "No, *you* referred to your wife as a vessel!"

The exchange continued to escalate, and I cannot remember exactly how it played out, but it concluded with me shouting at him, "Who the fuck do you think you are?!" Although I had planned on expressing emotions to break up the intellectualizing tone of the exchange, I had not planned on shouting profanities at him. I was embarrassed that I had done that, yet other graduate students were supportive after the meeting when we debriefed in private. We were all shaken by how arrogant and dismissive the professor had been. I was also troubled because my emotional exchange with Shubri became the highlight of the meeting; I felt that although my intentions were to be disruptive of the academic status quo by reacting emotionally, as a man, to the ideas and actions of Professor Shubri, I had unintentionally hijacked the meeting so that it became between the two of us, making everyone else auxiliary to our argument. Coincidentally, the date of the special gender workshop was also the date of our department holiday party held in the apartment of a faculty member. My concerns of having hijacked the meeting were confirmed when the first thing the professor did when he arrived at the party was come up to me and shake my hand. I know he meant well, but there was something decidedly masculine about the act, as if I had somehow earned his respect by having verbally sparred with him. The brief hand-shaking interaction struck me as something that would have been off limits to me had I been a woman.

Striving to Be Queer in the Academe

The events surrounding Carius Shubri's op-ed piece in *The New York Times* illuminate how challenging it can be to strive to be queer in both the content and form of what we say and do. Academic forms of interaction are supposed to be rational, reserved, and impersonal. Yet Shubri, because of his privilege, could share and have his experiences and views validated publicly in the pages of *The New York Times*.

Looking back, there were at least two interrelated influences upon my decision to take action. These factors provide some guidelines for academics who wish to challenge inequities in academia. First, I had read quite a bit of feminist scholarship because of courses I had taken that covered feminist theory, gender and reproduction, gender and the law, and family studies. I had also focused one of my comprehensive exams in the area of gender on my way to getting my PhD. This reading exposed me to the works of Audre Lorde and bell hooks, among many others. In Lorde's (1984: 113) classic essay on the "master's tools," she eloquently criticizes the pattern of marginalized groups having to educate privileged groups as "a diversion of energies and a tragic repetition of racist patriarchal thought." And bell hooks (1984: 24) explicitly defines feminism not as an identity, but as "a struggle to end sexist oppression." This means that to advocate for feminist ideals requires taking action, not merely identifying as a feminist.

Despite what I am sure they thought were their good intentions, men in the department were reinforcing a sexist pattern of behavior—doing nothing when they should have spoken out—that supported the status quo and, in turn, their (and my) own masculine privilege. Their inaction was an outgrowth of their own self-imposed ignorance. After all, one of the marks of privilege is that the privileged get to choose when to engage in social justice practice, if we choose to engage at all. Men's uncertainty about how to participate is itself a reflection of our collective privilege of not really having to be bothered with such thoughts. It is not surprising, then, that when confronted with an event that is patently racist, sexist, homophobic, or otherwise unjust, men (and other privileged group members) are often paralyzed by uncertainty.

The men's inaction highlights the dangers of understanding politics in terms of identity rather than action. For example, on the heels of the events surrounding Professor Shubri's op-ed piece, I had a telling exchange with a fellow graduate student, a friend who privately expressed his support for my actions. I asked him why he had not also participated in the exchange, and he indicated that he felt it was not his place to do so. Despite his generally egalitarian profeminist beliefs, he seemed paralyzed by the situation, unable to find a way into the conversation. In the end, his response, like that of all the other men in the department, was to do nothing. I suspect that disagreeing privately with Professor Shubri's actions left undisturbed my friend's identity as a "good guy." By framing their profeminist orientations as an identity I suspect many men in the department felt, like my friend, that the issue was not theirs to argue, even as potential allies of women in the department. This, of course, was a gendered pattern of (non)response that supported the sexist status quo. It also left undisturbed the general sense that people in the department and beyond really were divided along gender lines (the gender-wars framing of the issue). The good news was that the reality of the situation was that many men were potential allies in the struggle, that they framed their interests in ways other than the gender-wars approach. The bad news was that these men's support generally remained unspoken and therefore politically useless. Thus, a critical political opportunity to take queer action was lost.

The second and related catalyst for my decision to take action in response to Professor Shubri's essay was that I had read a lot of profeminist men's writings and had conducted research on profeminist male activists earlier in my graduate student career (O'Brien and Armato 2001). I found in these profeminist men models for antisexist practice. In one interview with an antiviolence activist, a man shared with me a mantra of one of the founders of his antirape organization: "We live in a society in which bad men rape, good men do nothing, and I can't tell the difference" (O'Brien and Armato 2001: 281). Other men I interviewed underscored the need for men to act more toward feminist goals. My knowledge that there were many men across the United States and beyond who had become allies in the struggle for social justice aided me in seeing that not only was it possible that I *could* participate, but also that I *should* take action in support of social justice in the academe, and that I should do so in a way that does not reproduce my privileged status. This last point gets at the heart of what it means to strive toward being queer. Academia—like the social world beyond—is a decidedly unqueer place. We live our lives within the categories that help constitute the socially produced inequalities of race, class, gender, and sexuality. We do so individually through our identities, interactionally through our face-to-face dealings with others, and collectively through our participation in and support of societal institutions.

As I have noted, striving to be queer refers to destabilizing those categories most people take for granted in everyday life. Striving toward queerness also means that I need to try to undermine the categories through *how* I choose to engage in my struggles toward social justice. Striving toward queerness while engaging with others is not easy to do because people, men and women, have trouble understanding me in any other way than through the heterosexist, racist, patriarchal categories that define (and privilege) me. For example, struggling for gender justice could be understood by others as me fighting on behalf of women in a way that enhances my status as a "chivalrous" heterosexual man, making me a "gentleman." This is not a queer approach.

No matter what my political beliefs may be, by default I am perceived of as a White heterosexual man as I move through the social world. This means I do not have to do anything in particular to receive the privileges associated with my dominant group statuses. When striving toward queerness, I must continually act in ways that undermine the categories of privilege and oppression. This is not merely about transgressing at the individual and interactional levels. It includes fighting institutional policies that marginalize specific groups of people.

Both of the factors that helped produce my decision to act when confronted with an unjust situation suggest that we, as academicians, can take actions that strive to queer the universities where we work. Below I conclude with some ideas for what we can do toward such ends.

As teachers, we can do much more to incorporate noncanonical and dissident voices into our curricula. We can also seek out examples from across historical time and place that destabilize commonly held knowledge about the world. My own exposure to feminist women's and profeminist men's writings and activism provided me with a framework for understanding and guidelines for taking action to oppose sexism in the academe. The insights garnered from this reading are central to the challenges I pose to racist, heterosexist, patriarchal, and classist practices. Providing our students with these materials also helps blur the line between academic work and political action. Academic feminism, especially recent work by women of color, has always been linked with activism. Similarly, marginalized peoples have long connected their understanding and critique of the world's injustices with the struggle to challenge those injustices. By incorporating noncanonical, liberatory scholarship into our classes, we also set an example for future generations of scholars while building up resources for our colleagues to make similar efforts. I was fortunate enough to have briefly studied under Joe Feagin, someone quite critical of the false distinction between academics and activism. Professor Feagin also exposed his students to the long tradition of critical, liberatory scholarship in our field (e.g., Feagin and Vera 2008; Vaughan, Sjoberg, and Reynolds 1993).

As researchers, we can take seriously the insights developed by marginalized peoples and resist the depoliticizing forces imposed upon us by our respective fields. This means that we keep power and inequalities central to our analyses. It also means remaining critical of how our concepts and frameworks may reproduce the inequities that we seek to redress by theorizing dominant group experiences as if they were universal (Collins 1990; Smith 1990). It also means that we make clear the links between our own research and its political implications. This includes discussing policy implications, but it likely also means unabashedly taking part in collective action for social change on and off campus.

Finally, as colleagues in our departments and on our campuses, we can strive to be queer in all the actions that produce inequalities on campus. Given how profoundly nonqueer institutions are in their everyday operations, there is no limit to the ways we can challenge inequalities. As a White heterosexual man, I volunteer to take on work that is often forced upon women through a generally accepted division of gendered labor in the academe that makes the work that women do invisible. In addition to undermining the gendered and racialized division of work by taking on more work, we can fight to get the work that others do acknowledged by administrators and our own departments. As colleagues, we can also strive to be queer by challenging the race-, gender-, class-, and sexuality-based assumptions that guide so much of our daily activities. This means that as dominant group members, we need to serve as allies in the struggles of our colleagues—faculty and staff—at our universities that do not share our privileged status. To do this effectively, we need to listen to the concerns of those who are marginalized and also take it upon ourselves to educate ourselves about key issues in their plight. We can no longer not act because of our ignorance or because we define ourselves as good liberals. We need to be committed to taking action to challenge inequalities in all their forms, even if it is inconvenient (or if we do not yet have tenure).

Notes

1   The name is a pseudonym.
2   Although the public response in my department was lacking, there was extensive online discussion in various feminist-oriented discussion groups and blogs. Professor Shubri also received huge numbers of e-mails from irate readers across the nation.

CHAPTER FIVE

One Activist Intellectual's Experience in Surviving and Transforming the Academy

Jose Guillermo Zapata Calderon

My survival in higher education has its roots in the connections between my lived experience as the immigrant son of farm worker parents and the lessons learned in overcoming systemic obstacles as a community organizer and intellectual activist. Whenever the road in academia got rough and I had to face another hurdle, I always remembered the difficulties that my immigrant farm worker family had to face. In this way, the problems I encountered in academia appeared smaller and more manageable. My struggles with learning English and growing up in a poor immigrant farm worker family became the foundations of language, labor, and immigration issues that I passionately took up in my organizing, teaching, and research as an activist intellectual in academia.

* * *

I have survived the ivory tower by being proactive in both finding and creating spaces that bridge the gaps between the academic world and community-based projects for action and social change. This has included organizing not only in the community, but organizing on the campus to validate the significance of the carpentry that it takes to build such spaces. In his article "College in the Community," sociologist John Wallace provides a glimpse of "what college education could be" if such spaces were created "with reality, with diverse disciplines, with a community of co-learners, with true self, and with purposes larger than the self" (2000: 762). For intellectual activists or organic public intellectuals who are tenacious in constructing such spaces in higher education, the obstacles are immense. It does mean creating a balance between the personal and political to advance ongoing educational and societal structural changes that recognize the significance of teaching and learning outside the traditional walls of academia.

The immensity of this endeavor has been recognized by the American Sociological Association (ASA). Through the efforts of 2004 president Michael Burawoy, a Task Force on Institutionalizing Public Sociologies (2005: 2) acknowledged that "despite the long-standing tradition of American public sociology going back to the nineteenth century, the work of public sociologists traditionally has not been recognized, rewarded, or encouraged in many of our sociology departments." A step in this direction is the task force's call to academia to recognize, validate, evaluate, and reward public sociology as both an applied and scholarly enterprise.

Public sociology has particular salience for historically excluded individuals from diverse racial, class, gender, and sexuality backgrounds, for whom the educational experience can be both an alienating and empowering experience. This chapter chronicles my journey in public sociology. It is a narrative about finding one's passion in one's lived experience as a foundation for overcoming obstacles in academia, connecting an engaged pedagogy to social activism, and advancing social change practices through learning, teaching, and research transformations.

Early Foundations of Academic Survival

As an immigrant who arrived in the United States at the age of seven, I did not know any English. I experienced the discrimination that many non-English-speaking students faced in the schools. My first six months in first grade were spent not understanding a word the teachers said. Everyone thought something was wrong with me. I learned how to organize every hour of my day at school so that I could make it through the day without speaking to anyone. I ensured that my bathroom breaks were after classes. To avoid interaction with anyone, I always ran home at noon for lunch. However, there were times during the winter when I was forced to bring my sack lunch to school. This practice stopped when a group of students made fun of the bean tacos my mother had made for me. After this experience, when the winter snows kept me inside, I quietly slipped away and hid in another room while my classmates ate their lunches.

I learned English with the help of a teacher who realized that there was nothing wrong with my ability to speak. She realized that I was silent most of the time because I did not understand the language. This teacher, Mrs. Elder, began to stay with me after school. She began by pretending to want to learn Spanish. In the process, she learned some Spanish and I learned to speak English. A half-dozen other Mexican students who were part of my first grade class eventually dropped out. They were not provided the same opportunity since, structurally, bilingual education had not been established at the time. Later, when I was a student at the University of Colorado, I went back and carried out research on these students, many of whom were working in low-paying jobs as waiters, truck drivers, and farm laborers. When I wrote a paper on these students, I realized that many of them had never learned English.

My research revealed the price I had had to pay for "making" it through the school system.[1] The school promoted assimilation, calling me the "good Spanish boy." Those who dropped out were called "Mexican." In my school, being called "Mexican" was a fighting word. The teachers had created a culture where being "Spanish" was acceptable and "Mexican" was not.

Unbeknownst to the teachers, I kept my Mexican culture, including the Spanish language, because of the persistence of my parents. They continued to emphasize that I was Mexican, that I should be proud of it, and that I should know my language. Knowledge of the Spanish language became a means of survival for me economically and academically. When I was in junior high school, I contributed to my family's finances by working as an interpreter in a local clothing store. In tenth grade, when everyone was required to take another language, I shined in Spanish classes and got straight A's. For the first time in my life, the Euro-American students were coming and asking me for help. My Spanish also helped me survive graduate school. When I was at the last steps of finishing my PhD, one of the requirements at UCLA was that one had to take a sociology exam in another language. The test required one to read excerpts from various sociology journals and answer multiple-choice questions based on the content. Many of these articles were difficult to understand in English, let alone in another language. I was able to whisk through the exam because of my Spanish.

Early Connections between the Academy and Social Change

Encouraged by a high school counselor to succeed in sports, I attended Northeastern Junior College in Sterling, Colorado, on a track scholarship. By my second year, I got involved in student government and decided to focus on my studies. I worked alongside other students in questioning why a meatpacking plant across from the library created such a bad odor that permeated the whole city. Some of us began to research the plant and found that the company had been cited for polluting a stream near the plant site. We took our research and turned it into action by organizing a demonstration that resulted in the closing of the plant until it dealt with its pollution problems. The significance of this first organizing experience is that I began to learn about the potential for turning research data into action for social change. Motivated by this discovery, I applied and was accepted to the University of Colorado (CU) as a major in communications.

At the University of Colorado, I survived by continuing to connect the classroom to social issues and by continuing my involvement in student government. I took various sociology and political science courses that introduced me to the debates that were going on about the war in Vietnam. In one sociology course, I challenged a professor who said that he had two positions on the war: one was his personal position and the other was his "institutional" position. My questioning led to a panel debate on the meaning of the word "integrity" in the class. Little by little, my convictions deepened my commitment to the antiwar movement. Subsequently, as vice president of the student government,

I joined the antiwar movement on campus and helped organize a rally of ten thousand students in support of a national student strike against the war in 1970. Instead of completely shutting down the university, we turned this action into a learning moment during the last two weeks of the spring quarter. By working collectively with dozens of students and faculty, I learned about the power of popular education and how it could be implemented in opening a new university that connected classes in the various disciplines with study and debate on the educational system and how it was affected by an unjust war. Subsequently, we had media students writing columns and letters to the newspaper, engineering students building peace domes, and art students creating murals and posters on the effects of the war. One of our efforts included placing various billboards throughout the city depicting a young dead soldier on the ground with an inscription reading "Dear Mom and Dad Your Silence is Killing Me in Viet Nam."

During my involvement in the antiwar movement, between 1968 and 1971, I also became active in the struggles to get more students of color on campus. I joined the United Mexican American Students in asking for funds to develop summer programs to prepare Chicano/a students to go to college. We occupied a building on campus when Board of Regents representative Joe Coors took a position that minority students were less qualified than other students to attend the university and that no funds should be used for their recruitment. The first summer programs were developed after we were able to show that there were dozens of qualified Chicano/a students who could be admitted to the university but who lacked the necessary resources to survive. Out of those summer programs, I met students who eventually went on to become social workers, teachers, lawyers, doctors, community organizers, and political leaders.

While organizing on campus, I met various students who were involved with a farm worker support group on the campus. In addition to getting the student senate to allocate funds for the group, I joined them in traveling to Center, Colorado, and joining striking lettuce workers on the picket line. It also led me to make connections between the farm worker movement and the antiwar movement. For one of my classes at CU, I wrote a paper called "Rhetoric of the Chicano Movement."

In looking at the persuasion strategies of leaders in the Chicano/a movement, I was most impressed with the strategies of Cesar Chavez. In carrying out the research, I was shocked to find that the Defense Department, under the Nixon administration, was buying tons of grapes when the farm workers were on strike (Del Castillo and Garcia 1995: 92). This really affected me since I had witnessed the burial of various friends who had died in the war. On the one hand, the labor of the farm workers was being used to increase the profits and power of large agribusiness corporations (Barger and Reza 1994: 22–25). On the other, the sons of these farm workers were being drafted in disproportionate numbers, representing 20 percent of those who died on the front lines (Gonzalez 1999: 211–213).

Feeling that I could do something about these injustices, I decided to go and learn firsthand about Cesar Chavez's union. With only $57 in my pocket, I caught a Greyhound bus that took me to Delano, California, where I observed the organizing strategies of Cesar Chavez and the violence being waged by the growers against the farm workers. I also heard a speech by Cesar Chavez that changed my life. In challenging the young students volunteering with the union, Cesar proposed that "we have only one life to live" and that "the highest level of using your life is in service to others." It was after this experience that I made the decision to return to northern Colorado and to use my education to organize against systemic injustices that had kept farm worker and immigrant communities at the lowest levels of the economic ladder. The sacrifices of farm worker organizers, including Cesar Chavez, who received only five dollars a week for their organizing efforts, inspired me in this direction.

Connecting Popular Education to Community Organizing

Galvanized by my experience with the farm workers, I returned to Ault, Colorado, where I had grown up, and began my organizing efforts. I first developed a community center out of a garage in my parents' backyard. Remembering the difficulties I had faced in not knowing English at an early age, I used the methods of Paulo Freire in teaching young Mexican children to speak English.[2] These educational strategies would later become a part of my teaching methods in the college classroom. I also used the research skills that I had obtained from my undergraduate education to discover that eight out of ten Mexican children who started in the first grade in Ault eventually dropped out of school. After learning this information, the students and their parents collectively used this research to appear before the school board to demand that bilingual education be instituted in the school district. The response of one school board member was that if we wanted bilingual education, we could "return to Mexico." This response led to a seventy-mile protest march from Ault to the state capital in Denver. Our efforts, coupled with organized student walkouts, led to an ongoing social movement in the region that resulted in the establishment of bilingual education programs and the hiring of bilingual teachers and administrators in many Weld County schools.

As a result of these organizing efforts in the next few years, I was asked to teach a class called "The Community" at Aims Junior College. The class was my first major experience in having students connect the classroom to community service and social change issues. Hearing about the successes of the class, the Sociology Department chair at the University of Northern Colorado asked me to teach a similar class there. Before long, without a master's degree, I was teaching as much as a full-time professor (on part-time pay). The experience of teaching sociology classes strengthened my affinity for the field of sociology. Simultaneously, it allowed me to experiment with various forms of using critical pedagogy and research by having students conduct research on migrant housing through the Colorado Migrant Council and volunteer at a community center that we developed in the north side of Greeley, Colorado. I did not know it then, but these organizing efforts laid the foundation I needed to complete my PhD and be a teacher and researcher at the college level. Like other activists of this time period, I began my teaching at the university without a PhD (Ichioka 2006: 281).

For the next twelve years, I survived on little income, but I was sustained by the spirit and passion of the farm worker, immigrant, student, and poor communities that I collaborated with. Working with various national organizations, such as the Workers Viewpoint, I was motivated to look beyond issues of race to working-class issues that affected low-income people from all racial/ethnic backgrounds. The unity of multiracial leaders who turned away from luxury to devote their lives to building a more just and equal society energized me.

Challenges to Economic and Activist Survival

In 1984, after marrying and having children, I faced the reality of looking for a long-term career that would allow me to meet my responsibilities to my family as well as allow me to continue my commitment to community organizing and social change. After coming across an announcement for a graduate fellowship at UCLA, I filled out an application and obtained recommendation letters from my former undergraduate professors. In June of 1984, I was accepted to UCLA. Although saddened at the prospect of leaving our friends and their families, my wife, Rose, and I agreed that that we could no longer survive on part-time jobs in the Greeley area and that we had to plan for the long term.

After saying good-bye to friends, we drove to Los Angeles in a U-Haul truck with our two young boys in the front and our belongings packed in the back. Rose obtained employment as an administrative assistant with the Mexican American Legal Defense and Education Fund, and I obtained a part-time job as a counselor with the Optimist Boy's Home in Highland Park. This highly demanding job involved implementing counseling projects to advance teamwork and leadership skills among one hundred young men who were primarily referrals from the County Department of Probation. My life consisted of managing the freeway from our apartment in El Sereno to classes at UCLA, working at the Boy's Home, studying at the library, and juggling home and day-care chores with Rose.

Unhappy with this new life, I longed to return to my life of community organizing in rural Colorado. At UCLA, I became part of a graduate student cohort group that focused on comparative and historical sociology. While enthralled by the readings, I was frustrated by the lack of connections between the classroom and community-based issues. I had envisioned UCLA's sociology graduate school program as one that was engaged with the urban problems faced by the mosaic of diverse communities in

Los Angeles, but my classes focused primarily on historical comparisons and theory that lacked grounding in participatory transformative social change. My involvement in various study groups and my teaching experience in Colorado had provided me with some understanding of the theories of power and conflict, particularly Marxism. I used this understanding to critique the arguments in the assigned readings. Rather than simply analyzing the authors' data, my arguments centered on whether the theories would be useful as agents of social change. The discussions in the class appeared to be polemical—so I made them polemical.

At the time, I didn't fully understand why the professors and some students would roll their eyes when I spoke. In the ensuing months, I learned that the task was to find "holes" in the authors' arguments regardless of what significance their arguments had to our lived experienced and practices in social justice organizing. It is this connection between intellectual activity and "the experience of human beings in a specific community at a certain moment in history . . . a social interaction involving both thought and feeling" that is often missing in the academic classroom (Shor 1992: 22). By the second semester, when I had begun to figure out what the professors wanted, I was already making plans to complete my master's degree and quit the PhD program to work in a union.

In the Optimist Boy's Home, I also faced the frustration of having to do "therapy sessions" with dozens of Latino and African American teenagers without any room to empower them or to create structural changes in the institution. Tired of the bureaucracy, I went to the campus employment office and found an internship with the city manager's office in the city of Monterey Park.

Connecting Research with Community Organizing

This internship led to my involvement in the city and fostered my survival in the PhD program. In the mid-1980s, Monterey Park was going through a dramatic demographic transformation that reflected the larger changes taking place in California. Monterey Park's population had gone from 85 percent Euro-American, 3 percent Asian and 12 percent

Latino/a in 1960 to 56 percent Asian American, 31.3 percent Latino/a, and 11.7 percent Euro-American in 1990. When I started working in the city manager's office, Monterey Park had just received a national designation as an "All-America City" for its innovative volunteer programs that reached out to new Chinese immigrants. At the same time, an organized backlash against the unbridled growth policies of the city council had begun. As part of blaming the "growth" problems on the new Chinese immigrants, an all-White city council passed an "English only" ordinance making English the official language of the city, calling for the local police to cooperate with the Immigration and Naturalization Service, and giving nonsupport to any city that advocated sanctuary for immigrants. As an intern in the city manager's office, I was assigned to carry out research on the passage of a similar ordinance in the city of Fillmore. I was almost fired by the city manager when I used the research to criticize the city council, at one of their open meetings, for passing such a racist measure. By the time my internship was coming to an end, I was already involved as a community organizer, resident, and cochair of a coalition to defeat the English-only initiative.

In 1988 and 1990, I complemented my organizing activities in the community by working as a researcher with Professor John Horton of the UCLA Department of Sociology and a seven-member local research team in a study of the politics of conflict and cooperation in Monterey Park.[3] My research, as part of the study of demographic transformations taking place in Los Angeles County, where racial minorities and new immigrants are becoming the majority, focused on the changing ethnic and class alliances between Latinos/as, old residents, and new Asian Pacific immigrants.

The Monterey Park research project brought together what I had been looking for in the academic world: a concrete connection between sociological theories and the lived experiences of diverse communities in an urban setting. The project also created a space for my passion as a former immigrant, an activist, and a researcher working for social change. The experience strengthened my commitment to finish my dissertation and provided a glimpse of how I could connect the academic world with community-based participatory research, teaching, and learning.

Rather than perpetuating the traditional idea that research-ers should not participate in the organizations they study, the project allowed for my involvement as an organizer and researcher in the com-munity. My data was gathered from field notes written from my lived experience as a resident in the community and from my participation in numerous community-based organizations.[4] I remained conscious throughout the process of representing the meanings and actions of the participants without discounting my own perspectives as a participant. After my thesis proposal was reviewed and accepted, I learned that the time between the proposal and the actual writing of the dissertation is crucial in finishing the PhD. I applied some of the recommendations from David Sternberg's (1981) *How to Complete and Survive a Doctoral Dissertation* for my own academic survival, including prioritizing my commitments to ensure a focus on the task at hand, ensuring a balance between my academic and family responsibilities, putting aside at least three hours a day to writing, organizing a personal file system, develop-ing a support network, and finding employment with a flexible environ-ment. My support network included employment as a graduate research assistant with the Chicano Studies Research Center and involvement with other Latino/a graduate students through the Raza Grad Student Organization. We organized the latter group to bring students together to share, socialize, mentor, and to survive the academy. We developed our own newsletter and at one point organized a demonstration to advo-cate for our rights as graduate students. To this day, I have close ties with many of these friends who are now colleagues in various colleges throughout the country.

In addition to these networks of support, there were various pro-fessors, such as John Horton, David Lopez, David Hayes-Bautista, and Edna Bonacich, who took the time to mentor me and other Latino/a students. They encouraged me to utilize my ability to tell stories as a vehicle for ethnographic research.[5] Another professor, Richard Berk, saved me from drowning in a required two-quarter statistics course by creatively integrating storytelling in his assignments. Rather than writing endless formulas from the textbooks on the board and moving ahead before we could explain our confusion, this professor connected statistical theories and formulas to data that involved compelling issues in our lives. Analyzing historical data on the death penalty taught us the meaning of "longitudinal concepts." I remember the excitement I felt when he complimented my analysis of statistical data on the economic conditions of farm workers in the United States.[6]

I survived the dissertation process, graduated from UCLA in 1991, and landed a position in sociology and Chicano Studies at Pitzer College in Claremont, California.[7] I had planned with my family to return to Colorado, but there were no jobs available there in my field at the time. Nevertheless, I was drawn to Pitzer by its ethos of advancing intercultural and interdisciplinary understanding in the context of social responsibility. It was the type of place that fit with my passion of connecting the academic world with social change.

For six years, I had driven twenty-five miles west from Monterey Park to UCLA. Now, I drove thirty miles east from Monterey Park to Pitzer in Claremont. The distance added to the difficulties of finding a balance between my teaching and committee work on campus and my family and organizing activities in the community. The only way I could do all this and still find time to conduct research was to continue to develop creative ways of connecting the classroom with the community and to write about it.

Connecting Teaching and Research to School Transformations

When a series of fights erupted between Latino and Chinese American students at a high school that my son attended, I joined with other parents in organizing a coalition, the Multi-Cultural Community Association, to resolve these conflicts. After numerous meetings between the leaders in the Latino/a and Asian Pacific communities, we successfully pressured school administrators to establish an official advisory group to the school board, the Alhambra School District Human Relations Advisory Committee.

In this committee, I worked in the dual roles of researcher and committee chair. As a researcher, I worked alongside the community representatives to counter the views of some administrators who blamed the conflicts on the "hormones" of the students. The survey showed that 86 percent of the students at Mark Keppel High School and a majority of the students at all three high schools in the district perceived racial tensions as a big problem.

At the same time, at Pitzer I collaborated with sociology professor Betty Farrell in developing a conflict-resolution service learning class. In addition to encouraging students to conduct research on a multicultural curriculum and ethnic conflict-resolution programs, this class provided students with a unique opportunity to help the Alhambra School District assess the effectiveness of its policies for dealing with racial and ethnic conflict (Calderon and Farrell 1996). The foundation of the program was the training the students received in ethnographic research and the literature related to ethnic conflict resolution. The students' research included the gathering of census data and information from the district's schools (e.g., ethnic makeup, dropout and expulsions rates, etc.) and interviews with students, teachers, and administrators that identified issues confronting ethnic/racial groups in the district.

Ultimately, the Alhambra School District's Human Relations Advisory Committee utilized the collaborative research of the coalition and Pitzer students to develop a policy on hate-motivated behavior and to implement a racial/ethnic sensitivity program for all teachers. As part of this policy, the school district institutionalized conflict-resolution classes as part of the curriculum and gave students the option of mediation as an alternative to expulsion (Calderon 1995).

Connecting Service Learning to the Farm Worker and Day Laborer Experience

In reflecting on my lived experience as a farm worker and the impact that Cesar Chavez had on my life, I sought to develop a class that would have the same influence that the farm worker social movement had on my life. Out of this passion and with the help of various farm worker contacts, I developed another service learning class called Rural and Urban Ethnic Movements. In this class, now in its seventeenth year, students learn about community-based organizing theories and how they apply to the civil rights, farm worker, immigrant, and contemporary social movements (Barger and Reza 1994; Broyles-Gonzales 1994; Bulosan 1984; Buss 1993; Del Castillo and Garcia 1995; Edid 1994; Ferris and Sandoval 1997; Ganz 2009; Rose 1990; Ross 1989; Scharlin and Villanueva 2006; Shaw 2008; Weber 1994; Wells 1996; Zavella 1987).

During the spring break, the class visits the historical sites of the United Farm Workers Union in La Paz (Keene, California) and Delano. The students learn from farm worker leaders about the history of the movement, particularly the strategies that the union has used to survive. In return, the students implement service projects based on the union's needs. In the first alternative spring break in 1994, alongside Filipino American leader Pete Velasco, the students planted one hundred roses at the gravesite of Cesar Chavez. In the following year they helped to clean up after a flood hit the community. Seven years ago the students carried rocks from a nearby creek to help build the foundation for a Cesar Chavez Memorial. That experience involved students from Vina Danks Middle School, located in the nearby city of Ontario, and day laborers from the Pomona Day Labor Center. This collaboration resulted in the painting of two murals, one at Vina Danks and one at the day labor center, led by community-based artist Paul Botello. More recently, the students traveled to Delano and began framing the pictures of sixty Filipino farm workers who, because of antimiscegenation laws in California, never married and passed away in an elderly farm worker village, Agbayani Village (Calderon and Cadena 2007).

When I began the service learning project with the farm workers, another opportunity for a service learning site came forward when the city of Pomona passed a resolution in 1996 that anyone caught on a corner asking for jobs could be fined $1,000 and spend six months in jail. The ordinance was clearly aimed at the community's growing day laborer population. I was teaching a class, Restructuring Communities, when immigrant rights activist and Pitzer student Fabian Nunez organized a coalition of students, day laborers, and community supporters to pack city hall. When the city council argued that it could not fund a center for undocumented workers, the students gathered research showing that many of the day laborers were also permanent residents. In 1998, these efforts led to the establishment of a nonprofit day labor center, $50,000 in funding from the Pomona city council, and an advisory board that included Pitzer students and faculty. Fabian Nunez, the nonprofit's first board chair, eventually ran for the California state assembly and became one of the most influential Latinos when he was elected as the speaker in Sacramento.[8]

Since the center opened in 1998, students from my classes have joined in collaborative programs with the day laborers in developing employment training programs, health referral networks, immigration rights counseling, and biweekly organizational meetings. In addition to holding language and computer classes every morning, the students have been instrumental in ensuring worker representation on the organization's board. Rather than allowing city officials or consultant "experts" to control the decision-making process, we have organized biweekly meetings to build the collective voice of the workers in running the center. As a result, two day laborers were employed as coordinators and the son of another day laborer is serving as an office administrator. In further advancing the historical partnership between Pitzer College and the day laborers, one of my former students, Suzanne Foster, was hired as the center's director.

In response to the city council's decision to minimally fund the day labor center in the future, we have utilized surveys, questionnaires, and focus groups to establish the amount of resources that the workers have and how they can be maximized.[9] Our collaborative research with the workers has resulted in the writing of various grant proposals to area foundations. One grant helped pay for a day laborer organizer and allowed us to develop a health referral program for the day laborers and their families. Another grant assisted in expanding language, computer, and job-training programs.

Surviving Promotion through Creating Transformative Spaces

I survived the joint appointment pressures and both my tenure and full professor reviews by relying on the support of collective action and by ensuring structural change in my lived environment. Flowing from the vivid examples presented to us by various union organizers in the region, I worked alongside my family, day laborers, students, faculty, and community friends to develop democratic "spaces" that exemplified the type of society we would like to live in. In our home, Rose and I created a culture where we all shared in carrying out the household chores. In the day labor center, the day laborers and students went beyond "charity" services to collaborating in organizing pilgrimage marches in support of driver's licenses for immigrants, pickets of employers who refused to pay, and community "fiestas" to build broad coalitions of support for immigrant rights.

One lesson I have learned in creating a democratic classroom and having students think critically about the social issues around them is that the students' growing conscience and engagement often lead to collective action. This was the case when some students at Pitzer, motivated by their experiences of working in service learning projects with unions, day laborers, and farm workers, joined the college's cafeteria workers in their efforts to obtain higher wages and better health benefits. As early as 1991, when I began as a professor at Pitzer, a collaboration developed between the cafeteria workers and various faculty and student leaders to address worker grievances. One student, Juan de Lara, who later became Pitzer's first Rhodes Scholar, met with cafeteria supervisors when the workers faced problems. This practice continued throughout the years until students and workers agreed that the grievances could be handled more efficiently through a union. After vocal demonstrations by the workers and students, the workers joined the Hotel Employees and Restaurant Employees (HERE) union.

The beauty of having a critical pedagogy turn into practical examples of social change can be exhilarating. On the other hand, it can affect the evaluation process when one comes up for tenure or promotion.

As a junior faculty member, I had to figure out how to publish enough work to ensure tenure. I did this by writing throughout the process of the service learning projects I designed. As a result, I published a number of articles based on my organizing work in Monterey Park, the Alhambra School District, the United Farm Workers Union, and the Pomona Day Labor Center (Calderon 2004b). I also joined a dialogue in the Pitzer Faculty Executive Committee to change the faculty handbook so that it was more inclusive of the teaching, research, and service activities of a public intellectual.[10] Today's faculty handbook includes

sections recognizing the contributions in this realm as part of the contract renewal, promotion, and evaluation process:

> effectiveness inside and outside the classroom,
> sponsorship of internships and other non-traditional
> means of teaching and learning, the supervising of
> student participation in research projects, evidence of
> applied research and/or action research, service to the
> wider community, and acting as an intellectual resource
> for colleagues, students, and the community (Pitzer
> College Faculty Personnel Policies and Procedures
> 2009, Section V-A).

The changes in the faculty handbook, together with the development of a core of faculty who supported service learning initiatives, ultimately helped me to obtain tenure and full professor status. Although
numerous professors supported me in this process, there were struggles
along the way. My ongoing support of the cafeteria workers' unioniz-
ing efforts resulted in a letter from the administration questioning my
involvement as an employee of the college. When I argued for an increase
in the number of underrepresented faculty at one faculty meeting, I was
stunned to hear a professor who considered himself progressive argue
that affirmative action "discriminated against White males." When
some students questioned why various art murals had been painted over,
I stood with the students in their efforts to ensure that designated spaces
were made available on college walls and columns for student-created
art pieces. Mindful that the negativity in these conflicts was stirred by a
small number of individuals, the collaborative governance structure at
Pitzer responded by developing an art committee that included the voice
of the students and changed the faculty handbook in support of specified
affirmative action goals.[11]

In 2004, after overcoming the "full professor" promotion hurdles, I
jumped at the opportunity to apply for a newly created revolving chair
position, the Michi and Walter Weglyn Endowed Chair in Multicultural
Studies, at Cal Poly Pomona University. I was drawn to the position
by the rich diversity among students on the campus, the requisite that
one had to only teach one class per quarter, and the reality that I would

have more time and resources for my service learning and participatory research work in the community.[12]

Moving to Higher Levels in Applying Participatory Service, Teaching, and Research

This two-year position expanded my history of connecting academic teaching and research with community organizing and social change initiatives. Michi and Walter Weglyn, for whom the endowed chair position was named, were examples of individuals who used their lives to carry out research and to use that research in service to the community and to advance social change policies. They were examples not only in the academic sense (with Michi Weglyn producing a book *Years of Infamy: The Untold Story of America's Concentration Camps* [1976]), but also in the participatory action sense. Hence, Michi Weglyn's book and efforts helped advance a movement that eventually led to reparations for more than eighty thousand interned Japanese Americans and exposed the kidnappings of thousands of Japanese Latin Americans who were forcibly held as prisoners of war during World War II.

Since I was the inaugural chair for the position, I had the opportunity to develop a plan and implement it in the context of the Weglyns' visionary commitment to turning learning, teaching, and research into civic engagement. Although I had been implementing aspects of critical pedagogy, multiculturalism, service learning, and participatory research in my academic work, the endowed chair position gave me the time and space to deepen my understanding of these concepts and their integration.[13] Working alongside Professor Gilbert Cadena, professors from the Ethnic and Women's Studies Department, and the Center for Community Service, we developed a faculty learning circle that met every other Friday.[14] The faculty learning circle was a foundation for deepening my study of the project-based approach as described by Randy Stoecker in *Research Methods for Community Change* (2005). It was also a catalyst for working with a diverse group of faculty and students at Cal Poly in developing various interdisciplinary projects at the Pomona Day Labor Center and organizing a campus-wide conference on service learning and participatory research.[15]

In connecting the reading materials in the classroom to the history of local communities, I also had the opportunity to experiment with service learning and participatory research projects that included the contributions of groups that our educational system has had a tendency to marginalize or exclude. As a Civic Scholar with Campus Compact, a national organization of colleges devoted to civic engagement, I had the opportunity to participate in a dialogue with other national scholars on how to make the classroom more a part of the civic realm and to encourage students' skepticism of traditional historical documents.

* * *

In this chapter, I have chosen to tell selected stories from my lived experience that include the lessons learned in surviving the educational system by making learning, teaching, research, and organizing part of a lifelong commitment to advancing social change and social justice. To survive, I have found my passion from reflecting on the "individual issues" that affected my family and working with others in linking these issues to what other oppressed groups have faced historically, placing these issues in a larger context, and implementing strategies for change through nontraditional forms of campus and community engagement.[16]

Along the way, I have had various mentors and teachers who helped me in overcoming academic obstacles: from the support of my family and Raza Graduate Students to various professors in graduate school who helped me make the positive connections between my activism and participatory research.

From graduate school to the present, I have steadily deepened my understanding and implementation of these connections. Through my involvement in the Monterey Park project, I was introduced to the use of ethnographic methodology. As a professor at Pitzer College, I learned to collaborate with other students and professors in applying both service learning and participatory research techniques in implementing solutions to racial conflicts in the schools. Through my work with the United Farm Workers Union and the Pomona Day Labor Center, I learned the importance of making a long-term commitment to a particular site and how service learning and participatory research could move beyond charity to social change and leadership empowerment initiatives. As an endowed chair at Cal Poly Pomona, I had the opportunity and time to work with a diverse group of students and professors in applying aspects of the project-based approach.

As my story has shown, there are spaces in the academy for those who connect their teaching, learning, and research with their passion for social justice. The creation of such democratic spaces takes the organized collective support of family, mentors, colleagues, and community activists who are supporters and participants in transforming the educational system to transform society. The application of a transformative pedagogy, rooted in a passion for overcoming systemic and historical injustices, can determine whether historically excluded individuals and groups can survive the traditional walls of the academy and can play a role in advancing long-term structural changes in the larger society.

Notes

1   For a more developed account of this life experience tied to Chicano history see Calderon 2004a.

2   I used Freire's *Pedagogy of the Oppressed* (2000) in implementing a style of teaching that asked students to express the words that best reflected the day-to-day experiences in their lives. I would write their words on square sheets made from cardboard boxes. On one side, their word was written in English and on the other in Spanish. Eventually, each student owned a box that included dozens of their "own" words. As the students shared each other's words, they began to develop a dialogue in English.

3   One result of this collective project was a book, *The Politics of Diversity* (Horton 1995), and a PBS film, *America Becoming*. Additionally, two other books connected to this project included Leland Saito's *Race and Politics: Asian Americans, Latinos, and Whites in a Los Angeles Suburb* (1998) and Mary Pardo's *Mexican American Women Activists: Identity and Resistance in Two Los Angeles Communities* (1998).

4   At the time, our research team used the ethnographic methodology as prescribed by John and Lyn Lofland in *Analyzing Social Settings: A Guide to Qualitative Observations and Analysis* (1984). At the same time, Linda Shaw trained our team using materials from a book that she would later coauthor with Robert Emerson and Rachel Fretz, *Writing Ethnographic Field Notes*.

5   I have always been good at telling stories. I grew up hearing stories about the history of Mexico through the lived experiences described by my mother. I resonated with author Gloria Anzaldúa's stories, in *Borderlands* (1987), about how her grandmother and father used *cuentos,* much like the indigenous people, to connect the "artistic" with "everyday life."

6   This moment of survival reminded me of another teacher in high school who saw that I was having problems understanding the sine, the cosine (cosecant), and tangent in a geometry class. Rather than ridiculing me in the class, he took me outside with another student and showed me how to measure between buildings. To this day, I have not forgotten those terms and their meanings. In later years, it also taught me the significance of "doing" sociology.

7   The thesis, "Mexican Americans in a Multi-Ethnic Community," was completed in the spring of 1991.

8   The early history of the center is documented in an article, "Organizing Immigrant Workers: Action Research Strategies in the Pomona Day Labor Center," published in the book *Latino Los Angeles* (2006) and written with the collaboration of two former Pitzer College students, Suzanne Foster and Silvia Rodriguez.

9   A dozen students have written their senior theses on the topic of the informal economy, while others have made presentations at the National Association of Chicana and Chicano Studies (NACCS), the American Sociological Association, the American Association of Higher Education, and the Pitzer College Undergraduate Research Conference.

10   Sociology professor Michael Burawoy, when he was president of the American Sociological Association, helped to bring to the forefront the need to appreciate a public sociology "that seeks to bring sociology to publics beyond the academy, promoting dialogues about issues that affect the fate of society" (2004: 104). In August 2004, the Task Force on Institutionalizing Public Sociologies (2005: 2) was developed by the American Sociological Association to develop proposals "for the recognition and validation of public sociology, incentive and rewards for doing public sociology, and evaluating public sociology."

11   Pitzer College adopted an affirmative action policy with the goal "of increasing, during the period 2001–2015, the overall size of the faculty and the proportion of women and persons from underrepresented minorities on the continuing Pitzer faculty from the 1994 31 percent of women faculty members to 50 percent or more, and from 1994 19 percent

of faculty members from underrepresented minorities to 50 percent or more" (Pitzer College Faculty Personnel Policies and Procedures 2001). These goals were met and new goals are being formulated for adoption in the academic year 2010–2011.

12 The endowed chair position allowed me to experiment with carrying out community-based teaching, research, and organizing without the tremendous workload exacted by being in a joint appointment. Most of the faculty of color at the Claremont Colleges, up until 2010 when the policy was changed, were hired in joint appointments that divided their teaching load with three-fifths in a primary discipline and two-fifths in a five-college department (Black Studies, Chicano Studies, Gender and Feminist Studies, or Asian American Studies). Ultimately, the many responsibilities of serving on many committees and having advisees from all five campuses cut into the amount of time that professors could devote to community-based research and service learning. The professors who do carry out these types of pedagogy in the community usually do it out of a deep commitment to the benefits of applied learning. At the same time, they do it with an understanding that this work is not valued as much as traditional academic activities and that it often has to be done above and beyond all the other typical responsibilities of a faculty member.

13 Over the years, I had invested many hours in studying the literature on these methodologies advancing from traditional ethnography to critical pedagogy, action research, participatory research, community-based research, and project-based research. The result has been an ongoing learning process of implementation and collaboration with others in what Randy Stoecker's project-based approach describes as a cycle of diagnosis, prescription, implementation, and evaluation.

14 The faculty learning circle held discussions on such books as *Empowering Education* (Shor 1992) and *Community-Based Research in Higher Education* (Strand et al. 2003).

15 Our version of implementing the project-based approach is described in Calderon and Cadena 2007.

16 C. Wright Mills, in the *Sociological Imagination*, wrote that many personal troubles cannot be solved merely as such, but must be understood in terms of public issues—and in terms of the problems of history making. Within that range the life of the individual and the making of societies occur, and within that range the sociological imagination has its chance to make a difference in the quality of human life in our time (Mills 1959: 226).

CHAPTER SIX

Activist-Scholar Alliances for Social Change

*The Transformative Power of
University-Community Collaborations*

DAVID NAGUIB PELLOW

Since 1985 I have been intimately involved in struggles against environmental racism and human rights abuses occurring in the United States and globally. My activism began with a youth movement organization in my hometown, Nashville, Tennessee, and continued with my participation and leadership in anti-apartheid, solidarity, animal rights, antiracist, global justice, and environmental justice movements. My parents' deep involvement in the civil rights movement in the U.S. South left an unmistakable imprint on my view of the world, and their wisdom continues to shape my thinking and political activities today.

My father recently retired from a successful career as a professor of world history and French literature. During a dinner conversation about social change and the university, he once remarked to me, "I turn out about twenty revolutionaries each year, because I'm teaching students to think critically and to engage the world in that way." I believe that is the greatest potential and power of education. In my own teaching, I strive to make sure my course syllabi, readings, exams, and assignments all push students to think critically about power relations, social hierarchies, and history and, finally, to imagine and actively produce radically different futures. My approach to research mirrors this pedagogical perspective as well—gathering, analyzing, and presenting data from social settings where inequalities are documented and challenged. In so doing, I aim to document and challenge such inequalities myself. What is frustrating for me, though, is that while scholars frequently direct their analytic eye outside the university, we often forget that the university itself can and must be a site of social change.

Some of the most profound social movements have been launched or supported by students, faculty, and staff at colleges and universities around the world. The anti-apartheid, antiwar, free speech, women's rights, civil rights, and third world liberation movements gained power through the influence and participation of people in institutions of higher education. But higher education must also be a site of social change because colleges and universities often participate vigorously in the continued oppression of communities of color, working-class and indigenous communities at home and abroad, through displacement, gentrification, militarization, and the development of scholarship that erases, distorts, and otherwise exerts control over the historical and contemporary realities of various peoples. All too often education has been consciously and deliberately used as a tool of control and social reproduction by political, cultural, and economic elites. In higher educational institutions, military recruiters tempt students with the chance to join the armed forces and be frontline participants in the killing machine that stands in for U.S. diplomacy. At many of these same institutions, the federal government has awarded millions of dollars to support research for war making in general and for the so-called "war on terror" in particular.[1] I once found myself in a briefing about a research program involving my university's personnel and federal resources to develop protections against terrorist bombings and biological warfare. I had the sense that I was present at something closer to a Pentagon briefing than a research update within the academy. And while I *was* in fact in a higher education setting, hundreds of thousands of other African American men like myself are (1) unemployed with few economic or career prospects, (2) fighting the wars for the U.S. empire, or (3) rotting in the prison-industrial complex (there are more African American males in prison than in college—Taylor 2005). Recognition of these practices has necessarily led me to forge progressive community-university collaborations because such partnerships seek to harness the creative power of—and ultimately to transform—both.

Considering the stark realities of institutional violence that people of color and the working classes in the United States and globally face every day, I believe we have an obligation to transform the academy and to work for social justice everywhere we find injustice, drawing on our skills as scholars and teachers. One way to begin this process is to participate in university-community collaborations for the production of sustainable knowledge and social change. Angana Chatterji, a colleague and friend of mine who is also an activist-scholar, once stated that "sustainable knowledge is one of the most important foundations of sustainable communities." I concur. Some of the most exciting research by scholars of social justice and social movements insists that we expand beyond the traditional social scientific fixation upon social movement mobilization, collective action frames, and political opportunity structures to embrace a focus on the production of alternative knowledge. In other words, social movements involved in producing and preserving ideas, ways of knowing, and alternative information systems are engaged in work that is as important to social change as any materially focused tactics and strategies activists may also be pursuing (Rodriguez 2006). "It is precisely in the creation, articulation, and formulation of new thoughts and ideas—new knowledge—that a social movement defines itself in society" (Eyerman and Jamison 1991: 55). If knowledge is at the core of what makes a social movement, then university-based activist-scholars are in a unique position to contribute to social change, since we make a living producing and communicating new knowledge to our students, colleagues, and the public.

Paulo Freire is probably the most famous advocate and architect of the theory and practice of scholar-community collaborations for social change. In his classic work, *Pedagogy of the Oppressed*, he rearticulates the meaning of both education and politics. His analysis pushes the reader to see that both are intimately and necessarily linked. Freire's framework requires that teacher and student, scholar and citizen, work together in as nonhierarchical a process as possible so that both may be transformed through this exercise. Other scholars have proposed much more specific programs for political education and social change.

For example, today there is a growing body of scholarship on university-community research and teaching partnerships. I focus on this topic because it involves efforts on the part of university scholars, students, and members of the public to produce new knowledge for mutually beneficial outcomes that are directed toward social change. Much of the writing on these collaborations addresses the difficulties of making such partnerships work, the dilemmas of the various hierarchies that persist between educational institutions and community-based organizations (CBOs) and among primarily European American middle-class male academics and a much less privileged and more ethnically diverse citizenry, and the mechanics of engaging various projects for the benefit of a broader community (see Cable and Hastings 2005; Knapp 1998; Maurrasse 2002; Nyden et al. 1997; Park and Pellow 1996; Shefner and Cobb 2002). However, not enough scholars working in the area of community-university partnerships discuss their work in terms that speak to (a) the possibilities for a broader transformation of the academy and/or (b) broader progressive movements for social justice.

In this chapter, I want to present the university-community collaborative as a method of transforming both community and the academy. I explore two cases in which I and other faculty members, students, and community leaders coordinated research and action efforts to achieve both educational and social change goals. These collaborations reveal how scholars and activists can shape public spaces and universities in positive ways. My personal involvement in both cases made it possible to develop an insider's viewpoint, but I also felt it was important to step back to reflect on the significance of these projects.

Transatlantic Initiative on Environmental Justice

Since 1992, my major research, teaching, and service energies have been focused on environmental justice movements and the problem of environmental racism. Poor and working-class people of all racial and ethnic backgrounds are frequently relegated to the least desirable neighborhoods with poor housing quality and often in close proximity to locally unwanted landfills, incinerators, and polluting factories (Pellow 2007), and they are often forced to work in the most dangerous, toxic, and low-paying jobs, when they can secure employment at all (Pellow and Park 2002). These populations are also routinely negatively affected by development and planning decisions around natural resource extraction and management. While these social and environmental insults dispro-portionately impact poor people around the world in general, they have a particularly intense impact on ethnic and racial minorities and indige-nous peoples globally. In the United States context, this includes Native Americans, Asian Pacific Americans, African Americans, and Latinos/as. Much of the research on environmental racism has emerged from col-laborations between scholars and activists, and I have drawn inspiration from these models of political education and activist scholarship (see Pellow and Brulle 2005).

Most of the scholarship on environmental racism focuses on the United States primarily, and secondarily on communities in Africa, Asia, and Latin America. Until very recently, environmental racism in Europe was not given much attention. Recently, scholars, activists, and lawyers from environmental and human rights organizations in Bulgaria, the Czech Republic, Hungary, Macedonia, Romania, and Slovakia came together to form the Coalition for Environmental Justice (CEJ) in cen-tral and eastern Europe (CEE). This coalition was developed with the expressed goal of combating environmental racism and human rights abuses directed at the Roma people of Europe. The Roma have for centu-ries been one of Europe's most despised ethnic groups, suffering continu-ous personal and mass violence at the hand of nation-states, institutions, and dominant cultural groups and individuals since the Roma migration into the area began in the twelfth century (Crowe 1996; Fraser 1995). With the emergence of a global discourse on environmental racism, activists and scholars in the CEE region began to link that language with the long-standing reality that Roma people have faced in the area. The Roma confront numerous environmental injustices in the region, including being forced to live on or near municipal waste dumps, poor access to clean water and sanitation, disproportionate exposure to toxins (e.g., abandoned mines), and heightened vulnerability to floods (e.g., living on islands on rivers).

CEJ members decided that, at that critical point in their movement's development, they would benefit from an exchange with U.S. environmental justice scholars, activists, and legal advocates, and they launched an effective global initiative to promote environmental justice in the region. This project was the first of its kind in that it specifically linked the situation of vulnerable peoples and threatened environments in the CEE region to the struggles of peoples in the United States.

I was asked to coordinate the U.S. delegation to the exchange meeting. So in October 2005, I organized a group of academics, activists, and lawyers from the United States to travel to Budapest, Hungary, to join with counterparts from CEE nations. The workshop was held at the Central European University and focused on reporting on case studies, building strategies for policy and legal change, and creating networks among scholars and activists for future collaborations. The group eventually decided to call itself the Transatlantic Initiative on Environmental Justice (TIEJ), which would serve as a network linking advocates on both sides of the Atlantic, sharing critical information, developing new knowledge, and supporting campaigns.

The TIEJ then decided to move forward to support a number of campaigns and to initiate collaborative projects. One of the outcomes of the meeting was a human rights campaign to bring attention to a dire situation facing Roma populations in Kosovo who—after having been displaced by the war in 1999—had been relocated by the United Nations to a toxic waste site where children were dying of lead poisoning.

For many years I have worked with Global Response, an organization that mobilizes letter-writing campaigns to bring attention to human rights and environmental justice abuses around the world. Letter writing focuses public attention on leaders, governments, and corporations involved in problematic policymaking, but it is also an important venue for creating and disseminating alternative knowledge that seeks to redefine a situation as a site of injustice. Drawing on this resource, I brought together Global Response (Colorado, USA) and the European Roma Rights Center (Budapest, Hungary) to launch an international letter-writing campaign to persuade the United Nations to relocate Roma families from a toxic waste site in Kosovo (see Global Response 2005). After hundreds of letter writers from around the world participated in this effort, the campaign secured an unprecedented response from the UN, which moved to create a relocation plan within a month's time. I also created a website that allows activists involved in this network to electronically publish their case studies of community struggles for environmental justice, and we have an Internet e-mail list that facilitates regular communication and information sharing across national borders (see California Cultures 2005). These were just two of the many projects that emerged from this exchange.

Funding for the Transatlantic Initiative on Environmental Justice came from the in-kind support of several grassroots and university organizations involved and from the Trust for Mutual Understanding, a New York–based foundation set up to support U.S.-CEE collaborations on important political and social issues. Without these sources of funding, the project would have been impossible. Even with this support, the task of bringing together so many people from across the planet to convene in a single space to build a consensus around the problem of environmental racism and agree on steps forward was, at times, monumentally difficult.

The TIEJ has, in a short time, mobilized individuals, organizations, and institutions to support the production of critical knowledge and action in support of social change for vulnerable communities in both the United States and Europe. The two institutions of higher education involved—the University of California and the Central European University—both contributed personnel, technical resources, and space to this initiative, and students and scholars have continued working on research projects and social change campaigns that emerged from the first meeting in 2005. This project speaks directly to the power of education and collaborative action by university scholars and community leaders to transform both the academy and the world around us. It is also a collaboration focused primarily on the power of *research* to facilitate the production of knowledge for social change. The next case is much more revealing of the power of *teaching* to pursue similar ends.

Teaching Social Change: Activist/Scholars Dialogue (ASD)

Joaquin "Quino" McWhinney is a social activist, cultural critic, and lead singer of the roots reggae band Big Mountain. Quino once told me and other professors at my university, "I just wish you all would write books that we could read!" He was speaking to the real frustration that many activists experience with scholarly writing that is all too frequently jargon-laden, absurdly abstract, and generally devoid of soul and use value for most people. This is a particularly acute problem for some disciplines that have emerged out of community struggles to make universities more relevant to marginalized populations and have in recent years become far removed from those communities. I agreed with Quino's point 100 percent, and his critique highlights the divide and mistrust that many people outside the academy feel about those on the inside.

It was the winter of 2003, and, as director of a center for the study of comparative cultures on my university campus, I was co-hosting our first "Activist/Scholars Dialogue" (ASD). The guiding question for the event was: How can students, professors/teachers, and grassroots community leaders work together to build stronger movements for social justice, peace, women's rights, indigenous rights, and environmental and public health?

The basis of the ASD rested on several premises: (1) colleges and universities have resources that can be shared with communities; (2) communities have resources that can be advantageous to universities; (3) such exchanges can produce better educational environments for students and improved social science research practices, leading to real improvements in the academy; (4) university-community collaborations can produce social changes in communities by providing skills and media through which community leaders' efforts can gain elevated visibility and political leverage.

Through the Activist/Scholars Dialogue at my university, I helped bring together community activists, professors, and students to engage in critical conversations about the need for people of color inside and outside the academy to work together. The conversation I facilitated recognized both the political and intellectual work that activists in communities of color do every day in theorizing problems and mobilizing to achieve solutions. The ASD also allowed us to tease out the potential public good within the university regarding how student and faculty knowledge, energy, skills, and other resources might be applied to advance the goals of social justice in communities of color. Ultimately, the goal was to move participants to link the conversation and ideas with other forms of action. To that end, there were substantial hurdles to overcome. For example, in some cases, activists stated that they had never been on the university campus before because no one had ever invited them and/or because our university had a reputation for being distanced from the city, both physically and in terms of its sphere of concerns and priorities. The "college on the hill" image may be idyllic for elite liberal arts institutions, but that symbolism reveals a significant physical and social distance from the public, and this is deeply problematic. I personally found that the university I taught in was an institution that was largely committed to reproducing elite structures of domination and inequality, so I was deeply motivated to challenge this. Through the ASD, we openly confronted these problems and argued for real linkages to social justice both inside and outside the university. Community activists participating in the ASDs have included leaders involved in antisweatshop, HIV/AIDS support, peace/antiwar, economic justice, environmental justice, domestic violence advocacy, immigrant and refugee rights, indigenous rights, and prisoner rights movements. Students and faculty who are engaged in community-based work have also been invited to speak.

Transforming Community, Transforming the Academy

During and after the ASD, students and faculty often developed partnerships and relationships with community activists to achieve a number of goals. For example, the executive director of a domestic violence support center in a heavily immigrant and refugee community of San Diego succeeded in gaining new volunteers, a new website, and equipment donations for his organization. In return, the university was able to send students to volunteer and serve as interns for academic credit. Perhaps more importantly, students were exposed to information about ongoing grassroots struggles they had been unaware of because few, if any, professors were teaching about these concerns in the classroom. The presence of community activist leaders on campus gave greater authority to their organizations and the issues they fought for, leading many students to demand changes in the curriculum and internship programs, thus potentially transforming the university. In fact, at least three campus programs offered student internships with the organizations whose representatives attended the ASD. Moreover, the campus initiative I directed offered grants to faculty, students, and community-based organizations when they joined and collaborated on social change projects. One of these grants helped support the above-mentioned relationship among students, a professor, and the domestic violence advocacy organization.

In another case, a faculty member involved in the ASD was asked to join the board of directors of an environmental justice organization that regularly participated in the event. That organization also recruited students to join its volunteer staff. Many of those students worked directly on "get out the vote" campaigns to urge citizens to push for public initiatives that would provide funding for sustainable economic development projects while successfully opposing the upgrade of a massive coal-fired plant in the city. Members of this organization then returned to campus to make additional presentations in classrooms, educating students about environmental and human rights concerns in their own "backyards" and recruiting more of them to work on various campaigns. This was transformative for many of the students because they heard a lecture and participated in discussions with community activists during class time, thus expanding the material and perspectives normally associated with campus course work. But there were other ways in which this experience was impactful.

One student remarked that hosting the ASD in the same room that normally hosts a weekly faculty research colloquium "was therapeutic for me, because we reclaimed and redefined that space, which for me is normally a space of restrictive and elitist thinking, that never even considers questions of how to apply our knowledge for the public good." Several students stated that "we should have an ASD every single quarter, every year!" Each ASD featured a standing-room-only audience because, as I recently stated to a colleague, there is a pent-up frustration, demand, and need on the part of students and faculty for a connection to something concrete and politically efficacious, particularly in this historical moment when the left is under attack, academic freedom is being targeted by the right, and U.S. domestic and foreign policy are so intensely oppressive. Since universities have historically been sites of major political disruptions, they are ideal locations for creative forms of dissent and productive methods of debating and engaging in social change. The ASD provided that opportunity for university members and for leaders and activists from the off-campus community.

The ASD was made possible primarily because of the support offered by the university's Cross-Cultural Center. That center's director has a reputation as a staunch ally of students of color and of the LGBTQ and indigenous communities on campus. With her support and the efforts of a faculty member who directs the Chicano/a and Latino/a Arts and Humanities Program, we made the ASD a reality. We secured a small grant to fund administrative costs and used other university funding to support new media work, including a television broadcast of the events on cable access TV titled "Growing Activism." The university administration never challenged the work we did, but as one faculty member told me, "it's certainly not a priority for them." Securing and maintaining sufficient funding for the project has been a serious challenge, so we relied primarily on volunteer labor among faculty, students, and staff.

The ASD project eventually evolved into a class that I cotaught with another faculty member and enrolled fifteen to twenty students. We taped and broadcast many of the classes, which are available on the Internet. Many students and faculty at other universities have seen the show on the Internet and contacted us for advice on how to set up similar projects elsewhere. The ASD served primarily as a teaching tool for students seeking knowledge about social movements and possible opportunities to engage community-based organizations. I believe it has been a great example of how education and collaboration become critical to building democratic movements. I also consciously designed the course to engender partnerships between my university and off-campus communities, in ways that are less hierarchical, nonexploitative, and transformative. Many other faculty members and students at the university have been inspired to propose additional courses similar to the ASD in order to move their departments and disciplines toward greater relevance and accountability to the broader community. Many students who participated in the ASD have since gone on to work full-time with progressive social change organizations or matriculated into graduate school programs with the intention of conducting research and teaching on the potential for social change within the academy. Perhaps small steps like the Activist/Scholars Dialogue will offer universities a push forward in the quest for engagement with communities of color that have been ignored for far too long.

* * *

Universities in the United States represent the promises and perils of education and democracy. On one hand, colleges and universities provide opportunities for upward mobility, financial and career stability, intellectual freedom, and democratic participation for many people, including members of the working class. On the other hand, institutions of higher education have become more class- and race-segregated and tend to support the status quo in this nation, strengthening systems of inequality. What is at stake here is the very purpose and mission of higher education and whether colleges and universities will serve as a source for democracy and popular empowerment or the maintenance of elite power and hegemony over the majority. Educational institutions have been some of the most important sites of radical social movements emerging in the United States and globally, and that power and rebellious potential of student movements must be nurtured and encouraged. University-community collaborations are one way to support sustained interest and skill building among students and faculty to pursue social change.

The Activist/Scholars Dialogue (ASD) and the Transatlantic Initiative on Environmental Justice are just two of many examples of university-community collaborations to work toward progressive change within and outside the academy. The ASD is a local initiative coordinated by faculty, students, and community activists in San Diego to produce both a respectful dialogue and a nonhierarchical, reciprocal relationship to amplify and sustain the work of local community groups while simultaneously improving the quality of the educational experience for students and faculty at the University of California, San Diego. And while it may be a local initiative, this project has inspired others to explore the possibility of doing the same on other campuses around the state and the nation. The ASD is also quite expansive because of its broad topical range, including immigrant rights, prisoners' rights, public and environmental health, domestic violence, global justice, indigenous rights, labor and economic justice, and peace movements. That breadth makes it possible for participants from a single university to reach out to a broad base of interests among many public stakeholders. Finally, the ASD is primarily focused on *teaching* and expanding the curricular offerings students have access to, because at a research university focused on national and global scholarship, faculty often ignore the political struggles of local communities.

The Transatlantic Initiative on Environmental Justice, by comparison, is broader in its geographic and spatial scope, but much narrower in its topical reach. By connecting U.S. and European stakeholders from universities, legal support centers, and community organizations, that project has taken on an organizing task that requires communication, travel, and mobilization across thousands of miles. Unlike the ASD, the TIEJ is largely focused on the power of *research* to illuminate and document social injustices, which can then empower campaigns in their efforts to challenge certain policies. In the time since the TIEJ was launched, several participants have produced reports, articles, and books focused on the links between environmental racism in the United States and in central and eastern Europe. But both the ASD and TIEJ reveal the importance of the creation of knowledge for challenging injustices and power relations. While those dynamics certainly involve the struggles of communities off campus, they also underscore the injustice of excluding these perspectives from university curricula and research agendas. In that sense, both projects sought different kinds of social and institutional changes that can reinforce one another: opening up new and expansive teaching *and* research agendas can produce and disseminate knowledge useful in further challenging exclusions within the university as well as placing the spotlight on situations far from campus that must also be addressed and transformed.

Education can be a tool for liberation and/or oppression. For far too long, universities have been used primarily for the latter: to create and preserve systems of race/class/gender/sexual/national domination, hierarchy, elitism, and privilege. Scholars in general, and social scientists in particular, have an obligation to challenge those hegemonies and to draw from the rich history of university-community alliances and scholar-activist collaborations that have cotransformed the largely private space of higher education and the public space of cities and rural areas where ordinary people with extraordinary ideas and energy live and work.

A reasonable critique of both these projects is that they are limited because they occurred within the conventional context of a major university. Perhaps. But that perspective overlooks the nature of the work itself. We made creative use of university and nonuniversity resources to do what a progressive educational institution *should* do: encourage students to think and act critically, and link university and community resources for social change and the production of sustainable knowledge. Ultimately, this kind of work has the potential to transform the nature and purpose of the university and of higher education. If there is anything I have learned in my time as a student and professor, it is that education is always political in its implications. Finally, I would like to think I am following in my father's footsteps by each year training numerous students who become critical thinkers and publicly engaged members of the world community.

Notes

1   Elite universities such as UC Berkeley, MIT, and Stanford are among some of the more infamous institutions associated with the military-industrial complex. While their presidents and chancellors are proud of their intellectual stature in the academy, each of these schools has been intimately involved with research and development of weaponry for warfare (see Pellow and Park 2002).

CHAPTER SEVEN

Transformative Disjunctures in the Academy

Asian American Studies as Praxis

Linda Trinh Võ

Nothing in my early childhood narrative indicated I would become a professor at an American university teaching about racial paradigms. During the Vietnam War, I lived with my grandmother in a rural village in South Vietnam, and she did her best to protect my sister and me from the ravages of warfare. We rarely saw my mother, who worked as a domestic in Saigon, where she met my Czech-Irish American stepfather, who grew up in the immigrant neighborhoods on the south side of Chicago. He worked for the U.S. embassy, and after their marriage they moved to Washington, D.C., where they managed to attain U.S. citizenship status for my sister and me. We joined them a year later in Japan, but the adjustment took time since we were literally living with strangers and urban life in Tokyo was in sharp contrast to life on the Mekong Delta. I attended an English-language all-girls Catholic school run by White nuns, where I learned English primarily from my Japanese and international classmates. We lived in the capitals of India, Indonesia, and Belgium before moving to Southern California, where I attended a racially divided public high school with African Americans, Latinos/as, and Whites, but only a handful of Asian Americans. During high school,

I learned lifelong lessons about the politics of de facto racial hierarchies and class segregation. As an undergraduate, I gravitated toward sociology as a major since it gave me the critical tools and theories to analyze the sociopolitical and economic structures of the countries I had resided in, including the colonial intervention that wreaked havoc on my "homeland."

By chance, in graduate school I became a grading assistant for a visiting lecturer, Wendy Ng, who was teaching a course on Asian American women, and for the first time in an educational setting, I learned about Asian American history. It was a transformative moment, for I entered the sociology graduate program intending to complete an area studies research project. At the campus library, I scoured the two rows of books on Asian Americans, most of them written by anti-Asian nativists or those depicting "Orientals" as passive victims of racism. In contrast, the literature I read on African Americans and other racialized communities portrayed them as proactive social agents transforming their lives and their communities. Undeterred by belittling comments from faculty and peers that focusing my research on Asian Americans was an obscure and unmarketable topic, I defiantly decided to write a dissertation on Asian American community mobilization.

I begin with the experiential since I readily admit that my personal biography has shaped my career trajectory. I suspect that my story, although a circuitous immigrant one, is not so unique for a scholar of Asian American Studies, many of whom are, in crude terms, products of U.S. colonialism. Ironically, were it not for Western imperialism in all its forms, we would have never left our homelands for America nor infiltrated academic institutions where we critique U.S. empire building. Yet our incorporation into the academy has hardly been a smooth process, and Asian American Studies continues to confront varying levels of skepticism in the process of finding a stable place in the academy (Butler 2001). In this chapter, I analyze the development of the field of Asian American Studies, focusing on efforts to institutionalize and professionalize the discipline, along with the multiple requirements and challenges scholars encounter in the academy, especially balancing their teaching and on-campus and off-campus service demands.[1] I contextualize these developments by intertwining these macro-micro dynamics with personal observations and experiences to demarcate some of the ways in which I have negotiated my own path in the academy.

Transforming Asian American Studies

The emergence of Asian American Studies has not been accidental, but deliberately struggled for and staunchly defended by scholars, students, and community members (Gee 1976; Tachiki et al. 1971).[2] "Orientals" have been the subject of earlier studies (Yu 2001), yet the formative beginnings of Asian American Studies were shaped by the oppositional politics of the civil rights movement and forged by the antiracist power movements and antiwar protests of the late 1960s and early 1970s (Espiritu 2003; Maeda 2009; Wei 1993). In addition, as Mazumdar notes, the Third World decolonization movements also "marked the crest of a worldwide struggle against racism, against capitalism, against bureaucratic socialism, struggles which exploded with the escalation of the Vietnam War" (1991: 39), which included student protests to transform curricula and universities. Over the years, in order to stabilize the discipline, Asian American Studies has become professionalized and institutionalized, albeit unevenly. New generations of scholars are challenging earlier epistemologies, ideologies, curricula, and historical markers (Davé et al. 2000; De Jesús 2005; Tchen 1999). The challenges of establishing Asian American Studies as noted in Chan and Wang's (1991) seminal work continue, such as the external debates—and internal divisions— about the vision of the discipline, how we define what constitutes "Asian America," and the parameters for evaluating scholarship in the field.

Communities of color have adjusted their organizing strategies as the composition of the group and structural circumstances have changed (Võ 2004). As a result of the 1965 Immigration Act and the post-1975 refugee flows at the end of the Vietnam War, Asian American communities have grown in size, and this has impacted the economic, social, political, and cultural terrain of this country. Along with this demographic growth, Asian American Studies as an academic discipline has blossomed, with an unprecedented increase in the number of scholars and a proliferation in scholarship. In other ways, much has remained the same, such as our continuing political marginalization, even in the sites where we are a demographically large population. As Asian American communities have expanded, they have faced resistance at the local level from unwelcoming neighbors, and they are still rarely included in the national political agenda, often perceived as the passive, perpetual foreigner. Asian American Studies programs continue to face barriers and experience stagnation, even in places where Asian bodies constitute a high percentage of the undergraduate population.

On principle, Asian American Studies should be implemented based on the premise that it is a significant intellectual endeavor, not based on the "critical mass" argument, namely the number of Asian American students on a college campus or changing demographics in the country. However, these substantial statistics should be an imperative to re-evaluate institutional choices and reconsider pedagogical configurations, such as diversifying the faculty ranks and the offerings of Ethnic Studies courses. The number of students of color has increased dramatically at both the University of California[3] and the California State University[4] systems, which have been instrumental in the creation of Ethnic Studies programs, yet these programs still grow slowly, continue to face uphill battles, and at times seem to be losing ground. Regardless, California still leads the nation in developing Ethnic Studies and training faculty of color. On the one hand, California can boast a "majority-minority" population with thriving communities of color throughout the state— rural, urban, and suburban. On the other hand, the number of faculty positions offered each year in institutions seeking specialties in African American, Asian American, Native American, Chicano/a and Latino/a studies or race relations is minimal. Institutions argue that in this era of financial cutbacks in education, traditional departments need to be protected, often at the expense of newer disciplines, such as Women's Studies and Ethnic Studies. In times of tight fiscal budgets, divide-and-conquer strategies are used to pit one group against another; for example, faculty have to decide between creating a new Asian American or a Chicano/Latino faculty position. Oftentimes these programs are vulnerable since newer programs are seen as expendable and opponents can use budget reductions in education as a cover to merge, weaken, dismantle, or even eliminate them.

There are few autonomous Asian American Studies departments, since Asian American Studies are typically programs that have less resources and fewer faculty than full-fledged departments or are merged into American Studies, Ethnic Studies, or even Asian Studies. There are interconnections between the distinct fields of Asian American Studies and Asian Studies, but treating the two as interchangeable poses major problems when administrators argue there is no need to develop Asian American Studies courses because there is already an Asian Studies curriculum. Most universities, if they have Asian American Studies classes, only offer a sprinkling of courses through traditional departments.[5] Hirabayashi and Alquizola recommend that "[t]he pursuit of and evaluation of what constitutes Asian American Studies should be self-determined by a collective body of Asian American scholars, committed to a range of theoretically informed practices" (1994: 361). Yet others argue that it needs to become a unified "discipline" in order to gain legitimacy (Miyamoto 1989), since managing this interdisciplinary theoretical and methodological merging is too unwieldy. This is also the reason skeptics argue against the establishment of Asian American Studies as a stand-alone unit, without also acknowledging that traditional disciplines, such as history and sociology, use multiple methodologies, perspectives, and theories, and the range of subjects covered are quite divergent as well. In my institutional journeys, I have been affiliated with American Studies, Asian American Studies, Ethnic Studies, sociology, Urban Studies, and Women's Studies programs or departments. Having a department is ideal but not imperative, since the most suitable placement of Asian American Studies curricula or faculty depends on factors such as the size and type of institution. I am currently a faculty member in an interdisciplinary Department of Asian American Studies housed in the School of Humanities that was originally established as a result of student and community protests in the early 1990s.[6]

Given the diversity of the group and interracial historical connections with other communities of colors and transnational linkages, the field has continuously mutated and been redefined. Immigration growth, ethnic differences, generational divisions, and regional context complicate the internal politics of the Asian American community (Osajima 1998). Transnational, diasporic, globalization, cultural, poststructural, postcolonial, postmodern, and Pacific Rim studies frameworks (Chan 2005: 193; Okamura 2003), along with feminist (Hune and Nomura 2003) and queer theories (Manalansan 2003), as well as developments in Ethnic Studies (Espiritu 2003), challenge the boundaries of what constitutes the study of "Asian America." For example, Asian immigrants from throughout Asia, Africa, Europe, the Caribbean, and Central and South America, along with an expanding multiracial population, are reconfiguring the boundaries of the field (Sumida 1998). Asian migration has influenced critical studies on capital and labor, ethnicization and racialization, and nation and citizenship (Das Gupta 2006; Ngai 2004). When the field was originally developed, the majority of Asian Americans were U.S.-born, whereas now the majority are foreign-born. Among them are immigrant or refugee scholars, some preferring to align themselves with hybrid deterritorialized or postnationalist identities rather than be merely situated within U.S. borders. These scholars have reshaped the field (Chan 2005: 189). For example, those who claim dual citizenship and spend more time outside the United States defy the simple straight-line assimilationist models, namely the narrative that immigrants and their progeny will become "American" once they come to our shores. The Ethnic Studies paradigm has shifted, yet there are adherents in the field unwilling to accept innovative theoretical, interdisciplinary, or multidisciplinary approaches (Butler and Walter 1991). They continue to promulgate an ethnic chauvinism agenda mired in "in/authentic" identity politics or tropes of cultural nationalism, disregarding multiple differences within our communities.[7] These debates have livened and enriched a field that continues to evolve, but some opponents have used these intellectual exchanges to question the legitimacy of the scholarship and argue for the dismantling of the discipline.

The Ethnic Studies project is part of larger contestations against "melting pot" assimilationist policies and a critique of American imperialism and nationalism (Gerstle 2001). In some cases, diluted versions of "multiculturalism" studies that focus on celebratory or contributionist histories of a people become the substitute for Ethnic Studies, and these attempts to co-opt and depoliticize the discipline have been effective in undermining it. As Lipsitz reminds us, "the question of which circumstances make it desirable to rally around a common *identity* and what circumstances make it desirable to rally around a common *ideology* or political *project*" is the challenge for multiethnic antiracist activism (2001: 130). The discipline of Asian American Studies is a product of this activism. Without comprehending the scope of the field, some scholars promote a conventional directive for Asian American Studies. For example, some simply count the number of immigrants entering the country each year rather than engage in critical analytical scholarship that examines the underlying socioeconomic determinants and political policies that impact who comes and why, or the complexities of postcolonial, diasporic, transnational cultural productions or identity formations. Some administrators can also deliberately or inadvertently undermine its establishment by hiring faculty untrained or mistrained in the field or by providing inadequate resources to empower the unit, which can be detrimental to both emerging and established programs (Chang 1999). For example, a traditional department that is allotted an Asian American Studies faculty line will hire a faculty member who has minimal knowledge or commitment in this area, but whose primary research is in another, more highly prized field, stunting the potential growth of Asian American Studies on that campus. These initial positions are crucial since they can advocate for additional resources for the field; otherwise the program will maintain the status quo and the university will do no more than hire one token faculty member who is marginally connected to the discipline to teach or misteach an obligatory introductory-level Asian American Studies course, which only reinforces the administration's belief that it is a stagnant field.

Focusing on Institutionalization and Professionalization

Currently, the majority of Asian American Studies scholars are of Asian ancestry, so the professionalization and institutionalization of the discipline centers on hiring and tenuring them.[8] The statistics on Asian Americans at the student, staff, and faculty level, if they are available, are deceptive, since most institutions do not disaggregate Asian Americans from Asian nationals, such as international students or scholars. As a result of the "brain drain" effect, which has led to the recruitment of skilled professionals from Asia, most faculty of Asian descent in U.S.

universities are Asian nationals in the medical, technological, and scientific fields, and sometimes they are perceived as "overrepresented" in the sciences, a perception that neglects Asian American underrepresentation in the arts, humanities, and social sciences (Hune 1998). The number of Asian American students at select public and private institutions across the country has grown, even to the point of alarm to administrators who have sought to restrict their admissions (Takagi 1992). These changes, however, are less visible among faculty and administrators. In the University of California system, Whites, who make up 43 percent of the state's population, hold 80 percent of all faculty positions, even as increasing numbers of students are Asian American (Campus Advisory Committee 2001).[9]

As "the first" or "one of the few," first-generation faculty of color and women faculty have had to navigate a formerly homogenous academic terrain that has not always embraced their presence. Kolodny (1996) notes the prevalence of "antifeminist intellectual harassment," which can be a "policy, action, statement, and/or behavior" that creates a stifling environment that is counterproductive to academic freedom and to their integration in the academy. Parallel dynamics of subtle but insidious forms of racism confront faculty of color. In one job interview on a Midwest campus, I distinctly remember a senior administrator asking me in a condescending tone, "Look around you, do you think you could feel comfortable here?" I later learned she was resistant to Ethnic Studies as a discipline. Quite frankly, she stated the obvious; how comfortable does a Vietnamese American female faculty member feel on any university campus, regardless of disciplinary training, where she most likely will be the only one, not to mention one of a small handful in the country? In the early years during job interviews, faculty made racialized and gendered judgments regarding my teaching abilities at predominantly White institutions. Often they did not even bother to hide their skepticism and constantly informed me that they had a center for teaching assistance, although I had worked extensively as a teaching assistant and lecturer while a graduate student at a predominantly White institution where I had won a teaching award. Experiences of being stigmatized and tokenized, in addition to overt forms of racial and gender discrimination, can create an inhospitable climate for faculty of color (Niemann 1999;

de la Luz Reyes and Halcón 1997), and this chilly climate has created a revolving door for Asian American women (Hune 1998). The reality is that academic salaries in the social sciences and humanities are modest, often incommensurate with the years of education and the stressful workload, so that scholars of color find other rewarding career paths in which they feel they can be more effective, without the racial tokenism.

At times, scholars may be working in environments that not only question their physical presence, but also the validity of their research and the placement of their publications (Williams 1997). Ironically, it seems the demands on tenure have become increasingly rigorous as more women and faculty of color are entering the academy. In many cases, junior faculty are being reviewed by senior faculty who often had lower expectations placed upon them during the promotion and tenure process. Rules for navigating the academy are often not transparent, and accountability is often lacking; the reality is that there are many informal rules as well as countless exceptions to the formal rules. Organizational structures often impede the successful advancement of women and faculty of color; for example, many tenure-track positions offered in these newer disciplines are joint appointments with traditional departments, which overburden faculty with excessive workloads and place them in a precarious position during their tenure process. In the promotion and tenure process, minority faculty, especially those working in newer fields, are expected to exceed in performance or are scrutinized more closely than their counterparts (Williams 1997). On smaller campuses, there are few faculty competent to evaluate their publications and, when working in an emerging field, there are fewer senior scholars off campus who can assess their research when external letters of support are needed for promotion. Efforts to increase the number of faculty of color, as well as women faculty, along with the development of Ethnic Studies programs, were implemented simultaneously with affirmative action programs in the late 1960s and early 1970s. In some cases, affirmative action programs initiated or strengthened policies that increased the diversification of the faculty and curriculum, and in other cases they were parallel occurrences. Critics have interlinked these transformations as undermining traditional educational standards, underscoring their suspicion of the field and of the qualifications of the faculty hired. Traditional structures and informal networks of power can impede career advancement for faculty of color, who as a result of their historical exclusion are essentially newcomers. Studies and reports show that women academics face disadvantages in being rewarded for professional achievements when compared to men (Valian 1998). According to organizational researchers who focus on career development, workplace relationships provide two crucial benefits, namely instrumental career assistance and emotional support (Gersick, Bartunek, and Dutton 2000). It is crucial that faculty are mentored through the academic process, but there are often few women or faculty of color—particularly women of color—in senior positions to mentor junior faculty, something I found to be the case when I had to match junior faculty with tenured faculty mentors in my administrative role.[10]

Each campus has idiosyncratic policies, and faculty have to maneuver through the maze of formal and informal policies (Chan 2005). Of course, there are generic strategies, such as being informed of institutional policies, asking lots of questions, finding powerful allies, and being selective in the battles one chooses to fight and with whom. It means being strategically proactive and remembering that one cannot assume that your department or colleagues, even other faculty of color or women faculty, will automatically assist or support you. While some faculty of color are equipped to maneuver through this process with ease, in many cases it has been incumbent on senior faculty and administrators savvy and dedicated enough to intervene against discriminatory institutionalized policies to prevent talented colleagues from leaving or being forced to abandon academia, never able to live up to their full potential. In other cases, legal strategists, political advocates, and community supporters have coalesced to fight against unfair denials of tenure or termination (Minami 1995).

Working in a field that encourages interdisciplinarity in teaching, research, and program building (Palumbo-Liu 2003) can be time consuming since it requires expertise in multiple fields and can limit scholarly productivity. Although trained as a sociologist, I find it restrictive, if not intellectually imprudent, to limit my study of ethnicity, race, or immigration to one discipline, even when my main affiliation was in a sociology department, although I realize that some shortsighted faculty still impose this discipline boundary model on current graduate students and penalize their peers and subordinates who choose not to conform. While doing interdisciplinary or multidisciplinary scholarship can be overwhelming, it is also intellectually enriching, and this cross-fertilization has continually reshaped my scholarship and teaching.

I pay attention to the personal experiences of scholars working in Ethnic Studies, making me acutely cognizant of how I am positioned and how to navigate the oftentimes treacherous terrain of academia. As a graduate student, I was extremely fortunate to be hired as a teaching assistant in the newly formed Department of Ethnic Studies at my institution and to receive a graduate fellowship at the University of California Humanities Research Institute and a postdoctoral fellowship at the University of California, Berkeley, where I met faculty mentors who validated and guided my intellectual interests. Nowadays, there are faculty who majored in Asian American Studies or Ethnic Studies as undergraduates, and as graduate students were mentored by faculty who themselves received generous training in these fields, compared to earlier generations who were self-taught or had to retool themselves (Chan 2000). Additionally, I have found it helpful to identify faculty on my own campus willing to provide mentorship and those from multiple disciplines on other campuses willing to share their knowledge of the personal politics of navigating institutions of higher education.[11]

Furthermore, regardless of the discourse of gender equity or the implementation of family-friendly policies, university cultures are inherently hostile or ambivalent to parenthood, especially motherhood, so balancing an academic career with childbirth and child rearing is challenging (Munn-Giddings 1998). Connecting with other women faculty of color to simply discuss strategies for balancing a demanding career and parenthood has been invaluable. I realized that for many people of color, it is not the intellectual demands of the profession that force individuals to exit the academy, but the hostility of academe, in all its forms and its psychological effects, that wears them down.

As I advance in my career, I find it disconcerting that there are even fewer faces of color and hardly any women of color, especially with children, in senior faculty positions and among administrators. I cannot help but notice that at meetings for department chairs that I am one of the few women and people of color in the room, and even White males will sometimes remark on the paucity of diversity. However, as cliché as this may sound, a small number are willing to take the initiative to reflect on how their behavior might be offputting, such as the preroga-tive they take to interrupt female colleagues when they are talking more so than male ones, or validating the ideas of male colleagues even if these ideas were originally suggested by female faculty. Few are coura-geous or committed enough to transform policies and workplace cultures that will create a pipeline that will change this inequity. Although many feel that we are overrepresented at the undergraduate ranks, the reality is there are no high-ranking Asian American administrators, male or female, at my current institution and there are a limited number in the nation, especially ones that can serve as mentors for the next generation of scholars.

Challenging Teaching and Service

While most of my training as a teacher comes from the University of California system, it has also been shaped by experiences in other loca-tions. Teaching at a small private liberal arts college in the Midwest with a history of progressive politics taught me that even in a place where the structures of power are supposedly more egalitarian, although not so transparent, change can be slow. Coalitions of vocal students had been struggling to institute Asian American Studies courses there for twenty-five years. I was the first professor hired as a visiting faculty to teach such courses,[12] and many of the students in my classes were non-Asians who were supportive of the new curriculum. I also worked at a large public institution with few students of color in a rural area of the Pacific Northwest. Many of the White students came from small towns and had limited contact with individuals who were racially, politically, culturally, and religiously unlike them. I imagine that most had no inter-personal contact with Vietnamese or Asians previously, especially one in a position of authority. There was incredible resistance to learning about race and ethnic relations; the students had been taught simplistic notions such as "It happened in the past, so we should forget about it, especially since it isn't my fault" or had adopted color-blind defensive postures such as "I've never seen racism, so it doesn't exist."[13] I learned important lessons about race relations and the climate of racial hostility in this country, particularly that the rhetoric of de jure egalitarianism still allows for de facto racist ideologies and practices to be easily transmitted from one generation to the next in the post–civil rights era.[14]

Now I teach at a large public institution with an undergraduate population that is more than 50 percent Asian Americans, the highest percentage in the continental United States, so the material I teach reflects their lived experiences. However, some of the students are uninterested in Ethnic Studies and they take the ethnic and racial diversity around them for granted, denying that discrimination impacts them. They often do not seem to notice the lack of diversity at the faculty or administrative levels on campus or the racial hierarchy within the state. Sometimes, ethnic groups are more conscious of inequality when they are a numeric minority as compared to those who live in large ethnic communities (Portes and Manning 1986). Students at the Midwest and Pacific Northwest institutions were more forthcoming of how visible racial markers forced them to constantly articulate and defend who they were to others and justify why they belonged in the university setting. Unfortunately, seemingly benign questions such as "Where are you from?" in which it is expected that we will name some country in Asia, highlight the racist perceptions that Asian Americans are foreigners. On college campuses where students experience overt forms of racial discrimination and where Asian bodies and curricula are largely absent, there can be a greater awareness of racial inequalities and clear incentives to contest racial barriers.

Race and gender are codified in the classroom, which adds more complexity when faculty are teaching "difference" in an attempt to encourage students to move beyond reductive and essentialized notions of social groups. "Counterpower harassment," a term coined by Katherine Benson, refers to the ways students draw upon gender-based power, which can be overt and public or indirect and anonymous, to undermine and subvert a female professor's legitimacy in the classroom (1984). A common example of this is addressing male colleagues as "Dr." or "Professor" and female faculty as "Ms.," "Mrs.," or by their first name. Faculty of color and women faculty can encounter mere disinterest or confrontational resistance to the cultural histories they teach, which manifests itself in opposition to their professorial authority (Bauer and Rhoades 1996) or even physical intimidation. As the scholars in this collection can attest, harassment can also be based on ethnic, racial, sexual orientation, and religious factors and is more commonplace for those engaged in feminist, antiracist, or queer pedagogies. How students react to decentering Whiteness or male privilege in the curricula and the classroom setting varies according to student perceptions of the gender and race of the faculty member (TuSmith and Reddy 2002). Students are socially imbued with the exotification of racialized, gendered bodies, namely the stereotypes of Asian women through the media, and this socialization reveals itself within the classroom setting as well (Hune 1998). The reality is I am not perceived the same way in the classroom as an older White male colleague or male faculty of color, and I do have to work harder to exert my authority in large lecture classes, regardless of the ethnic or racial composition of the students. These experiences can be productively and skillfully incorporated into a dialectal classroom discussion, as Chatterjee (2000) illuminates, but they can also be intellectually distressing and emotionally draining, especially when they detract from the time faculty should expend on research and writing.

Anecdotal evidence and official reports indicate that women and minority faculty spend an inordinate amount of time on service obligations for their programs and working with undergraduate and graduate students (Fogg 2003; Niemann 1999). Ethnic Studies faculty, even untenured ones, are frequently asked to establish new programs and serve on numerous committees, often as the token "diversity" representative, and I, along with many others, have done more than our share of "representing." Historically, students of color have been denied access to higher education at both the undergraduate and graduate levels, so incoming cohorts are disproportionately composed of first-generation students. A fair percentage of Latino/a and Asian students come from immigrant or refugee families, so they often lack parental guidance through the academic labyrinth, and students from low-income families and crime-ridden neighborhoods face additional challenges.

Finding appropriate assistance is often linked to their ability to stay in school and these students of color gravitate toward faculty of color who they perceive can serve as mentors. This challenge is heightened for women of color faculty, who are sought out as mentors with the assumption that they are more nurturing. The materials we teach resonate with ethnic, queer, women, working-class, and immigrant/refugee students, and as a result they come to us for guidance and support (TuSmith and Reddy 2002). It is common for students to share with me their struggles regarding eating disorders, racist incidents, domestic violence, addiction problems, gang pressure, generational conflicts with their immigrant/refugee parents, sexual violence, etc.[15] As a first-generation college student who also faced educational challenges, I feel an obligation to support these students. Beyond those one formally advises on thesis or dissertation projects, the time spent unofficially advising undergraduate or graduate students outside of the classroom context, whether assisting them with their personal problems or providing them with career advice, and even helping them contend with the racism they experience from other faculty, is not officially tabulated and thus rarely recognized in retention, promotion, and tenure evaluations. Students continually gravitate toward faculty who volunteer to guide student groups, give talks to their organizations, or speak up on their behalf, so these faculty continue to do a disproportionate amount of service work.

Therefore, faculty of color shoulder an unfair share of mentoring work that is not compensated or credited, particularly because this invisible labor is not easily quantifiable. At research institutions, this service is not valued compared to tangible publications in prestigious presses or journals or acquiring major grants, nor is it considered as important as service work on university committees, preferably not related to "diversity" issues. Graduate and undergraduate students avoid faculty, including faculty of color or women faculty, who have an aversion to mentoring, which allows these colleagues more time to devote to grant writing, research, and publishing. Simply put, faculty who focus on mentoring are penalized, but those who avoid it are rewarded for their publishing productivity. The number of Asian American students has grown on many campuses, but the faculty ranks have not increased proportionately, so those that serve as mentors and advocates find a high demand on their time. Ironically, students at large public institutions, where many students of color attend, that need the most individualized attention are often the ones who seem to receive the least amount of guidance.

Mentoring students can be productive since it helps faculty become more knowledgeable teachers who are attuned to the intellectual needs of their students. Teaching is not simply about imparting theories and formulas, but involves the application of appropriate pedagogical strategies and finding ways to connect students to the materials. Faculty have the ability to expand and transform a student's life choices, educational and career trajectories, and political perspectives. This potential resonates with the vision of Asian American Studies when it was established (Hirabayashi 1998); unfortunately, many faculty in the field have lost sight of the discipline's origins.

Balancing the Ivory Tower and the Community

Some Asian American faculty are not fully aware that faculty positions and programs owe their existence to student and community protests. Others disavow themselves from the political struggles of the Asian American community or from the politics of the discipline, envisioning their scholarship as apolitical. In some cases this is because their research is more abstract in nature or they feel that engaging in these struggles makes their research biased (Võ 2000). They may justify that the community work they engage in is with the students in their classes and they rarely interact with the "community" outside of the ivory tower (Chan 2000). In contrast, some scholars have explicitly called for researchers and community activists to collaborate with community organizations (Loo and Mar 1986). Sucheng Chan, a pioneer in the field, encourages "the necessity of engaging in *both* scholarship and political action" whether that be within or outside the campus (2005: 190).

However, there is no singular blueprint or strategy for involvement with a range of organizations and grassroots groups; rather it should be a reciprocal effort dependent on location, needs, interest, and available expertise and resources. Lipsitz articulates the connection between these community groups and the development of Ethnic Studies, explaining that "[t]he institutional spaces we occupy exist because community activists and organizations won them through sustained collective struggle"

(2001: 119). Given the often tenuous position of Asian American Studies within the academy, having the support of the community in certain aspects can help it flourish.[16] As academics became professionalized, focusing on theories and publications that bring them scholarly accolades, they are being accused of abandoning applied, collaborative, community-based research that benefits the community and of isolating themselves from the groups that led to the fruition of their disciplines. It is often more complicated than this, since tenure-track positions and programs are not always directly linked to a particular community protest (Chang 1999), but these criticisms are based on valid points.

There are national, state, and local groups and organizations that continue to advocate for a redistribution of resources and power and challenge injustices and inequalities such as unfair social programs, police harassment, educational setbacks, environmental hazards, and unjust immigration and deportation policies, which warrant more input from and involvement by academics. Graduate students and faculty can use their expertise to work with community groups to conduct systematic assessments, statistical analysis, and in-depth ethnographic studies that can be implemented for advocacy and public policy purposes. The *AAPI Nexus: Asian Americans & Pacific Islanders Policy, Practice and Community Journal*, established in 2003 and published by the UCLA Asian American Studies Center, includes as its mission "the explicit goal of reinvigorating Asian American Studies' traditional mission of serving communities and generating practical research," signaling a need to refocus on community-university partnerships in applied research.[17] For the most part, more sustained collaborations are based on individual faculty efforts, not necessarily funded or sanctioned by their universities.[18]

I have never considered myself a career community activist, although I have been engaged in community projects of one form or another, from civic engagement to collective protest, over the years. This has given me opportunities to collaborate with individuals from diverse backgrounds and areas of expertise who are committed to creating sustained transformations, and at times this involvement has overlapped with my research projects and enhanced my teaching pedagogies.[19] Perhaps I am drawn to these projects as a counterbalance to institutions where really fine ideas can get lost in the quagmire of an academic bureaucracy that does not value campus projects directed at communities of color. Engaging in the camaraderie of social justice activists who focus on various forms of social agency and resistance allows me to counterbalance the sometimes depressing nature of researching, writing, and teaching about the disempowering violence of oppression. Faculty can utilize their privileged position within the academy to help community members navigate the university and can bring the "community" to the campus and vice versa, though the latter seems to be more complicated.

Faculty can incorporate academic community service learning projects in their courses to bring students into the community as well as to connect community members to the classroom. Through my research classes, students have been engaged in a variety of projects, such as ones related to domestic violence, mentoring at-risk youth, advocacy or policy work, electoral politics, labor organizing, artistic or cultural productions, and public health campaigns. Through this praxis model, students can apply theories of inequality, social stratification, and race relations, as well as learn pragmatic lessons on social change that have an enduring impact on them beyond their years at the university. Students can be idealistic in their quest to change the world, so when well-coordinated with intellectually rigorous readings, these experiences can be epistemologically enriching and can provide them practical lessons about the challenges of social justice work. The imperative that Kiang (1989) emphasized more than a decade ago is still relevant—the need to expose students, many of them immigrants and refugees or the children of immigrants and refugees, to a variety of meaningful professional and activist choices. Yet without university staff assistance, it is challenging to coordinate service learning, as well as arrange site visits, to ensure that students participate appropriately at designated sites, and to help organizations provide sufficient guidance throughout the quarter/semester (Osajima 1998).

Projects that Ethnic Studies faculty are involved in defy simple categorization during the merit and promotion process; some are related to their research and further advance the field, although in indirect and subtle ways. My participation has included helping to create a web portal from my university library's special collection,[20] consulting for a public national radio project, participating in documentaries, advising on exhibits, organizing film festivals, supporting humanitarian organizations, consulting on oral history projects, and assisting political campaigns. Some involve writing reports or textual materials, raising money, or creating networks, but overall they are about "educating" the public, raising awareness of community issues, improving opportunities for youth, or addressing public policy agendas. Admittedly, these tasks are beyond the professional requirements of presenting one's research at academic conferences or invited talks at college campuses, and they all take an inordinate amount of time and require skills not acquired during my graduate education.[21] Beyond assisting the community and contributing to the implementation of change, there are definite benefits to community work since faculty who are involved in the community can assist their Asian American Studies or Ethnic Studies majors—a nontraditional option—to place them in internships and assist them in finding employment.

Unlike my faculty career, which was mapped out more or less, my engagement in the community has been piecemeal experimentation and has evolved organically. I intended for my research and publications on Asian American mobilization, on which I was rewarded with tenure, to provide a critical and practical analysis of the instrumental role of community organizations in mediating and enacting social change. Just as meaningful to me, and beyond the purview of my training as a social scientist, has been my direct involvement organizing the biennial Vietnamese International Film Festival, which provides a platform for us to showcase "our stories" and provides counterhegemonic representations to contest the stereotypical Hollywood Vietnam War filmic narrative that depicts us an inhumane savages.[22]

The pressure by the institution on faculty to confine their service work to campus committees, especially academically oriented ones, is a disincentive to community involvement (Williams 1997).[23] Generally, faculty are inadequately rewarded for these efforts, unless it brings in major recognition such as donations or grants to the university. Besides the lack of institutional support, there are faculty of all backgrounds clinging to the ideals of "objective detachment," who advocate disassociating research from activism and who discourage and disapprove of graduate students or faculty engaging in social justice campaigns. As a graduate student, this disinvestment in "the community" model was drilled in me, and early in my career I conformed to these practices. The biggest challenge for many faculty of color is balancing community and advocacy work, other academic demands, and one's personal life (Delgado 2003). This balancing act is especially difficult for women faculty with children, particularly single parents, who already have to contend with an academic environment that is unsupportive of motherhood. Each can be time-consuming and stressful, and combined they can hinder research productivity and can be detrimental to one's mental health. My community work, even if it will not contribute to my next promotion, brings me personal gratification and counters the isolation I experience in the university. The struggles we mount in the ivory tower are interlinked to larger struggles against institutionalized racism and exclusion.

The goal of "serving the community," which was the mantra of the Ethnic Studies movement of an earlier period, has been set aside in favor of the demands of professionalization and institutionalization (Sanchez 2008). Additionally, some faculty eschew community involvement, since they are unwilling to contest the hazardous internal politics common in most Asian American communities.[24] When making requests of faculty or critiquing the depoliticization of the discipline in research institutions, community members need to recognize that faculty are under intense pressure to "publish or perish" and have to devote themselves to the administrative tasks of building or sustaining their academic programs. Faculty who are involved in community projects and creating linkages, disproportionately women and people of color, are making a conscious political choice to do so, not because it is required by the academy. Balancing the needs of the academy and the community is a precarious endeavor that involves the constant negotiation of obligations, reciprocity, benefits, and autonomy.

* * *

After almost thirty-five years, labeling Asian American Studies as a new academic discipline of intellectual inquiry seems passé. Despite the expansion of Asian American and Ethnic Studies, they are still considered marginal by those who continue to question their legitimacy in the academy and refuse to incorporate them into the canon, a repudiation typically aligned with their fears of the balkanization of the American nation (Yamane 2001). They continue to doubt its validity despite the vast range of scholarly publications on the topic, including prestigious university press book series that focus exclusively on or include Asian American topics.[25] Additionally, attendees at the Association for Asian American Studies and the American Studies annual conferences continue to increase and the presence of scholars working on Asian American projects at conferences organized by traditional disciplines has risen as well.[26] Since the late 1960s, the transformation of invisibility into activism has fostered the teaching of a more inclusive history as well as the diversification of the student, staff, faculty, and even administrative population. Configurations of Ethnic Studies will continue to mutate as it faces continuing challenges from the neoconservative right, which considers the curriculum and discourse on diversity as polarizing, as well as from the radical left, which considers the discipline as too institutionalized.

New generations of faculty, myself included, have benefited from the foundation laid by earlier pioneers in the field. But we continue to struggle to find our place in the academy and in the community. Some Asian American Studies programs and departments are crumbling because of ideological infighting, which is compounded by scarce resources and institutional indifference and neglect. In the 1980s, terms used to describe the prospects for the few Asian American Studies programs were "crisis," "stagnation," and "lost" (Loo and Mar 1986; Okihiro et al. 1988; Omi 1988). In the 1990s, there was more optimism about the robustness of the field (Monaghan 1999), yet there are still only a small number of programs that can be described as moderately stable and on course.[27] In the contemporary period, a new generation of scholars and activists who are beneficiaries, though not direct participants of the Asian American movement of the late 1960s and early 1970s, are reconfiguring the interconnections between the academy and the community. Ideally this necessitates envisioning a discipline able to critique the current strains of postidentity and postracial discourses in an era of renewed American imperialism and a field expansive enough to prioritize its political commitment to scholarly productions that encompasses the multiple needs of the community.

Without a doubt, I have experienced firsthand and vicariously my fair share of disillusionment with the field and with academia, but I have chosen to remain an optimistic, albeit at times a weary, stakeholder. As a pragmatist, I recognize that in praxis the implementation of Asian American Studies or Ethnic Studies, like the struggles to build an equitable society, is marred by multiple disjunctures, but I prefer to focus on the transformative moments and critical interventions that have created the foundation for expanding the academy.

Notes

1   I focus more on public institutions, especially on the West Coast, and recognize that there are other ways to imagine the field of Asian American Studies according to discipline and region, and that individual faculty experiences may differ according to their own background and their educational affiliations.

2   My discussion focuses on Asian American Studies and does not incorporate Pacific Islander Studies, which has a distinct intellectual and institutional development that would involve a more extensive analysis, although some programs combine the two. There are larger debates about the problematic lumping together of these umbrella groups.

3   The University of California consists of ten campuses with more than 220,000 students and approximately 170,000 faculty and staff. University of California webpage, http://www.universityofcalifornia.edu/aboutuc/welcome.html (accessed January 12, 2011).

4   The California State University System has twenty-three campuses with almost 433,000 students and 44,000 faculty and staff. California State University webpage, http://www.calstate.edu/ (accessed January 12, 2011).

5   The only College of Ethnic Studies is at San Francisco State University. For more extensive discussion of where Asian American Studies should be housed, see Espiritu 2003.

6   The African American Studies Program is housed in the same school, while the Chicano/Latino Studies Department is located in the School of Social Sciences. These distributions are hardly ideal in terms of resource sharing or intellectual exchanges and are a result of political negotiations by key faculty and administrators.

7   The central theoretical and ideological debates about the manifold directions and the porous boundaries of the field highlighted in Omi and Takagi's landmark special issue of *Amerasia Journal* still maintain their relevancy (1995).

8   I recognize that professionalization and institutionalization involve implementing curricula, programs, and departments, etc., but for the purposes of this chapter, I focus on faculty development, especially the demands and expectations placed on tenure-track faculty.

9   White persons non-Hispanic. Source U.S. Census Bureau: State and County Quick Facts, 2006. http://quickfacts.census.gov/qfd/states/06000 .html (accessed January 8, 2009).

10   On my campus, I served as an equity advisor for the School of Humanities, working as a faculty assistant to the dean to improve gender and ethnic diversity in the professoriate, focusing on equal opportunity and equity practices in hiring, mentoring, and retention. I coordinated a mentoring program in which faculty can select the type of mentor they would like and I did my best to find a match. I recognize that any faculty member can serve as a mentor, but my informal assessment indicates that it is more productive and rewarding if a mentor shares similar personal experiences and/or scholarly interests with a mentee.

11   Once an intimate gathering for scholars, the Association for Asian American Studies (AAAS) reached a thousand members in 2010. Since the mid-1990s a subgroup calling itself East of California (EoC), indicative of the need to differentiate it from the dominance of California in the field, has its own annual gathering for collegial support and mentorship of graduate students and professors. Since my graduate schools years, the AAAS, and briefly the EoC while I was in the Midwest, provided me with crucial networks and invaluable friendships that have nurtured my career.

12   The year before I arrived, Peter Kwong commuted from another state to teach an Asian American Studies course for one semester. Two of the five courses I was hired to teach were Asian American ones.

13   I refrain here from repeating the barrage of racist stereotypes students articulated in class and in their writings. In one large introductory class, when one of the few students of color in the class who had been outspoken in contesting these comments became silent in the second half of the semester, I asked him about this and was dismayed to learn that he was being verbally and physically harassed in the dormitories for being the "teacher's pet."

14 As hopeful as I am about Barack Obama's presidency in what some have labeled the postracial era, the election of one mixed-race individual to the White House does not automatically transform entrenched forms of systematic racism that impedes the lives of so many in our nation. See Võ 2010.

15 Since they entrust me with personal matters that are often beyond my range of professional expertise, when appropriate I direct students to services, such as the on-campus professional counseling center or legal center.

16 I recognize that not all faculty need to engage in community work or conduct participatory research.

17 See the first issue, *AAPI* 1(1) (Summer/Fall 2003), especially the "Message from the Editors: To Serve, Help Build, and Analyze" by Paul Ong and Don Nakanishi (iii–vi), and "Opportunities for Community-University Partnerships: Implementing a Service-Learning Research Model in Asian American Studies" by Melany de la Cruz and Loh-Sze Leung (47–66).

18 In 2005, led by Paul Ong, faculty representatives from all the University of California campuses created a UC Asian American and Pacific Islander Multi-Campus Policy Initiative, but with limited institutional funding, its sustainability is tenuous.

19 For example, my involvement with the Vietnamese American community in Orange County has given me greater insight into the social, economic, and political complexities of the community, which has also stimulated and reshaped my research projects.

20 This project was funded by a $208,000 grant from the National Endowment for the Humanities.

21 Additionally, speaking at community forums or workshops, serving on working boards or committees of community organizations, and participating in local political events and projects are regular engagements.

22 This eight-day festival is held at UC Irvine, Little Saigon (Orange County), UCLA, and other community sites. www.vietfilmfest.com.

23 Some private liberal arts colleges and state colleges are more favorable toward community outreach projects.

24 I know from firsthand experience that working on projects with the Asian American community involves personal and professional risks. For example, the Vietnamese American community is primarily a first-generation refugee population that has suffered decades of colonialism, a civil war, postwar trauma, and forced displacement and relocation, and this infuses their political lives in the United States.

25   Temple University Press is notable for having almost sixty books in their Asian American History and Culture series, which I serve as a series editor. Others publishers with noteworthy collections of Asian American Studies books are Duke University Press, New York University Press, Rutgers University Press, Stanford University Press, University of California Press, University of Hawai'i Press, University of Illinois Press, University of Minnesota Press, and University of Washington Press.

26   An average of six to seven hundred attend the annual Association for Asian American Studies conference. Steven Sumida was the 2002–2003 president of the American Studies Association and Evelyn Nakano Glenn was the 2010 president of the American Sociological Association, both of whom helped to establish the field of Asian American Studies. There are active Asian American sections, subgroups, or caucuses in traditional disciplinary associations.

27   I acknowledge that this is a subjective statement. I make this judgment based on my observations of the field and discussions with scholars across the country, focusing particularly on new faculty hires in recent years, the ratio of tenured versus untenured faculty, number of majors and minors, program versus departmental status, consistent course offerings, collegiality of faculty, range of programmatic activities, etc.

CHAPTER EIGHT

Queering the Ivory Tower

Tales of a Troublemaking Homosexual

BRETT C. STOCKDILL

It's Queer to Me: Being Gay Is Not Enough

> I think it's okay if we have a gay professor, but I don't think we want a gay AIDS activist professor going around and getting arrested.
>
> —Professor at a Research 1 university

This reaction to my research presentation on prison AIDS activism during a job interview illuminates the complexity of homophobia and anti-activist bias in the ivory tower. Being gay *and* being an activist, a prison AIDS activist no less (think anal sex, intravenous drug use, prisoners, etc.), in the academy provokes feelings of fear, uneasiness, and anger. Protesting—disrupting business as usual, especially getting arrested—is perceived to be the problem, *not* the lack of HIV prevention or health care for prisoners living with HIV/AIDS (Stockdill 1995). My experiences of the academy have often meant being seen not just as a gay man, but as a "troublemaking homosexual." Though I am often met with hostility, I embrace my identity as a queer activist-educator-scholar. Being openly gay is not enough. Fighting homophobia alone (or any other singular form of oppression) is insufficient. In this chapter, I examine the development of my own brand of queerness; I utilize a queer political perspective to illuminate overt and covert forms of inequality and possible strategies for change in higher education. My queerness has been profoundly shaped by the analysis and activism of Black lesbian feminists, including the Combahee River Collective (1983: 272):

> we are actively committed to struggling against racial, sexual, heterosexual, and class oppression, and see as our particular task the development of integrated analysis and practice based upon the fact that the major systems of oppression are interlocking.

The term "queer" is a contested one that has different meanings for different people. Historically used as a term of self-identification for some as well as a pejorative term to attack lesbians and gay men, some "queers" have reclaimed the word to defy homophobia and other forms of oppression. More politically conservative LGBTQ (lesbian, gay, bisexual, transgender, and queer) folks detest the term. Younger LGBTQ people are more likely to embrace it, some without much political reflection. Some LGBT activists of color have critiqued queer as a "White thing" while others have enthusiastically added the "Q" to LGBT (Johnson and Henderson 2005). Queer theory has blossomed in the academy, producing scholarship that is often provocative but often inaccessible.

While I currently embrace queer as an identity, I am wary of reifying the term. Actively and regularly subverting hegemonic ways of thinking and being is more important than the term itself. That being said, we use language to make sense of our social worlds. Just as there is a difference between *woman* and *feminist*, we must distinguish between *gay* and *queer*.

Queer is a collective identity and a political perspective that critiques and resists the status quo. The term is inclusive of lesbian, gay, bisexual, transgender, and intersex people. Queers interrogate taken-for-granted claims and categories. Being queer means rejecting dominant views of what it means to be a "boy/man" and "girl/woman" as well as dominant norms around sex and relationships. Queers reject the idea that LGBTQ people should conform to heterosexist society, and instead celebrate being queer and, optimally, challenge all forms of oppression

(Crimp 2004; Kumashiro 2002). Queer activists organize against a multitude of injustices including the death penalty, police brutality, globalization and war, violence against women, homelessness, and gentrification.

In contrast to dominant notions of social change shaped by Eurocentric and heteropatriarchal ideas,[1] queer political consciousness and struggle encompass not only the analytical (dissecting systemic oppression and imagining more humane and just values and institutions), but also the emotional (despair, rage, and, always, hope) and the strategic (protest, both individual and collective). Thus, a queer politic traverses both private and public situations, unmasking and defying the power differentials in the heterosexist, racist, sexist, and classist social order that shape all of our lives—every day. At its core, queer activism reflects the acknowledgment that progressive change occurs when we make conscious, deliberate choices to engage in struggle rather than acquiesce. In the words of the late Black gay activist Joseph Beam (2008: 181), "Aren't all hearts and fists and minds needed in this struggle or will this faggot be tossed in the fire?"

My queer identity, born of isolation, anger, and dreams, compelled me to make sense of the world, to survive the academy, and to work for social change. As a student, researcher, educator, and colleague, my identity as someone who transgresses boundaries and viscerally feels injustice has led me to confront the ways in which dominant institutions perpetuate ideologies and practices of exclusion and marginalization.

There are many reasons to make trouble in the ivory tower in 2012. Many institutional leaders tout "diversity" as a valued goal in the post–civil rights movement era, but diversity campaigns are often diversity charades because of the lack of direct dialogue and action on inequality and injustice. While far too long to list here, a few examples highlight the persistence of inequality and injustice in academia:

- African Americans and Latin@s,[2] who make up approximately 28 percent of the U.S. population, accounted for only 12 percent of doctorates awarded in 2008 (National Science Foundation 2009).
- Between the years of 2001 and 2008, the *American Sociological Review*, considered by some to be the premier sociology

journal, published only two articles on LGBT issues (American Sociological Association 2009).

- Reflecting national patterns, University of Miami president Donna Shalala received compensation of $630,000 in 2003–2004 while University of Miami janitors' average wages were between $6.40 and $7.53 an hour—less than $15,000 a year (June 2006).

- An estimated 20 to 25 percent of women in higher educational institutions will experience "completed or attempted rape victimization" during their college years (Fisher, Cullen, and Turner 2000: 10).

- Six percent of students from the lowest-income families completed bachelor's degrees by age twenty-four in 2002—the same percentage as 1970 (Sacks 2007).

Diversity initiatives typically ignore or downplay these and other structural problems, and, consequently, institutional inequities go unscathed (Brayboy 2003). Inequities in higher education reflect and reinforce broader societal inequalities. The workforces of multinational corporations are often very diverse, but racial, class, and gender hierarchies are such that affluent White men disproportionately occupy CEO positions and spots on boards of directors (Domhoff 2009), while people of color, especially women, occupy the lowest-paying, least secure, most boring, and most dangerous jobs (Pellow and Park 2002).

Queers and others who speak out forcefully and consistently against such institutional inequalities are subjected to negative sanctions from both conservative and liberal colleagues. The ways queers behave— or misbehave—determines how both straight and many mainstream LGBTQ members of the campus community receive us. There are parallels for feminist, antiracist, and leftist scholars/educators—all overlapping groups. While still an institution that perpetuates White supremacy, economic injustice, patriarchy, and homophobia, the university has long been a site of exciting struggles for progressive and, optimally, radical social change (Boren 2001). Those of us who have the privilege of gaining entrée into academia have a responsibility to "make trouble," to agitate for change both within and outside the ivory tower. Below I highlight different ways in which social inequalities shape university policies and practices, curriculum and teaching, and the production and evaluation of scholarship, as well as the processes of professionalization, hiring, retention, tenure, and promotion. I emphasize complicated queer challenges to these inequalities—sometimes successful, sometimes not—but always with lessons for the future.

There are pitfalls in synthesizing the personal, political, and analytical. Because there are a seemingly infinite number of examples of reprisals targeting agents for change in the ivory tower, deciding upon which to describe is difficult. Even articulating such experiences—and, in particular, the accompanying emotions—may not be seen by some as a "sociological" or "academic" enterprise. But these perceptions are part and parcel of marginalization in the academy and precisely why it is critical to carry on the long struggle to transform the ivory tower.

Being Gay, Becoming Queer: Antiracist Activism as a Launching Pad

> You have grown up with a great deal of privilege and opportunity. As an adult, you now have the responsibility to use your privilege to help others.
>
> —My father

I embraced queer activism in the early 1990s during my involvement in ACT UP (AIDS Coalition to Unleash Power)/Chicago.[3] While this period marked my first explicitly queer endeavors in activism, teaching, and scholarship, my queer consciousness was rooted in earlier experiences of privilege and oppression as well as putting—and failing to put—beliefs into practice. Condensing even a segment of a life history has its pitfalls, but my main point in this section is to acknowledge that becoming a queer activist-educator-scholar was not inevitable; it was an extension and transformation of earlier experiences of life, particularly antiracist activism. One is not born queer, one chooses to be queer, and it is a daily, lifelong practice. This is the case for any activist identity—we make choices to take action or not.

My introduction to translating commitments into practice began with the teachings of my parents, who catalyzed my sense of social responsibility. Simultaneously, the wounds of homophobia led to intense alienation. I responded to these forces as well as to the privileges of being a middle-class White male with both conformity and rebellion. In many ways, I led a double life marked by assimilation and defiance as I grew up. This winding path expanded my understanding of the social world, sowing the seeds of my queer leftist activism.

My parents, born to White, working-class, and rural families during the Great Depression, imparted to me a strong work ethic and a sense of social responsibility. Often on my father's shoulders, I attended civil rights and antiwar rallies in Washington, D.C., in the late 1960s and early 1970s. My parents modeled vocations in creating social change, my father in community mental health and my mother in education. Thanks largely to their influences, I idolized "lefties" like singers Joan Baez and Phil Ochs and author James Baldwin, and I came to despise the antidemocratic practices of the Republican Party, the CIA, the U.S. military, and the Catholic Church. Thanks to the civil rights movement, I attended racially integrated schools in the 1970s and 1980s that provided me with an embryonic understanding of race and racism.

My family, however, was a contradictory space that facilitated my concern for certain social justice issues while also perpetuating my experience of homophobia and heterosexism. This paradoxical dynamic proved to be a key ingredient in the development of my own queer identity as my sense of alienation and experiences of homophobia, combined with my involvement in liberal causes (e.g., marching for the nonproliferation of nuclear weapons), fostered empathy for the experiences of other marginalized groups.

Homophobia and heterosexism pervaded my education from preschool through graduate school. I cannot count the number of times I have heard and read the words "faggot" and "fag," sometimes directed at me, sometimes heard in passing, at school over the past four decades.[4] I had no openly gay teachers until I was in graduate school (and then only one, outside my department). My twenty-four years of formal education were virtually devoid of any lessons beneficial to me as a gay person.[5] The educational system, the media, the church, and other institutions prevented me from knowing that millions of other LGBTQ people had similar experiences and that many had found peace with themselves.

Heterosexist socialization and education also denied me, during my youth, rich histories of queer resistance, histories I have since discovered and applied to my teaching, scholarship, and activism.

Homophobia kept me in the closet during my adolescence, stalling my emotional and political development. My early troublemaking typically centered on nonsexuality issues, but this resistance glimpsed my future queerness. I knew at a young age that things were awry in the world. At twelve, after learning about the Holocaust, I began to question the morality and the existence of God. I butted heads with authority figures—teachers, principals, my parents, and others. Beginning in fourth grade, I expressed fiery indignation toward teachers and administrators whose teaching or disciplinary styles were arbitrary or unfair. My sixth grade report card reveals my lowest grades were in the area "Observes rules and regulations." In junior high school, I quickly came to despise President Ronald Reagan. In high school, I had heated arguments with peers in which I challenged nuclear weapons, interpersonal racism, and the U.S. invasion of Vietnam.

Much of my rebellion was "without a cause." I drank heavily, participated in adolescent pranks, and honed my sarcasm in the face of the snotty conformity of high school. Despite (or perhaps because of) my sadness and anger, I continued to excel academically and in extracurricular activities. In many ways I was a "model" student, active in student government, church, and sports and largely oblivious to my privileges as a middle-class White male. The turmoil of my double life remained largely internal.

I promised myself that I would come out when I left home for college, my middle-class privilege mediating my experiences of heterosexist oppression. I came out during my first and second years of college and began to challenge interpersonal forms of homophobia. I engaged in antiracist and anti-apartheid organizing, but I was a gay antiracist activist, not a queer antiracist activist . . . yet. My own sexual identity was not interwoven into the realm of political struggle, but antiracist—and, to a lesser extent, feminist—activism laid a critical foundation for me to see the interconnections among oppression and privilege and the importance of social location. When I turned to examining and resisting homophobia and heterosexism, I was building upon the deep work I had already done.

After being disenchanted campaigning for Democrats Walter Mondale and Geraldine Ferraro in 1984, my political consciousness blossomed with my participation in anti-apartheid and antiracist movements at the University of Michigan, Ann Arbor. Vibrant, intense interactions with other progressive and leftist students—particularly African American feminists—catalyzed my efforts to confront racism. These activist experiences gave me a vocabulary and conceptual framework to examine my own prejudices, privileges, and complicity in systems of racial, gender, and class oppression. They galvanized my feeling of responsibility to fight inequalities as a White middle-class man. While difficult and painful at times, making sense of my own social location— how I fit into the larger world—was liberating. During this time period, I moved from a liberal, interpersonal understanding of discrimination and prejudice to a leftist understanding of systemic oppressions.

I learned several key things as an antiracist student activist. As a member of the Free South Africa Coordinating Committee (FSACC) and the United Coalition Against Racism (UCAR), I participated in meetings that went for hours, writing newsletter articles, occupying buildings, exposing racist comments made by administrators, and reading historical and political analyses I rarely found in my syllabi.[6] Learning about the historical and systemic character of racial, class, and gender inequalities laid the foundation for my analysis of heterosexual oppression. The Eurocentric, male, and heterosexual biases were—and are—so ubiquitous across the university curriculum that most students and faculty did not even see them, let alone challenge them. In my adolescent psychology class, finding no research on gay youth, I wrote an analysis of Edmund White's novel *A Boy's Own Story* and handed it in, half hoping that my professor would give me a bad grade so I could rail against homophobia in mainstream psychology. I got an A. I learned that solid, critical scholarship is sometimes seen as such and has the potential to challenge bias. While my challenges to homophobia were primarily on the interpersonal level and were rarely centered in my activism, the seeds of my queer identity and activism had been planted.

I learned the necessity of working collectively to effect social change. For example, UCAR forged an extensive campaign against

racism in the university's faculty hiring and student recruitment practices, curriculum, financial aid policies, support services for students of
color (or lack thereof), and other areas. While many of our demands
were not fully met, such activism forced the university to make concrete changes, and we brought the skills we gained to other struggles for
progressive change.

I also learned about the reprisals that face groups working for change.
Many mainstream White students lashed out at UCAR members verbally,
and sometimes physically. Administrators used campus police to attempt
to intimidate us, distorted our demands and actions, and attempted to co-
opt student activism by instituting cosmetic changes such as "Diversity
Day." Sexist and homophobic Black male activists referred to UCAR's
Black feminist leaders as "bitches," "dykes," and "ho's," deepening my
understanding of intracommunity/group divisions and conflict. Such
attacks, blatant and subtle racism among White students, and the practices of the university, helped me to see the connections between multiple
forms (racism, sexism, homophobia, classism) and dimensions (historical,
ideological, institutional, personal) of oppression.

The extensive reading and research, intense political debate, and
writing contributed greatly to my intellectual growth. My work compil-
ing and writing about incidents of racist violence for UCAR's publication, *Racism Alert*, later provided much of the data for my second year
paper (equivalent to a master's thesis). Years of studying and protesting institutionalized racism, and to a lesser extent sexism, classism, and
homophobia, ultimately led me to leave psychology and pursue a doctorate in sociology to utilize my experiences, skills, and social privileges to
teach, research, and write about oppression and resistance.

My work in FSACC and UCAR taught me that social change
occurs when people collectively disrupt business as usual. Whether
it was racist recruiting practices, shrinking financial aid packages,
Eurocentric and sexist curricula, a racist comment by a campus radio DJ,
or the exploitation of campus workers, we felt morally obligated to speak
out. Reinforcing the teachings of my parents, one overarching lesson
from my undergraduate years is that we choose our political actions—or
inactions. As a White activist, I recognized antiracism as a choice, a

crucial lesson in my journey toward even more inclusive political analyses and strategies.

Being out and loud about racism, classism, and sexism served as a launching pad for my explicit queer identity in the late 1980s and early 1990s. By the time I left Ann Arbor in 1989 to attend Northwestern University, I was just as vocal in challenging homophobia as I had been in challenging racism and other inequalities in and outside the academy. I was no longer just gay. I was also queer.

Integrating Dissent into the Learning Process: The Problem with—and the Promise of—Graduate School

> We seem to have a problem on our hands . . . the (largely racial) tension which marred the beginning of the 90/91 academic year has not abated. . . . It seems clear that no expression of support of solidarity is sufficient to satisfy . . . [Daniel, Sharon,[7] and Brett], and they have seen fit to characterize the department and fellow students as less than enlightened on matters of racial equality. The problem arises, however, in the open, public manner in which these three students have shown their displeasure. . . . I believe the militant students should be informed (if they need be) of the serious impact their actions are having on fellow students.
>
> —Sociology Department Graduate
> Affairs Committee memo

Along with two progressive African American students, I was the third "militant" in the memo above. We had challenged the lack of representation of women and people of color in a modern social theory syllabus as well as Eurocentric/racist, sexist, and homophobic biases in other classes and facets of Northwestern University's Sociology Department. My queer agitation as a graduate student was bolstered by my undergraduate activist experience and the solidarity of other graduate students who were committed to combating not only racism but also sexism, homophobia, and classism. We viewed oppression as the problem, including inequitable institutions of higher education. With the privilege of attending graduate school came a responsibility to speak out and resist on multiple fronts, particularly within our own department. We enjoyed relative privileges and inhabited spaces that were created by those who had struggled before us. We felt it our responsibility to build on this legacy. How could we understand and combat social inequality in the world outside the ivory tower without doing so from within?

Circulated to all faculty members, the memo quoted above illustrates the common practice of labeling protest and protesters as "problems" by those supporting the status quo. Many—graduate students, faculty, and administrators—minimize or even deny the pervasiveness of inequality in the academy. Challengers of injustice are often labeled as threats that must be contained if not eliminated, as seen in DePaul University's denial of tenure to leftist, antiracist scholar Norman Finkelstein in 2007 (Howard 2007). Both liberal and conservative academics attempt to delegitimize and sanction dissenters. Simultaneously, those who are silent and/or acquiescent are rewarded. While the costs of dissent take a significant toll on queer, antiracist, feminist, and other activist graduate students, the short- and long-term gains demonstrate not only the power of graduate student organizing, but the absolute necessity of agitating for change within the ivory tower (Lopez 2001).

Denial of institutional inequalities is underscored by the lengthy memo's focus on the actions of the "militants," which deflected attention away from the systemic inequities entrenched in the department and reinforced by the larger university. As we organized to diversify the faculty (in particular to hire women of color), expand course offerings, and improve recruitment and retention of students of color, we found support from some graduate students and a few faculty. But we were met with not only indifference and defensiveness, but with hostility from many faculty members and graduate students.

The memo asserts that our vocal challenges "threatened the intellectual and social atmosphere of the entire department." Given the image of academics as open-minded, free thinkers, it may seem ironic that many in higher education assume the same reactionary stances as other elites. But it makes sense. The hierarchical and elitist socialization of graduate school (and the tenure/promotion process) elicits the labeling of dissent as a threat. And in some ways, it is a threat: A threat to the decorum, the expectations, the sense of entitlement and expertise that swell the egos of those with the letters "PhD" after their names. A threat to that face of the academy that claims detachment from the ugliness of the world, a claim that in reality feeds the ugliness of exclusion, violence, and poverty (Chomsky 2003). Naming White, male, and heterosexual privileges did indeed make the "atmosphere" uncomfortable, something that those in privileged groups—particularly straight, White, male sociologists—had historically not felt in the workplace, in stark contrast to people of color, LGBTQs, and women.

As we studied theories of norms and deviance, we who transgressed were labeled, a la Howard Becker's labeling theory (1997), our labelers seemingly oblivious to their role as authority figures sanctioning political deviance, thereby igniting the palpable "tension."[8] Our "open, public" challenges to racism and other forms of inequality had broken the unspoken rule that sociologists need not reflect on their own complicity in the everyday reproduction of oppression. Some topics of inquiry were off-limits. In a department in which faculty and grad students gloried in ripping each other to shreds during sociological debates, there was virtually no vocabulary for—or emotional investment in—reflecting critically on race, class, gender, and sexuality *within* the department and the discipline itself. Our failure to adhere to the norms led many to view us as "disrespectful," our disrespect located in our raising, according to the memo, "polemical (and substantially irrelevant?) statements regarding the failure of the theorists to address issues of race."

Such attempts to shift the responsibility for conflict onto marginalized voices are linked to a classic liberal (and increasingly conservative as well) diversity trope. Having bodies that are LGBT, women, people of color, etc.—is acceptable, even desirable, as long as there are not *too many* and, perhaps more importantly, as long as they remain silent or parrot the historically dominant voices that echo throughout the ivory tower. As Rick Bonus (this volume) discusses, this notion of diversity denies the existence of difference and power. Yet many members of oppressed groups (and some principled allies) do misbehave and demand equality. Despite being proponents of conflict theory, which posits that power differentials between groups shape the social world, many White (or male or straight) sociologists respond to such demands from their standpoints of privilege rather than from an understanding of social life and social conflict. This disconnect between sociological knowledge and social behavior parallels a broader pattern in which academics often think of themselves as outside the social world they claim to study, as if to say, "I am not a part of this."

The Graduate Affairs Committee memo reflects broader attempts to delegitimize progressive and radical voices in academe.[9] Throughout my time at Northwestern, faculty and some graduate students strove to intimidate, malign, and discredit the rabble-rousers. In closed meetings, faculty members derided me as "not serious" about sociology. One faculty member predicted—wrongly—that Daniel would never get his PhD. The academic performance and potential of antiracist, feminist, and queer students was constantly called into question.

The gatekeepers of the ivory tower label perspectives challenging the status quo as "unsociological," "not empirically based," or "biased." A classic strategy for denying positions (or tenure, promotion, etc.) to scholars whose work subverts dominant ideas—particularly folks in marginalized groups—is to argue that their work is of "insufficient quality and/or quantity." This expression of inequality, whether conscious or unconscious, persists today, as seen in the denial of tenure in 2008 to Andrea Smith, an indigenous feminist scholar and activist, by the University of Michigan (Aldarete 2007; Pharr 2008; see also Thomas and Hollenshead 2001; Turner and Myers 2000).

While the disruption of practices of domination embedded in the professionalization process was quickly labeled problematic and political, the faculty and student mobilization against this disruption, which defended institutionalized inequalities, was framed as objective, reasonable, and apolitical. White students catalyzed this mobilization, complaining that they felt uncomfortable speaking in class: "the militant students should be informed (if they need be) of the serious impact their actions are having on fellow students." The quick legitimacy and reassurances given to these students underscore the privileges that accrue to not only White students, but also straight students and male students. These privileges encompass having one's lived experiences valued and integrated into readings, lectures, discussion, research projects, social interactions, and so on. Added to these are rewards linked to conformity. Complacent students—whether they belong to privileged or oppressed groups—do not lose study time while writing a petition on racism in hiring, do not face the ire of professors who have just been confronted on their sexist language, do not encounter resistance for integrating activism and research, and so on.

Progressive and leftist activist students, particularly those in oppressed groups, experience great frustration on top of the typical pressures of graduate school. We must recognize and address the impact of such psychosocial realities in pursuing a graduate degree and simultaneously fighting programmatic inequalities—alienation, dropping out, self-destructive behavior, mental health problems, increased time to degree, mistrust of faculty members, etc. The sheer time and energy involved in organizing takes time away from coursework, writing a thesis or dissertation, etc. In part due to the paucity of women, people of color, and LGBTQ faculty, many graduate students in these and other subordinated groups have served as teachers and mentors for undergraduate students and more junior graduate students. In addition, many graduate student activists are also political organizers outside the university.

While time-consuming and frustrating, the conflict that emerged resulted in not only negative sanctions but also positive change on both individual and institutional levels. I believe that most of us gained much more than we lost. Viewing political struggle and education as inseparable is a core value embodied in social movements throughout history. The university has been a site of political conflict and social change for centuries. Choosing to frame graduate school—and all academic endeavors—within this context made it more than just a place to gain credentials, but an incredible opportunity to gain new perspectives, ideas, and skills that could then be used to work for justice and equality as activists, scholars, and teachers.

The collective struggles of graduate students—and a few faculty—at Northwestern exposed sheltered, middle-class White students to the entrenched racism and elitism of the academy. Debates about homophobia and sexism compelled heterosexual and male students to listen. Some of these students, including myself, gained valuable lessons in working for not just diversity, but equality in academia and beyond. Solidarity forged between students helped us to survive grad school and to mobilize for future departmental battles. These battles led to concrete, albeit sometimes temporary, changes in the curriculum. Graduate student political agitation dovetailed with our search for more critical and inclusive scholarship. The exchange of cutting-edge ideas and research among graduate students had a profound impact on our own education, research, and teaching. Graduate students spearheaded a course on Black feminism. In a department entrenched in heterosexism, graduate students organized a seminar on the social construction of sexuality and queer theory.[10]

While the full panoply of isms are alive and well in the ivory tower in 2012, course offerings are more inclusive, and some departments have hired more women, people of color, and openly LGBTQ faculty. The caveat here is that while more radical "troublemakers," building upon generations of resistance, have pushed to create spaces in the ivory tower, these spaces are often filled with academics who are women, people of color, and/or LGBTQ, *but* whose intellectual agendas serve to maintain the status quo. Elites—whether university administrators, corporate CEOs, or U.S. presidents—have learned it is good practice to have politically assimilated gays, women, and people of color in positions of power to deflect charges of homophobia, sexism, and racism stemming from persistent unjust collective beliefs, policies, and practices. We must continue to increase the numbers of marginalized groups in academe, but we must also transform the rules of the game as we do so. This involves creative challenges to racist, sexist, and heteronormative criteria that are used to evaluate teaching, research, and service.

The marginalization of women, people of color, and LGBTQ people in academia, as well as sanctions against leftist activist educators and scholars, has led to distorted political, cultural, and economic narratives. Consequently, queers and others use nontraditional research and teaching approaches—including activism—to generate more complex, inclusive, and accurate examinations of the world, whether in the humanities, social sciences, or the natural sciences.

Confronting the False Dichotomy of Scholar and Activist: Carving Out Transformative Space as a Graduate Student

> You cannot be both a scholar and an activist.
>
> —Faculty member on my dissertation committee

My professor's reprimand reflects debates over what kind of scholarship is viewed as legitimate and more generally what the role of a university should be. Activism had given me a sociological perspective before I had ever taken a sociology course, and the idea that I could somehow study social injustice without taking an active stand against it seemed hypocritical. My parents' teachings, lessons from my undergraduate years, and my emerging queer political consciousness urged me to defy this directive. Sociology, despite its flaws, appealed to me precisely because it could be used to catalyze social change. As a queer graduate student, I felt compelled to negotiate the contradictions of the academy to gain the skills, ideas, and credentials to more effectively work for change both within and outside the ivory tower. I continued to see the university as a site of *both* oppression *and* resistance.

While there is a rich tradition of activist-scholarship in sociology (from pioneers like W.E.B. Du Bois and Jane Addams to contemporaries including Al Gedicks and Martha Thompson; see Pellow, Calderon in this volume), hostility toward activism permeates sociology and other disciplines. This antagonism is rooted in the perception of sociologists and other academics as rational, objective, and unbiased observers of the social world (Jayaratne and Stewart 1991). The ivory tower itself is seen as separate, apart from the social world and untainted by its systemic oppressions. In contrast, feminist scholars (Bordo 1989; Spender 1980) have argued that this claim of neutrality and separateness is part and parcel of structured inequalities embedded in the production of knowledge. Unmasking, analyzing, and uprooting these inequalities are necessary tasks in struggles for social justice and equality because academic inequalities are intertwined with inequalities in the so-called "outside world," not divorced from them. Graduate students whose research deviates from conventional topical, theoretical, and methodological norms face many systemic obstacles, but tackling these obstacles head-on produces more critical scholars who blaze new paths in research and teaching.

Given the historical dominance of affluent, heterosexual, White, and/or male faculty, antipathy toward academic activism is logical. Such faculty have been socialized throughout their lives to behave in ways that serve their collective class, racial, gender, and/or sexual interests. They are professionalized to teach and conduct research from dominant perspectives that ignore, distort, and dismiss alternative modes of thought (hooks 1994; Ladner 1998; Ng 1993). Homophobia and other isms in sociology and other disciplines overlap with anti-activist sentiment. One consequence is the paucity of adequate mentors for graduate students whose interests go against the grain.

When I began graduate school in 1989, there were very few faculty mentors who were willing and able to support graduate students pursuing LGBTQ-related research in sociology departments across the country.[11] Few if any faculty at Northwestern were familiar with sociological research on sexuality, HIV/AIDS, and the intersections of sexuality, race, gender, and class. Some members of my dissertation committee expressed marked homophobia and/or heterosexism. One commented to another graduate student that he could clearly tell I was gay by the way I walked. I had to convince another professor that homophobia was indeed a form of social inequality, reflecting the frequent demand that queers have to justify the importance of studying and combating homophobia. Navigating the dissertation process without any queer or activist faculty mentors in my department and grappling with the heterosexism of my committee members was frustrating.[12] I learned to distinguish between, on the one hand, heterosexist and anti-activist feedback and, on the other hand, constructive feedback that focused on improving my skills as a scholar (writing a solid literature review, conducting in-depth interviews, interpreting data, etc.).

In turn, heterosexist research and theoretical frameworks are another barrier for graduate students pursuing LGBTQ-related topics. As a queer graduate student doing research on AIDS activism, activism spearheaded largely by LGBTQ communities, I found minimal resources in mainstream sociological scholarship as I conducted my literature review. Between 1986 and 1999, the *American Sociological Review*, the *Journal of American Sociology*, and *Social Forces* (the most prestigious sociological journals in the eyes of some) published zero articles on HIV/AIDS (Lichtenstein 2001). During this time period, millions of people worldwide died of AIDS.

My AIDS activism and research required attention to the interactive facets of homophobia, racism, sexism, and classism. However, I encountered a paucity of intersectional analyses within sociological scholarship in general and social movement literature in particular. Race, class, and gender were typically treated as separate forces rather than mutually reinforcing oppressions. Sexuality was seldom addressed in the discourse, and homophobia was (and is) often reduced to the interpersonal level, its interconnections with White supremacy, patriarchy, and capitalism ignored.

As my professor's admonition illustrates, mainstream academics often label those who challenge the status quo—particularly those situated in oppressed groups—as "not objective." They question the validity of our scholarship by pointing to our status in outsider groups as indicators of our "bias." Yet the objectivity of men, White people, heterosexuals, and/or academics with middle- and upper-class backgrounds is much less likely to be questioned—particularly when their work defends current power arrangements. Part of privilege is being seen as objective (Rich 1976). In a perverse logic, Whiteness, maleness, heterosexuality, and affluent socioeconomic status are conveniently unnamed and thus not seen as grounds for "bias."

Naming one's standpoint, and taking other standpoints into account, is more objective than believing that one can jettison all biases and values when studying social phenomena—as graduate students have often been taught. Being an activist-scholar requires critiquing the ways assertions of objectivity have historically been used as a smokescreen for methodologies, theories, paradigms, etc. that reinforce inequitable power arrangements (e.g., the patently racist *The Bell Curve* by Hernstein and Murray). This includes exposing the ways that inequalities convolute academic enterprises from their inception (Blauner and Wellman 1998).

Ingrained prejudices shape hegemonic research questions frequently presented as being objective (Duster 1987). As a young activist-scholar,

I learned to critique not only racist, classist,[13] and sexist but also heterosexist research questions. For example, the popular question "What causes homosexuality?" is often predicated on the idea that "homosexuals" are abnormal, unnatural, deviant, diseased, mentally ill, etc., and need to be cured (or perhaps aborted as fetuses!). Even the seemingly sympathetic position that we were "born this way" implies that if given the chance we would be "straight," reinforcing the stigma attached to LGBTQ sexualities. Another research question is "Are the children of lesbians and gay men more likely to be lesbian/gay themselves?" The underlying premise, that "raising" a lesbian/gay child is a negative outcome, is patently homophobic. Research based on such questions both reflects and reinforces broader patterns of homophobia.

A more critical line of thinking leads to provocative questions that destabilize essentialist notions of sexuality that are part and parcel of homophobia: Asking "What causes heterosexuality?" allows us to explore how sexuality is socially constructed. If we ask "How do heterosexual families teach their children to be homophobic?" we are able to explore the social roots of homophobia in various dominant institutions, including the family, as well as the many forms of heterosexual privilege. This type of queer query can be extended to critique the family and other intersectional institutions that play crucial roles in larger society: "How does the family (or school system, religion, media, etc.) reinforce patterns of heterosexual, gender, racial, and class domination?" Posing these counter questions can lead to confusion and defensiveness, but they also generate discussions that unmask the subjectivity of research questions and help us better understand the roots and impacts of homophobia and other inequalities. In turn, this dialogue catalyzes the re-evaluation of common, often exclusionary, notions of sexuality, parenting, family, community, and love.

These critical perspectives were gained by applying lessons learned as an undergraduate; I continued to look outside of traditional literatures and beyond disciplinary borders to sustain my research, teaching, and activism. Outside of the discipline of sociology (and its elitist "top" journals) I gravitated to analyses attentive to the interlocking oppressions shaping the AIDS crisis (ACT UP/New York 1992; Beam 2008; Corea 1992; Hammonds 1992). These provocative and compassionate works were frequently written by activists, particularly those at the inter-sections of oppressed groups—women of color, gay men of color, and lesbians (both of color and White)—and served as models of activist scholarship. I discovered most of these pivotal writings working with other antiracist, feminist, and queer students at Northwestern and radi-cal queer AIDS activists in ACT UP/Chicago. While I was relatively alone politically in my cohort, I found comrades in other cohorts and departments and outside the university. Such lessons illustrate both the frustrations felt and the achievements made when students feel com-pelled to teach themselves.

Challenging the hypocrisy and limitations of "objective," "value-free" research is essential in the production of ideas—expressed through teaching, research, writing—that can be applied to dismantling inequal-ities and generating positive social change (Feagin and Vera 2008). Activism generated my knowledge of institutional and ideological ineq-uities, so it would not make sense to disengage it from my scholarship as my advisor demanded. My research and activism have often been intertwined. My second year paper drew heavily on data collected as an undergraduate antiracist activist and as a member of the Taskforce to Confront Police Violence in Chicago. As I began my dissertation research, I joined ACT UP/Chicago's Prison Issues Committee because I wanted not only to study, but also to protest, the interactive oppressions igniting the AIDS crisis.

Rather than cloud my "objectivity," being an activist and a scholar provided me with multiple perspectives that proved indispensable in con-ducting my research. This knowledge was grounded not only in esoteric social movement literature, but lived experiences as a social movement participant. As an AIDS activist (not just a "participant observer"), I came to know the different players, factions, and organizations in the AIDS movement in Chicago and, to some extent, nationally. I had access to documents, conference calls, and informal discussions that shaped my understanding of the AIDS crisis and AIDS activism and thus my inter-view questions. Both my undergraduate and ACT UP activist networks facilitated vibrant interviews in Chicago, Los Angeles, and New York City. My status as an activist, not just another doctoral student writing a dissertation, promoted trust as respondents detailed their battles with

not only dominant institutions, but also with community-based HIV/
AIDS and other social service agencies, churches, and other activists—
some within their own organizations.

My familiarity with these common rifts in oppressed communities
as well as activist groups provided me with an understanding of intersec-
tionality that served as the conceptual foundation for my dissertation. As
a member of ACT UP/Chicago's Prison AIDS Committee, advocating
for prisoners affected by HIV/AIDS brought the abstraction of intersec-
tionality into sharp focus. For example, many middle-class White lesbians and gay men, including AIDS activists, did not consider prisoners
worthy of support in the face of the epidemic (Stockdill 2003: 89–90):

> AIDS activists are not immune to stereotypical images
> of prisoners. Mainstream AIDS activists were frequently
> caught up in the "law and order," "three strikes, you're
> out" mentality that has guided our society's approach to
> crime and punishment in recent decades.

This dynamic as well as other manifestations of the oppressed as oppressor (homophobia in churches of color, sexism among gay male activists,
etc.) reveal the contours of interlocking systems of inequality that operate on institutional, organizational, community, and interpersonal levels.

My graduate school experience demonstrates that activist-scholars
typically must not only understand and critique their respective canons
and "classics," but must also seek out and utilize oppositional scholarship frequently dismissed by mainstream scholars. We must take advan-
tage of our academic skills and privilege to center marginalized ideas,
theories, and methodologies. As I acted up in the streets, conducted my
research, and analyzed my findings, I refused to acquiesce to the false
activist-scholar dichotomy, and my dissertation committee came to treat
my area of research, my methodology, and my analysis as serious scholarship. With their guidance I finished my dissertation and later revised it
into a book exploring how interlocking oppressions affect community
organizing (Stockdill 2003). As Feagin and Vera (2008) explain, being
a participant who draws on multiple viewpoints, not just a detached
observer, engenders a much richer, more complex understanding of the
social world. Such a critical approach generates research that is optimally

useful in changing bigoted attitudes, behaviors, and public policies as well as transforming hegemonic culture and social institutions. You can be *both* an activist and a scholar. Combining these has made me a better activist, scholar, and teacher.

Acting Up in the Academy: Navigating Power Paradoxes as a Troublemaking Junior Professor

> Dr. Stockdill has raised the issue of homophobia, alleging that it biased the RTP [Retention, Tenure, and Promotion] Committee deliberations. These allegations are not evident in Committee recommendations and are not, in any event, within the purview of CRTP evaluation.
>
> —College Retention, Tenure, and
> Promotion Committee

Status quo faculty present homophobia and other inequalities as outside the "purview" of retention and tenure evaluations, while simultaneously perpetuating these very oppressions. This creates a paradoxical situation that is all too common in the ivory tower: it is difficult to substantiate "allegations" of inequality if such inequality is deemed irrelevant or nonexistent. While I received positive recommendations for each of my annual retention reviews at California State Polytechnic University, Pomona (Cal Poly Pomona), senior faculty members used such reviews as another arena in which to express their antipathy toward my queer politics. Their attacks, and the complicity of those who sat quite literally in silence, reflect broader efforts to stymie challenges to inequalities in the department and university.

Queer and other activist faculty members' contributions as educators, scholars, and colleagues are often downgraded, distorted, and delegitimized by their departments, colleges, universities, and disciplines. The incidents leading up to the college committee's comments above illustrate how dismissing "allegations" of bigotry ensures that bigotry continues to be very much within the "purview" of many departments, colleges, and universities—both in sociology and other disciplines. Identifying and analyzing particular instances of inequality and resistance in academia are necessary to pierce the façade of open-mindedness and fairness and galvanize solidarity among dissident faculty.

During my second year as an assistant professor, Proposition 22, which stated that only a heterosexual marriage would be recognized by the state, was put on the ballot in California. Christian fundamentalists covered the Cal Poly Pomona campus with signs supporting the proposition. A professor from another department said that in the weeks leading to the March 7, 2000, election, she felt like she "was in Nazi Germany" as she walked by the dozens of "Yes on 22" signs on campus. A group of LGBTQ students was harassed and taunted with epithets including "faggot" on campus the week before the election. LGBTQ people and antihomophobic heterosexuals challenged the proposition.

Within this context, I came upon a flyer in the Behavioral Sciences (Psychology and Sociology) Department office doorway that read,

Vote Yes on Prop 22

'Only marriage between a man and a woman is valid or recognized in California.'

. . . if there were no restrictions on marriage and feelings were all that mattered, fathers could marry their own daughters or brothers could marry their sisters. Any person, of any age, could marry anyone he wished—a close relative, three young children, etc.

Posted at the entrance to the departmental office, the flyer's message equating homosexuality with incest and pedophilia appeared to be the department's official position. While not a supporter of the patriarchal institution of marriage, I was so outraged by this blatant homophobia that I complained to my department chair about the flyer—which had been posted by a departmental secretary—pointing out its prejudicial content and problematic location. The chair told me there was nothing he could do. I told the secretary that the flyer was hateful, bigoted, and fostered a hostile work and learning environment for students, staff, and faculty. And I got in trouble.

My open defiance of homophobia was seen as decidedly more problematic than homophobia itself. While blatant displays of racism and, to a lesser extent, sexism have become less acceptable in many parts of U.S.

society, overt homophobia continues to be widely tolerated. In this case, faculty and administrators felt that the secretary's rights to free speech, particularly her religious beliefs, trumped my right to free speech and the rights of LGBTQ students, staff, and faculty to work and study on a campus where homophobic harassment is prohibited. My departmental retention evaluation described me as "unprofessional" and acting "inappropriately." In fact, some heterosexual faculty depicted me as guilty of sexual harassment; some compared me to a heterosexual man who had kept a gun in his office and made explicit sexual threats to female faculty. The protection of heterosexual privilege was clearly indicated in retention evaluation letters written by tenured faculty. One, an advocate of the work of the modern eugenicist Arthur Jensen, wrote, "I believe that Dr. Stockdill's behavior caused tension in the department and made it difficult for the secretaries, some professors (including myself), and some students to feel comfortable here." In violation of the faculty union contract, the department's Retention, Tenure, and Promotion (RTP) committee included the secretary's letter in my permanent RTP file, in which she exclaimed, "[Brett] was not very tolerant of my position." The department chair and college dean ordered me to write a letter of apology to the secretary.

While some faculty and administrators openly reprimanded me, there was a virtual blanket of silence among others that was in many ways more chilling than the antigay flyer itself. Silence, a form of denial and complicity, is common when issues of inequality are brought to light. If inequality can be imagined as nonexistent, it is easy to reject responsibility for challenging it. To preserve their (false) sense of enlightenment and open-mindedness, folks in higher education rely on the denial of oppression within the ivory tower. ("We aren't homophobic, so this must not be homophobia here.") In another revealing statement, the chair of the college level RTP committee dismissed my claims of homophobia because one of the most senior members of the department was an openly gay man. Yet members of oppressed groups can and do participate in the censure of their "own." In his evaluation of me, this same gay professor admonished me for not being a "team player" because I responded publicly to these and other problems in the department.

Senior faculty members made no attempts to have departmental discussions about homophobia. Two tenured professors who harshly criticized my lack of "professionalism" made no efforts to speak to me in the seven months between the incident and my receipt of their letters in my RTP evaluation. One was my assigned "mentor." Senior professors found it particularly distasteful that the incident took place "in public" (in the departmental office). This desire to avoid any acknowledgment of conflict perpetuated a climate antithetical to dialogue, democratic decision making, learning, and social change. On several occasions, the advice I received from the chair and other tenured faculty members was to *not* respond to homophobia and other inequalities in the department.

Systemic denial and silence are linked to norms sanctioning public expressions of emotionality. Faculty members chastised me in writing for expressing "anger," and the departmental retention evaluation stated that my "demeanor, loud tone, and persistence in continuing the discussion were unprofessional." As so-called objective academics, we are socialized to avoid expressions of strong emotions. However, personal thoughts and feelings are linked to larger systems of privilege and domination both within and outside the academy. Patriarchy, Eurocentrism, and classism in higher education foster anti-emotionality (hooks 1984). The pain and frustration expressed by marginalized groups in academia and in society in general are often turned against us. Lorde (1984) describes how White women often depict Black women who challenge racism as overly sensitive, angry, combative, etc., a dynamic that prevents meaningful antiracist dialogue. In the eyes of my colleagues, the problem was not homophobia, but my public, emotional response to homophobia. Yet the emotions—fear, hatred, disgust—underlying the unjust actions and complicity of those in privileged groups are seldom acknowledged.

Of all the tenured faculty members who signed off on my RTP evaluation, only one, an African American woman, actually expressed solidarity. While her support was only offered in private, the act of sharing her own pain and anger stemming from racism and sexism in the department lessened my sense of isolation. We must challenge the tendency among academics to dismiss or downplay feelings of pain, anger, and frustration. In the words of the Latina Feminist Group (2001: 14), acknowledging pain helps "to unveil the workings of power in institutional cultures, its human costs, and the ways in which individuals can and do overcome the ravages of power dynamics and abuses."

I had tremendous emotional and strategic support from my colleague and friend Mary Danico as well as feminist senior professors in other departments. The director of the campus LGBTQ Pride Center, along with many students—both LGBTQ and straight—were enraged by the treatment accorded me, and their rage was inspirational and supportive. This support was critical in helping me to forcefully name and articulate the injustice in not only this case, but in other instances of homophobia in the department. Our collective efforts provoked the university RTP committee to conduct an investigation that concluded that "[t]he department and dean have included statements, opinions and documentation that violate section 15.2 [of the California State University/California Faculty Association Contract]. Their commentary and statements are beyond the scope of RTP review, prejudicial to the candidate and should be removed." While the department and dean did not follow this directive, this decision demonstrated the potential impact of individual and collective resistance.

This type of resistance has positive, concrete effects. Over the course of two job searches, tenured male professors asserted that they did not think it would be a good move for the department to hire a "feminist." Tenured female professors critiqued feminist job candidates' demeanor—criticizing the way one walked and sat, and the outfit and hand movements (while lecturing) of another. Male candidates' clothing, mannerisms, etc. were not discussed. Despite this sexism, vocal junior faculty were able to push both of these outstanding candidates to the number two position, and when the number one picks declined the job offers, both women were hired.

Some faculty members seemed perplexed that I would focus on instances of homophobia, racism, and sexism rather than the overall positive retention evaluations of my teaching, research, and service. I was repulsed by the thought that challenging inequality should wait until I was retained, promoted, granted tenure, etc., particularly when as an assistant professor I had much greater autonomy and privilege than the majority of the members of the campus community. There is never a completely safe or comfortable time to confront injustice.

As I continued to challenge ingrained patterns of racism, sexism, homophobia, and elitism in the department and the broader university, most often with my comrade Mary, the costs of being a troublemaker were evident. When I was preparing to apply for early tenure, a recently tenured professor suddenly withdrew her previous offer to share her tenure application with me. My ideas on "nonpolitical" issues were often ignored or given short shrift. On more than one occasion, I completed major projects for the department and was not given credit. In other cases, I was falsely accused of failing to do assigned duties.

Though I received overwhelmingly positive teaching evaluations, some colleagues disparaged my efforts to center the experiences of oppressed groups in the classroom. After observing my Introductory Sociology course, one tenured professor wrote, "I wondered if—in his decision to emphasize the sexist, racist, white hegemonist, et cetera, view of things—it might appear to some students that he is a bit too repetitive (and possibly overbearing)." As the topic that day was U.S. social movements, it seems difficult to imagine not focusing on race and gender (as well as class, sexuality, etc.). If I had let these omnipresent sociological forces lie quietly (or loudly, depending on one's perspective) in the classroom, thereby reinforcing dominant ideology, it seems doubtful that I would have been criticized for *not* speaking about them. Such comments reflect broader efforts to maintain exclusionary curricula and other departmental policies and practices.

While such conflicts sucked up much of my energy over the course of five years at Cal Poly Pomona, they are quite instructive. When something unjust—either individual or collective—occurs, it is imperative to respond directly, thoroughly, and thoughtfully. First, it is crucial to document everything in a detailed manner, using existing institutional language or policies to reinforce one's case. Through this incident I learned about my own job contract as well as departmental, college, and university strategic plans, policies, etc. Documenting acts of bigotry was something I learned to do as an activist, but each institution and situation is unique. The knowledge I gained was useful to me in the ensuing years as a junior faculty member and an activist on campus. Second, when such events occur, reach out for collective support. Alone, I doubt I could have endured five years in that department. Despite the intransigence of many tenured faculty members in the department, I thrived as a teacher, scholar, and activist at Cal Poly Pomona because of progressive and leftist allies—faculty, staff, and students across the university and outside the university. It is crucial to cultivate this brand of solidarity in the face of the vulnerability of queer academics in their bids for retention, tenure, promotion, and so on.

Taking these steps, being out and open, is scary, but it also ensures that people know that you will fight back. In this sense, my queerness, my passion and troublemaking, have given me a sense of protection. In addition, I'd like to think the critical tension helped some in the department to rethink their views. What I do know is that in vocally naming and challenging homophobia, I contributed to broader struggles that reduce the isolation so commonly experienced by LGBTQ people and fuel feelings of pride.

At Cal Poly Pomona, I worked with other faculty as well as staff and students to raise awareness around various social justice issues on and off campus. I served as the cochair of the CPP Pride Alliance, an organization that provided support for LGBTQ faculty and staff, and I collaborated frequently with the campus's vibrant LGBTQ Pride Center, speaking at protests and doing workshops as an openly gay, HIV-positive faculty member. As I supported the personal development and collective action of LGBTQ students, I marveled at how courageously out many of these students were, much more so than I had been as an undergraduate.[14] I raised critical issues relating to sexuality and homophobia and emphasized the necessity of simultaneously confronting racial, gender, class, and anti-immigrant bigotry. Participating in building coalitions between queer, feminist, leftist, and antiracist students was the most exciting aspect of my activism at Cal Poly Pomona. Such alliances were seen vividly in the struggles of two radical political forces on campus, Chican@ students in MEChA (Movimiento Estudiantil Chicana/o de Aztlan—Chicano/a Student Movement of Aztlan)[15] and Native American students in Red Nations.

Collective Protest on Campus: Organizing with Students and Janitors

7 Basic Janitor Demands

1. Reinstate all workers that have been wrongly dismissed, fired, and or affected to Cal Poly Pomona.
2. Provide safe and decent working conditions.
3. Provide a living wage with health benefits.
4. Immediately eliminate Varsity Contractors, Inc. as a contractor of Cal Poly Pomona without affecting present workers.
5. Freedom to organize, choose a union, and exercise their legal rights.
6. Promote education in the workplace, in lieu of discriminating.
7. Provide a respectable and just workplace to all workers in the university.

—Student, Staff & Faculty Coalition in
Support of Janitors, Cal Poly Pomona

In 2001, the students of MEChA and Red Nations allied with campus janitors to launch one of the most vibrant political struggles in which I have participated. As immigrants or the children of immigrants and astute analysts of radical social movements, the members of MEChA and Red Nations felt strong solidarity with the janitors, predominantly immigrants from Mexico and El Salvador and largely women. The janitors' courage to take on the university and the corporate contractor that employed them reflects the broader reinvigoration of the U.S. labor movement by Latin American immigrants (Gonzalez 2001). Working with this dynamic, sharp, and daring group of janitors and students, supporting the most vulnerable and exploited group on campus was where I, as a queer activist, felt at home. My participation reflects the role that faculty can play in struggles for change within the ivory tower and beyond.

I felt a kinship with this younger generation of student activists and supported their struggles to gain more resources for students of color on campus, build coalitions between campus and community (including grassroots efforts to support low-income students of color to get into and stay in college), fight against racist/classist California state propositions, as well as protest globalization (e.g., NAFTA) and the war in Iraq. The traditional dichotomy of professor/teacher and student/learner was broken down. We shared political perspectives, strategies and tactics, activist networks, and traditions of resistance. I lent the resources I had as a tenure-track faculty member and my experiences as an antiracist and queer activist. I respected their willingness to expand their political consciousnesses, specifically to grapple with sexism and homophobia. In turn, this sophisticated, fiery group of students helped me to expand my own consciousness around issues facing youth of color in Southern California and to maintain my involvement in direct action activism.

After an initial protest in which janitors spoke out against horrific working conditions, we formed the Student, Staff and Faculty Coalition in Support of Janitors and met regularly with many of the janitors. In meetings conducted in Spanish and English, janitors and coalition members documented exploitative labor practices. For years, Cal Poly Pomona had contracted with Varsity Contractors, Inc., a corporation notorious for its exploitation of its janitorial staff. Janitors received about $6.00 an hour to mop floors, scrub toilets, scrape gum off of desks, and so on. They had no health insurance or paid vacation days and were not provided adequate safety equipment or first aid kits. Numerous janitors were injured on the job and denied overtime pay. They worked late at night, kept out of sight as they cleaned up the mess left by students, faculty, and staff. Varsity supervisors verbally abused janitors and sexually harassed female janitors.[16]

The coalition utilized fliers, letters to the student newspaper, e-mails, and rallies to educate students, staff, and faculty about these workplace conditions, many of which were blatant violations of labor laws. We conducted research on other janitor campaigns at other universities and worked to get the campaign in the media. We received critical advice and moral support from a Los Angeles–based Justice for Janitors organizer—a hardcore immigrant activist and former janitor himself—and the janitors were warmly welcomed into the SEIU (State Employees Industrial Union) local.

As punishment for speaking out, janitor leaders were given the most strenuous and labor-intensive jobs. As they began to voice their demands for higher wages and better working conditions, janitors were threatened with dismissal and deportation for forming a union. When several were fired in retaliation for their activism, the coalition started a support fund to collect money, food, clothing, and employment information for the janitors and their families. We exposed the retaliatory firings to further raise awareness on and off campus. More than seven hundred students, staff, and faculty signed a petition in support of the janitors. The janitors—including those who had been fired—continued to speak out publicly, and their personal stories were pivotal in putting a human face on the struggle.

Direct action protest, including a march to the doorstep of the university president's plush campus home, had a decisive impact. A crucial demonstration occurred at the June 2001 outdoor graduation ceremony for the College of Letters, Arts, and Social Sciences. As the graduating seniors, faculty, and administrators filed in, students and janitors stood alongside the walkway with banners proclaiming "Justice for Janitors," and as the ceremony began, students unfurled another enormous banner from the top floor of an adjacent building.

The campaign eventually forced the university to sever its contract with Varsity, Inc., and create new unionized janitorial positions with a living wage and full health benefits. The administration subsequently violated key agreements, resulting in several of the janitors not being rehired.[17] While this victory was bittersweet, it was a victory nonetheless. The campaign directly confronted not only the inequitable power structure of the university, but the racist, sexist, and anti-immigrant labor practices of a large corporation. Its success supports Black, Chicana, and other multiracial feminist calls for confronting multiple, interlocking oppressions. The struggle highlights the importance of both nurturing and following the leadership of both young people and the most exploited groups in society as well as forging alliances on and off campus to better agitate for change.

I still feel tremendous solidarity with the janitors and student activists, and along with other battles over the years this struggle solidified my dedication to queering the ivory tower. This requires organizing on an ongoing basis with the most radical members of the university community—most often students—against undemocratic university practices and policies. Because progressive and leftist student activists are typically the first ones—often the only ones—to take on the most ingrained forms of exclusion and marginalization, I continue to find sustenance working with them. In many cases, there has been a synergistic effect between my allying with student activists and my teaching. Nurturing and supporting the potential of students to act as agents of social change is the cornerstone of my teaching.

Making Connections in the Classroom: Teaching Critically, Teaching Passionately

> After the first lecture in my American Society course—in which I announced the class would focus on LGBTQ people in the U.S.—two born-again Christians expressed their fears about staying in the course because they had been taught that homosexuality was wrong, sinful and unnatural. On the last day of class, full of smiles, they both gave me warm hugs and thanked me.

I invite students to make the classroom a site of resistance and change. As a teacher I can facilitate that process, but students have to choose to actualize it. And the vast majority do. While many faculty and administrators often sadly see their education as complete, students, by and large, go to college because they want to learn. Teaching from a queer perspective is a challenge, but it fuels the emotional, intellectual, and political growth of both students and teachers.

Challenging hegemonic ideas and centering the perspectives and experiences of oppressed groups ignites change in students' minds. Students sometimes view blatant discrimination and abuse of oppressed groups as either isolated or as a thing of the past. Many are not familiar with the concrete manifestations of homophobia, and some believe that LGBTQ folks are not oppressed. Concrete examples and empirical evidence of homophobic violence, negative media portrayals, discrimination in housing and employment, police abuse, biases in the criminal justice system, lack of civil rights protection, and other inequalities targeting LGBTQ individuals and communities dispel this myth. Because LGBTQ people are also women, immigrants, people of color, poor people, etc., teaching about mutually reinforcing systems of oppression is a critical task. Teaching *queerly* about controversial topics such as HIV/AIDS, addiction, and prostitution requires squarely examining homophobia, racism, sexism, and economic injustice. For example, transgender sex workers of color face systemic police brutality that is simultaneously racist, sexist, classist, and transphobic (Ritchie 2006).

Empirical evidence and analysis must be coupled with the humanization of different social groups, showing their complex responses to systemic inequalities. Firsthand perspectives from myriad groups stimulate more excitement among students. Literature, poetry, novels, music, films, guest speakers, and field trips spark students' sociological imagination—making sense of where they fit and how other individuals and groups fit into the social world. A variety of multiple pedagogical approaches including lecture, discussion, interactive exercises, and student presentations maximizes the depth of learning in the classroom (Thompson 2008).

This process at its heart requires both teachers and students to relate course material to their own lives. In the words of bell hooks (1994: 89), "combining the analytical and the experiential is a richer way of knowing." Optimally, teachers help students recognize their relationships to systemic oppressions—both privileges and abuses. I use my own life experiences as a teaching tool. I highlight the impact of homophobia in my life as well as the benefits of my maleness, Whiteness, and middle-class status. In one class, I caught my students and myself speaking about dating dynamics without consciously recognizing that we were limiting our discussion to heterosexual relationships. I used this as an example of heterosexism at work.

Utilizing sociological analysis in concert with personal experience facilitates the interrogation of common misperceptions about race, class, gender, and sexuality. For example, when students downplay or dismiss the impact of homophobia by arguing that "gay people can pass," I point out that many of us cannot "pass" (e.g., butch lesbians, drag queens, etc.). Sharing both research on social isolation, mental health problems, addiction, and suicide among queer youth and adults as well as my own adolescent responses to homophobia—depression, self-hatred, binge drinking, and suicidal thoughts—elucidate the nightmares of the closet.

I ask students to consider the social pressure to repress and conceal vital and rich aspects of our core identities (i.e., alleged "passing") as a central manifestation of homophobic oppression. What would it be like to be forced to hide one's racial or ethnic identity, religion, etc. for fear of prejudice and violence?[18]

While it is essential to delineate the distinctions between different forms of oppression, teasing out the commonalities between homophobia and other inequalities can be quite productive. For example, drawing out the ways violence has been used to maintain the subordination of women, people of color, and sexual minorities helps students better understand both the similarities and the differences between sexism, racism, and homophobia.

Being out in the classroom puts a human face on groups seen as deviant—gays,[19] people living with HIV, and leftist activists in my case. Coupled with naming ones' privileges, this strategy invites critical discussion and support for students grappling with their own multifaceted identities—in both oppressed and oppressor groups. These teaching strategies encourage critical reflection among students. In my Senior Seminar in Sociology class, Joanna discussed how she experiences sexism as a woman and xenophobia as a Polish immigrant with an accent, as well as White privilege. In Social Inequalities, Emiliano examined his encounters with racism and classism as a working-class Mexican immigrant and acknowledged his complicity in sexism and homophobia. Liberatory sociology also contextualizes perspectives on and experiences with myriad social problems including sexual assault, the criminalization of addiction, gentrification, incarceration, and so on. This includes analyzing and celebrating individual and collective resistance to social inequalities. Patricia told me in office hours that learning about the systemic roots of social inequalities as well as the rich legacy of collective resistance to these inequalities (in my Social Movements course) helped her understand her own experiences of domestic violence and helped empower her to become an advocate for other survivors.

When students are not merely taking notes as the professor drones on and on from the podium, they are more likely to not only think, but also to *feel* about new perspectives, histories, and ideas. While students like those mentioned above typically feel both challenged and liberated by critical sociology, some resist critiques of their assumptions about the social world. Crystal, a heterosexual student in my Sociology of HIV/AIDS class, asserted, "Lectures were leaving the majority of the class feeling guilty or angry at their sexual orientation, a subject I feel is personal." hooks (1994: 43) writes, "[T]here can be, and usually is, some degree of pain involved in giving up old ways of thinking and knowing and learning new approaches." Though Crystal's reaction was negative, her comments reveal that she was very much engaged. It is crucial to remind students that learning is often a frustrating, uncomfortable process as they/we confront ingrained prejudices, blind spots, and unknown complicity in patterns of exploitation and structural violence. Like hooks, I respect that pain and acknowledge it regularly when teaching. In class we take time to examine multilayered feelings of frustration, anger, hope, solidarity, and liberation that emerge when the classroom is a site of resistance.

Crystal's comment reveals a perception common among many students and faculty that sexuality is merely a *private, personal* issue that should not be discussed in public, a perception that is a cornerstone of heterosexist oppression. Showing students that homophobic oppression is very public (e.g., gay bashing) and is rooted in the policies and practices of dominant institutions (e.g., police entrapment of gay men having public sex, anti–gay marriage laws) debunks the myth that sexuality is merely a "private, personal issue." For me, being a queer educator means, to use the classic adage, the personal is political—and therefore public.

There are obstacles and risks in teaching queer. I have had to teach not just students, but also heterosexist faculty that homophobia is indeed a form of oppression. As a graduate teaching assistant for a social inequality class, I was asked by the professor to give a guest lecture. When I suggested my lecture focus on homophobia, he told me I would have to convince him that this topic was relevant to the class. I did, and more than a hundred undergraduate students heard a sociological analysis of homophobia and LGBTQ resistance. Though the ignorance of the professor frustrated me, preparing a thorough argument justifying that homophobia is indeed a form of inequality not only had a concrete, immediate payoff, but it also made me a better educator. I have had to engage in similar conversations on a regular basis in the classroom, departmental and university meetings, and public forums. For example, I have applied this lesson in legitimizing why teaching about other marginalized perspectives (e.g., prostitution from sex workers' perspectives, the criminal justice system from prisoners' perspectives) is essential.

We run the risk of being labeled as biased by students and faculty when we teach critically about homophobia and LGBTQ issues. While heterosexual faculty's mention of spouses, families, etc. (sometimes ad nauseam) rarely evokes negative student evaluations, coming out in the classroom and teaching about homophobia sometimes leads to student evaluations like Crystal's in which we are accused of persecuting heterosexual students (or White, male, affluent, etc. students). Homophobic colleagues may seize upon such rare instances and depict them as representative of student feedback.[20]

However, exposing students to a sociological perspective critical of homophobia and other inequalities and inclusive of LGBTQ lives and the lives of women, poor people, people of color, undocumented people, etc. is more than worth the difficulties and reprimands. When we are *out* (and not just in terms of sexuality), we help our students to be *out:* to support a grandmother living with HIV/AIDS, a brother in prison, a teenage daughter coming out in a hostile school setting; to educate family members about social inequality and social movements; to provide holistic services to homeless Iraq veterans and other populations in need; to teach children to think critically; and, most importantly, to organize collectively against injustice. There are days when teaching leaves me feeling raw, vulnerable, and bruised emotionally. Nevertheless, teaching students to apply knowledge to their social worlds, particularly when this application takes the form of activism, is at the core of my work as a queer educator, intellectual, and activist. Along with other campus troublemakers, I feel both a moral obligation and a liberatory joy in struggling collectively to transform the ivory tower and the world of which it is a part.

Notes

1   Andrea Smith (2006) argues that patriarchy and heteronormativity are interconnected with white supremacy and are core components of U.S. imperialism.

2   I use the nonsexist terms Latin@s and Chican@s to include multiple genders often collapsed into "Latinos" and "Chicanos."

3   ACT UP (AIDS Coalition to Unleash Power) described itself as a "diverse, nonpartisan group of individuals united in anger and committed to direct action to end the AIDS crisis. We meet with government officials; we research and distribute the latest medical information. We protest and demonstrate; we are not silent" (Carter 1992: 1).

4   See reports from the Gay, Lesbian and Straight Educational Network (GLSEN) revealing high rates of harassment and violence targeting LGBT youth in school (http://www.glsen.org/cgi-bin/iowa/all/research/index.html).

5   Children's books, word problems in math, narratives in social studies and history texts, and biology classes virtually always represented heterosexual individuals, couples and families, and bodies, reinforcing compulsory heterosexuality (see Rich 1986). My teachers modeled heterosexist, and often homophobic, behavior, as most teachers still do so today.

6   We gathered inspiration from learning about the struggles of many organizations including the ANC (African National Congress), SNCC (Student Nonviolent Coordinating Committee), SDS (Students for a Democratic Society), the Black Panther Party, and AIM (American Indian Movement), as well as the work of radical feminists, particularly feminists of color such as Angela Davis (1983), Barbara Smith (1983), and Gloria Anzaldúa (1987).

7   Names of all students in this chapter are pseudonyms.

8   Ironically, Howard Becker was on Northwestern's faculty when I began my graduate studies.

9   A classic example is the derision targeting C. Wright Mills, author of *The Sociological Imagination* (1959), who was never awarded the rank of full professor.

10   Though there were a number of openly out lesbian, bisexual, and gay graduate students, there were no openly LGBTQ faculty or any visible efforts to address LGBTQ sexualities, politics, cultures, and histories by faculty members when I entered the program.

11   There are more such faculty mentors today, but LGBTQ graduate students continue to face many obstacles (American Sociological Association 2002, 2009).

12   The faculty member that I found to be most supportive of (and active in) antiracist and leftist activism, and who served on my second-year paper

committee, reportedly decided to end his half-time appointment in the Sociology Department and increase his position in African American Studies from half- to full-time.

13   For example, much contemporary research focuses on "neighborhood effects" that ostensibly explain racial and class inequality: "What is deficient about low-income communities of color that keeps them mired in poverty?" A more critical line of questioning asks, "In what ways do dominant institutions (government, economy, schools, media, criminal justice systems, etc.) sustain economic injustice and racism?"

14   I felt a profound sense of hope and pride as I watched LGBTQ students and straight allies celebrate at the annual CPP Lavender Graduation. Many were also working-class, first-generation students of color, and they had struggled on many levels to make it to graduation day.

15   Many students in CPP MEChA at the time viewed Chicanismo as a political identity and consciousness, and therefore there were at times "Chicanas/os" of non-Mexican descent, including those with Central American, South American, and Filipina/o heritage.

16   The working conditions of many janitors as well as the repression Justice for Janitors activists faced in organizing unions is vividly depicted in the fact-based film *Bread and Roses*.

17   For example, because a racist university hiring policy required janitors to take an English proficiency exam, we demanded there be a probationary period in which the former Varsity janitors be given the chance to learn English (students had already started tutoring some of the janitors). The administration agreed, but then reneged and refused to hire a number of the janitors with years of experience.

18   When students rationalize (or justify) homophobia using their religious beliefs or patriarchal political nationalism, I emphasize that both conventional religion and narrow nationalism exclude and alienate not only LGBTQ people, but also women—the majority of people in any particular faith or community.

19   Straight educators can be "out" by challenging homophobia, integrating LGBTQ perspectives and issues into their courses, and making the classroom safe for LGBTQ students.

20   See Ng's (1993) analysis of her experience with racism and sexism in the classroom.

REFERENCES

ACT UP (Aids Coalition to Unleash Power)/New York Women and AIDS Book Group.1992. *Women, AIDS and Activism*. Boston: South End Press.

Aguirre, Adalberto J. 2000. *Women and Minority Faculty in the Academic Workplace: Recruitment, Retention, and Academic Culture*. San Francisco: Jossey-Bass.

Aldarete, Adriana. 2007. "Perspectives: Current Tenure Process Deters Minority Women Professors." http://diverseeducation.com/article/10416/perspectives-current-tenure-process-deters-minority-women-professors.html.

Allen, Tammy D., and Lillian T. Eby. 2007. *The Blackwell Handbook of Mentoring: A Multiple Perspectives Approach*. Malden, Mass.: Blackwell.

American Association of University Professors. 2006. *The State of the Faculty at the University of Washington: Report Card for 2006*. http://depts.washington.edu/uwaaup/state_faculty.htm.

———. 2008. *2008–09 Report on the Economic Status of the Profession*. Washington, D.C.: American Association of University Professors. http://www.aaup.org/AAUP/comm/rep/Z/ecstatreport08–09/.

American Sociological Association. 2002. *Report on the Status of Gay, Lesbian, Bisexual, and Transgender Persons in Sociology*. Prepared by the Committee on the Status of Gay, Lesbian, Bisexual and Transgendered Persons in Sociology. July 16, 2002.

———. 2009. *Report on the Status of Gay, Lesbian, Bisexual and Transgender Persons in Sociology*. Prepared by the Committee on the Status of Gay, Lesbian, Bisexual and Transgender Persons in Sociology. May 28, 2009.

Anzaldúa, Gloria. 1987. *Borderlands/La Frontera: The New Mestiza*. San Francisco: Spinsters/Aunt Lute Book Company.

Anzaldúa, Gloria, and Cherrie Moraga. 1983. *This Bridge Called My Back: Writings by Radical Women of Color*. New York: Kitchen Table Press.

Aragon, Steven R. 2000. *Beyond Access: Methods and Models for Increasing Retention and Learning Among Minority Students*. San Francisco: Jossey-Bass.

Ayers, William C., Janet Miller, and Therese Quinn. 1998. *Teaching for Social Justice: A Democracy and Education Reader*. New York: Teachers College Press and The New Press.

Baez, Benjamin. 2000. "Race-related Service and Faculty of Color: Conceptualizing Critical Agency in Academe." *Higher Education* 39: 363–391.

Banks, James, ed. 1996. *Multicultural Education, Transformative Knowledge, and Action: Historical and Contemporary Perspectives.* New York: Teachers College Press.

Bannock, Graham, R. E. Baxter, and Evan Davis. 1999. *The Penguin Dictionary of Economics.* New York: Penguin Books.

Barbezat, Debra A., and James W. Hughes. 2005. "Salary Structure Effects and the Gender Pay Gap in Academia." *Research in Higher Education* 46: 621–640.

Barger, W. K., and Ernesto M. Reza. 1994. *The Farm Labor Movement in the Southwest: Social Change and Adaptation Among Migrant Farmworkers.* Austin: University of Texas Press.

Bauer, Dale, and Katherine Rhoades. 1996. "The Meanings and Metaphors of Student Resistance." In *Anti-Feminism in the Academy,* ed. V. Clark, S. Garner, M. Higonnet, and K. Katrak, 95–114. New York: Routledge.

Beam, Joseph. 2008. "Brother to Brother: Words from the Heart." In *In the Life: A Black Gay Anthology,* ed. Joseph Beam. Washington, D.C.: Red Bone Press.

Becker, Howard. 1997. *Outsiders.* New York: The Free Press.

Benjamin, Lois, ed. 1997. *Black Women in the Academy: Promises and Perils.* Gainesville: University Press of Florida.

Bennett, Lerone. 1993. *Before the Mayflower: A History of Black America,* 6th ed. New York: Penguin.

Benson, Katherine. 1984. "Comment on Crocker's 'An Analysis of University Definitions of Sexual Harassment.'" *Signs* 9: 516–519.

Bernal, Dolores D., and Octavio Villalpando. 2002. "An Apartheid of Knowledge in Academia: The Struggle over the 'Legitimate': Knowledge of Faculty of Color." *Equity & Excellence in Education* 35: 169–180.

Blauner, Robert, and David Wellman. 1998. "Toward the Decolonization of Social Research." In *The Death of White Sociology: Essays on Race and Culture,* ed. J. Ladner. Baltimore: Black Classic Press.

Bonilla-Silva, Eduardo. 2006. *Racism without Racists: Color-Blind Racism and the Persistence of Racial Inequality in the United States.* New York: Rowman & Littlefield.

Bonus, Rick, and Caroline C. Simpson. 2005. The U.W. Minority Faculty Collective: Resources for Diversity Project (The Minority Faculty CORD Project). Unpublished grant proposal.

Bordo, Susan R. 1989. "The Body and the Reproduction of Femininities: A Feminist Appropriation of Foucault." In *Gender/Body/Knowledge: Feminist Reproductions of Being and Knowing,* ed. A. Jaggar and S. Bordo. Rutgers, N.J.: Rutgers University Press.

Boren, Mark E. 2001. *Student Resistance: A History of the Unruly Subject.* New York: Routledge.

Brayboy, Bryan M. 2003. "The Implementation of Diversity in Predominantly White Colleges and Universities." *Journal of Black Studies* 34(1): 72–86.

Brittan, Arthur, and Mary Maynard. 1984. *Sexism, Racism, and Oppression.* New York: Basil Blackwell.

Brown, M. Christopher II, Michael L. Lomax, and RoSusan D. Bartee, eds. 2007. *Still Not Equal: Expanding Education Opportunity in Society.* New York: Peter Lang.

Brown, Victoria Bissell. 2007. *The Education of Jane Addams.* Philadelphia: University of Pennsylvania Press.

Brown-Glaude, Winnifred R., ed. 2008. *Doing Diversity in Higher Education: Faculty Leaders Share Challenges and Strategies.* Piscataway, N.J.: Rutgers University Press.

Broyles-Gonzales, Yolanda. 1994. *El Teatro Campesino: Theater in the Chicano Movement.* Austin: University of Texas Press.

Bulosan, Carlos. 1984. *America Is in the Heart.* Seattle: University of Washington Press.

Burawoy, Michael. 2004. "Introduction." In "Public Sociologies: A Symposium from Boston College," by M. Burawoy, W. Gamson, C. Ryan, S. Pfohl, D. Vaughan, C. Derber, & J. Schor. *Social Problems* 51(1): 103–130.

———. 2005. "2004 Presidential Address." *American Sociological Review* 70: 4–28.

Buss, Fran L. 1993. *Forged Under the Sun/Forjado Bajo del Sol: The Life of Maria Elena Lucas.* Ann Arbor: University of Michigan Press.

Butler, Johnnella E., ed. 2001. *Color-Line to Borderlands: The Matrix of American Ethnic Studies.* Seattle: University of Washington Press.

Butler, Johnnella E., and John C. Walter, eds. 1991. *Transforming the Curriculum: Ethnic Studies and Women's Studies.* Albany: State University of New York Press.

Cable, Sherry, and Donald Hastings. 2005. "Mission Impossible? Environmental Justice Activists' Collaborations with Professional Environmentalists and with Academics." In *Power, Justice, and the Environment: A Critical Appraisal of the Environmental Justice Movement,* ed. D. Pellow and R. Brulle, 55–75. Cambridge, Mass.: The MIT Press.

Calderon, Jose. 1991. "Mexican Americans in a Multi-Ethnic Community: The Case of Monterey Park, 1986–1990." PhD diss. Department of Sociology, University of California, Los Angeles.

———. 1995. "Multi-Ethnic Coalition-Building in a Diverse School District." *Critical Sociology* 21(1): 101–111.

———. 2004a. "Inclusion or Exclusion: One Immigrant's Experience and Perspective of a Multicultural Society." In *Minority Voices: Linking Personal*

Ethnic History and the Sociological Imagination, ed. John Myers, 106–120. Boston: Allyn & Bacon.

———. 2004b. "Lessons From an Activist Intellectual: Participatory Research, Teaching, and Learning for Social Change." *Latin American Perspectives* 31(1): 81–94.

Calderon, Jose, and Gilbert Cadena. 2007. "Linking Critical Democratic Pedagogy, Multiculturalism, and Service Learning to a Project-Based Approach." In *Race, Poverty and Social Justice: Multidisciplinary Perspectives through Service Learning*, ed. J. Calderon. Sterling, Va.: Stylus Publishing LLC.

Calderon, Jose, and Betty Farrell. 1996. "Doing Sociology: Connecting the Classroom Experience with a Multi-Ethnic School District." *Teaching Sociology* 24: 46–53.

Calderon, Jose, Suzanne Foster, and Silvia Rodriguez. 2006. "Organizing Immigrant Workers: Action Research and Strategies in the Pomona Day Labor Center." In *Latino Los Angeles*, ed. E. Ochoa and G. Ochoa. Tucson: Arizona State University Press.

California Cultures in Comparative Perspective. 2005. *The Transatlantic Initiative on Environmental Justice: Papers.* http://calcultures.ucsd.edu/transatlantic_initiative/papers.htm.

Campus Advisory Committee for Asian American Affairs. 2001. *Asian Pacific Americans at Berkeley: Visibility and Marginality: A Report to Chancellor Robert Berdahl.* University of California, Berkeley.

Carson, Clayborne. 1996. *In Struggle: SNCC and the Black Awakening of the 1960s.* Cambridge, Mass.: Harvard University Press.

Carter, George M. 1992. *ACT-UP, The AIDS War and Activism.* Westfield, N.J.: Open Magazine Pamphlet Series.

Center for Advancement of Racial and Ethnic Equity. 2004. Reflecting on Twenty Years on Minorities in Higher Education and the ACE Annual Status Report. Paper presented at the American Council on Education. Washington, D.C.

Chamberlain, Mariam K., ed. 1988. *Women in Academe: Progress and Prospects.* New York: Russell Sage Foundation.

Champagne, Duane, and Jay Stauss, eds. 2002. *Native American Studies in Higher Education: Models for Collaboration between Universities and Indigenous Nations.* Lanham, Md.: AltaMira Press.

Chan, Kenyon S. 2000. "Rethinking the Asian American Project: Bridging the Divide between 'Campus' and 'Community.'" *Journal of Asian American Studies* 3(1): 17–36.

Chan, Sucheng. 2005. *In Defense of Asian American Studies: The Politics of Teaching and Program Building.* Urbana: University of Illinois Press.

Chan, Sucheng, and Ling-chi Wang. 1991. "Racism and the Model Minority: Asian-Americans in Higher Education." In *The Racial Crisis in American Higher Education*, ed. P. Altback and K. Lomotey, 343–368. Albany: State University of New York Press.

Chang, Mitchell J. 1999. "Expansion and Its Discontent: The Formation of Asian American Studies Programs in the 1990s." In *Journal of Asian* in *Asian American Women: A Frontiers Reader*, ed. L. Võ and M. Sciachitano, 214–239. Lincoln: University of Nebraska Press.

Chatterjee, Piya. 2000. "De/Colonizing the Exotic: Teaching 'Asian Women' in the U.S. Classroom." *Frontiers Journal* 21(1 & 2): 87–110.

Chauncey, George. 1994. *Gay New York: Gender, Urban Culture and the Making of the Gay Male World, 1890–1940*. New York: Basic Books.

Chilly Collective. 1995. *Breaking Anonymity: The Chilly Climate for Women Faculty*. Waterloo, Ont.: Wilfred Laurier University Press.

Chomsky, Noam. 2003. *Objectivity and Liberal Scholarship*. New York: The New Press.

Chronicle of Higher Education. 2009. "Number of Full-Time Faculty Members by Sex, Rank, and Racial and Ethnic Group, Fall 2007." April 24, 2009. http://chronicle.com/article/Number-of-Full-Time-Faculty/47992/.

Chuh, Kandace, and Karen Shimakawa, eds. 2001. *Orientations: Mapping Studies in the Asian Diaspora*. Durham, N.C.: Duke University Press.

Cohen, Cathy J. 1999. *The Boundaries of Blackness: AIDS and the Breakdown of Black Politics*. Chicago: The University of Chicago Press.

Collins, Patricia H. 1990. *Black Feminist Thought: Knowledge, Consciousness, and the Politics of Empowerment*. Boston: Unwin Hyman.

Combahee River Collective. 1983. The Combahee River Collective Statement. In *Home Girls: A Black Feminist Anthology*, ed. B. Smith. New York: Kitchen Table Press.

Connell, R. W. 1997. "Why Is Classical Theory Classical?" *American Journal of Sociology* 102(6): 1511–1557.

Connerly, Ward. 2000. *Creating Equal: My Fight against Race Preferences*. San Francisco: Encounter Books.

Cooper, Joanne E., and Dannelle D. Stevens, eds. 2002. *Tenure in the Sacred Grove: Issues and Strategies for Women and Minority Faculty*. Albany: State University of New York Press.

Cooper, Tuesday L. 2006. *The Sista' Network: African-American Women Successfully Negotiating the Road to Tenure*. Boston: Anker Publishing.

Corea, Gena. 1992. *The Invisible Epidemic: The Story of Women and AIDS*. New York: Harper Collins.

Crimp, Douglas. 2004. *Melancholia and Moralism: Essays on AIDS and Queer Politics*. Cambridge, Mass.: The MIT Press.

Crowe, David M. 1996. *A History of the Gypsies of Eastern Europe and Russia*. New York: Palgrave Macmillan.

Danaher, Kevin. 2001. *Democratizing the Global Economy*. Boston: Common Courage Press.

Danico, Mary Yu. 2004. *The 1.5 Generation: Becoming Korean American in Hawai'i*. Honolulu: University of Hawai'i Press.

Das Gupta, Monisha. 2006. *Unruly Immigrants: Rights, Activism, and Transnational South Asian Politics in the United States*. Durham, N.C.: Duke University Press.

Davé, Shilpa, Pawan Dhingra, Sunaina Maira, Partha Mazumdar, Lavina Shankar, Jaideep Singh, and Rajini Srikanth. 2000. "De-privileging Positions: Indian Americans, South Asian Americans, and the Politics of Asian American Studies." *Journal of Asian American Studies* 3(1): 67–100.

Davis, Angela. 1983. *Women, Race, and Class*. New York: Vintage Books.

De Jesús, Melinda L. 2005. "'A-walkin' fo' de (Rice) Kake': A Filipina American Feminist's Adventures in Academia, or a Pinay's Progress." In *Pinay Power: Peminist Critical Theory, Theorizing the Filipina/American Experience*, ed. M. De Jesús, 259–274. New York: Routledge.

de la Luz Reyes, Maria, and John J. Halcón. 1997. "Racism in Academia: The Old Wolf Revisited." In *Latinos and Education: A Critical Reader*, ed. A. Darder, R. Torres, and H. Gutierrez. New York: Routledge.

DeBenedetti, Charles. 1990. *An American Ordeal: The Antiwar Movement of the Vietnam Era*. Syracuse, N.Y.: Syracuse University Press.

Del Castillo, Richard Griswold, and Richard A. Garcia. 1995. *Cesar Chavez: A Triumph of Spirit*. Norman: University of Oklahoma Press.

Delgado, Héctor. 2003. "Reflections on the Intersection of Research and Politics in Academia." In *Our Studies, Ourselves: Sociologists' Lives and Work*, ed. B. Glassner and R. Hertz, 24–34. New York: Oxford University Press.

Dews, C. L. Barney, and Carolyn Leste Law, eds. 1995. *This Fine Place So Far From Home: Voices of Academics from the Working Class*. Philadelphia: Temple University Press.

Dill, Bonnie T., and Ruth E. Zambrana, eds. 2008. *Emerging Intersections: Race, Class, and Gender in Theory, Policy, and Practice*. New Brunswick, N.J.: Rutgers University Press.

Domhoff, G. William. 2009. *Who Rules America? Challenges to Corporate and Class Dominance*. New York: McGraw Hill.

Dovidio, J. F., and S. L. Gaertner. 1996. "Affirmative Action, Unintentional Racial Biases, and Intergroup Relations." *Journal of Social Issues* 52: 51–75.

Duster, Troy. 1987. "Purpose and Bias." *Society* 24(2): 8–12.

Edid, Marilyn. 1994. *Farm Labor Organizing: Trends & Prospects*. Ithaca, N.Y.: ILR Press.

Emerson, Robert M., Rachel I. Fretz, and Linda L. Shaw. 1995. *Writing Ethnographic Field Notes*. Chicago: University of Chicago Press.

Espiritu, Yen Le. 2003. "Asian American Studies and Ethnic Studies: About Kin Disciplines." *Amerasia Journal* 29(2): 195–209.

Exum, William H., and Robert J. Menges. 1983. "Barriers to the Progress of Women and Minority Faculty." *Journal of Higher Education* 54(2): 123–144.

Eyerman, Ron, and Andrew Jamison. 1991. *Social Movements: A Cognitive Approach*. University Park: Pennsylvania State University Press.

Fausto-Sterling, Ann. 1985. *Myths of Gender: Biological Theories about Women and Men*. New York: Basic Books.

Feagin, Joe R., and Hernán Vera. 2008. *Liberation Sociology*, 2nd ed. Boulder, Colo.: Paradigm Publishers.

Ferris, Susan, and Ricardo Sandoval. 1997. *The Fight in the Fields: Cesar Chavez and The Farmworkers Movement*. Orlando, Fla.: Paradigm Productions.

Fisher, Bonnie S., Francis T. Cullen, and Michael G. Turner. 2000. *The Sexual Victimization of College Women*. National Institute of Justice and Bureau of Justice Statistics.

Fogg, Piper. 2003. "So Many Committees, So Little Time." *The Chronicle of Higher Education* 50(17): A14.

Fone, Byrne. 2001. *Homophobia: A History*. New York: Picador.

Fraser, Angus. 1995. *The Gypsies*, 2nd ed. Cambridge, Mass.: Blackwell.

Freire, Paulo. 2000. *Pedagogy of the Oppressed*, 30th Anniversary ed. New York: Continuum International Publishing Group.

Ganz, Marshall. 2009. *Why David Sometimes Wins*. New York: Oxford University Press.

Gay, Geneva. 2000. *Culturally Responsive Teaching: Theory, Research and Practice*. New York: Teachers College Press.

Gedicks, Al. 2001. *Resource Rebels: Native Challenges to Mining and Oil Corporations*. Boston: South End Press.

Gee, Emma, et al., eds. 1976. *Counterpoint: Perspectives on Asian America*. Los Angeles: UCLA Asian American Studies Center.

Gersick, Connie J., Jean M. Bartunek, and Jane E. Dutton. 2000. "Learning from Academia: The Importance of Relationships in Professional Life." *Academy of Management Journal* 43(6): 1026–1044.

Gerstle, Gary. 2001. *American Crucible: Race and Nation in the Twentieth Century*. Princeton, N.J.: Princeton University Press.

Giroux, Henry A. 2005. *Border Crossings: Cultural Workers and the Politics of Education*, 2nd ed. New York: Routledge.

Global Response. 2005. GRAction #4/05: Rescue Children from Contaminated Camp/Kosovo. http://globalresponse.org. Boulder, Colorado.

Goldberg, David Theo. 1993. *Racist Culture: Philosophy and the Politics of Meaning*. Malden, Mass.: Blackwell.

Gonzales, Manuel G. 1999. *Mexicanos: A History of Mexicans in the U.S.* Bloomington: Indiana University Press.

Gonzalez, Juan. 2001. *Harvest of Empire: A History of Latinos in the America.* New York: Penguin Books.

Gould, Stephen J. 1996. *The Mismeasure of Man*. New York: W. W. Norton & Co.

Hale, Frank W. Jr., ed. 2004. *What Makes Racial Diversity Work in Higher Education: Academic Leaders Present Successful Policies and Strategies*. Sterling, Va.: Stylus.

Hammonds, Evelynn. 1992. "Missing Persons: African American Women, AIDS and the History of Disease." *Radical America* 24(2).

Hernstein, Richard J., and Charles Murray. 1994. *The Bell Curve: Intelligence and Class Structure*. New York: Free Press.

Hirabayashi, Lane R., ed. 1998. *Teaching Asian America: Diversity and the Problem of Diversity*. Lanham, Md.: Rowman & Littlefield.

Hirabayashi, Lane R., and Marilyn C. Alquizola. 1994. "Asian American Studies: Reevaluating for the 1990s." In *The State of Asian America*, ed. K. Aguilar-San Juan, 351–364. Boston: South End Press.

Hong, Grace K. 2001. "Past Legacies, Future Projects: Asian Migration and the Role of the University under Globalization." *Diasporas* 10(1): 123.

hooks, bell. 1984. *Feminist Theory: From Margin to Center*. Boston: South End Press.

———. 1994. *Teaching to Transgress: Education as a Practice of Freedom*. New York: Routledge.

Horne, Pauline J., and C. Fergus Lowe. 1996. "On the Origins of Naming and Other Symbolic Behavior." *Journal of the Experimental Analysis of Behavior* 65: 185–241.

Horton, John (with Jose Calderon, Mary Pardo, Leland Saito, Linda Shaw, and Yen-Fen Tseng). 1995. *Politics of Diversity*. Philadelphia: Temple University Press.

Howard, Jennifer. 2007. "DePaul U. Turns Norman Finkelstein Down for Tenure." *The Chronicle of Higher Education*. June 11, 2007. http://chronicle.com/article/DePaul-U-Turns-Norman/123066/.

Howell, Annie, and Frank Tuitt, eds. 2003. *Race and Higher Education: Rethinking Pedagogy in Diverse College Classrooms*. Cambridge, Mass.: Harvard Educational Review.

Hune, Shirley. 1998. "Asian Pacific American Women in Higher Education: Claiming Visibility and Voice." Paper presented at the Association of American Colleges and Universities. Washington, D.C.

Hune, Shirley, and Gail Nomura, eds. 2003. *Asian/Pacific Islander American Women: A Historical Anthology*. New York: New York University Press.

Ichioka, Yuji. 2006. *Before Internment*. Stanford, Calif.: Stanford University Press.

Jayaratne, Toby Epstein, and Abigail J. Stewart. 1991. "Quantitative and Qualitative Methods in the Social Sciences: Current Feminist Issues and Practical Strategies." In *Beyond Methodology: Feminist Scholarship as Lived Research*, ed. Mary Margaret Fonow and Judith A. Cook. Bloomington: Indiana University Press.

Johnson, E. Patrick, and Mae G. Henderson. 2005. *Black Queer Studies: A Critical Anthology*. Durham, N.C.: Duke University Press.

June, Audrey W. 2006. "Janitor's Strike Grows at University of Miami." *The Chronicle of Higher Education* 52(28): A41.

Kiang, Peter N. 1989. "Bringing It All Back Home: New Views of Asian American Studies and Communities." In *Frontiers of Asian American Studies: Writing, Research, and Commentary*, ed. G. Nomura, R. Endo, S. Sumida, and R. Leong, 305–314. Pullman: Washington State University Press.

Knapp, Michael S. 1998. *Paths to Partnership: University and Community as Learners in Interprofessional Education*. Lanham, Md.: Rowman & Littlefield.

Kolodny, Annette. 1996. "Paying the Price of Antifeminist Intellectual Harassment." In *Anti-Feminism in the Academy*, ed. V. Clark, S. Garner, M. Higonnet, and K. Katrak, 3–34. New York: Routledge.

Kumashiro, Kevin. 2002. *Troubling Education: Queer Activism and Anti-Oppressive Pedagogy*. New York: Routledge.

Ladner, Joyce. 1998. *The Death of Black Sociology*. Baltimore: Black Classic Press.

Langford, R. Everett. 2004. *Introduction to Weapons of Mass Destruction: Radiological, Chemical, and Biological*. Malden, Mass.: Wiley Interscience.

Latina Feminist Group. 2001. *Telling to Live: Latina Feminist Testimonios*. Durham, N.C.: Duke University Press.

Lee, Sharon S. 2007. "In Defense of Asian American Studies: The Politics of Teaching and Program Building" (review). *The Journal of Higher Education* 78(6): 720–723.

Lengermann, Patricia, and Jill Niebrugge-Brantley. 1998. *The Women Founders: Sociology and Social Theory, 1830–1930*. New York: McGraw-Hill.

Leonardo, Zeus, ed. 2005. *Critical Pedagogy and Race*. Malden, Mass.: Blackwell.

Lesage, Julia, Abby L. Ferber, Debbie Storrs, and Donna Wong, eds. 2002. *Making a Difference: University Students of Color Speak Out*. Lanham, Md.: Rowman & Littlefield.

Lichtenstein, Bronwen. 2001. "The AIDS Epidemic and Sociological Enquiry." *Footnotes* 29(4): 9.

Lim, Shirley G., and Maria Herrera-Sobek, eds. 2000. *Power, Race and Gender in Academe: Strangers in the Tower?* New York: The Modern Language Association of America.

Lipset, Seymour Martin. *Rebellion in the University*. 1993. New Brunswick, N.J.: Transaction Publishers.

Lipsitz, George. 2001. *American Studies in a Moment of Danger*. Minneapolis: University of Minnesota Press.

Lofland, John, and Lyn Lofland. 1984. *Analyzing Social Settings: A Guide to Qualitative Observation and Analysis*. Belmont, Calif.: Wadsworth Publishing.

Loo, Chalsa, and Don Mar. 1986. "Research and Asian Americans: Social Change or Empty Prize?" *Amerasia Journal* 12(1): 85–93.

Lopez, Iris O. 2001. "Reflection and Rebirth: The Evolving Life of a Latina Academic." In *Telling to Live: Latina Feminist Testimonios*. Durham, N.C.: Duke University Press.

Lorde, Audre. 1984. *Sister Outsider: Essays and Speeches*. Freedom, Calif.: The Crossing Press.

Lowe, Lisa. 2001. "Epistemological Shifts: National Ontology and the New Asian Immigrant." In *Orientations: Mapping Studies in the Asian Diaspora*, ed. K. Chuh and K. Shimakawa, 267–276. Durham, N.C.: Duke University Press.

Maeda, Daryl J. 2009 *Chains of Babylon: The Rise of Asian America*. Minneapolis: University of Minnesota Press.

Manalansan, Martin F. IV. 2003. *Global Divas: Filipino Gay Men in the Diaspora*. Durham, N.C.: Duke University Press.

Marable, Manning. 1986. *W.E.B. DuBois: Black Radical Democrat*. Boston: Twayne Publishers.

Margolis, Eric, and Mary Romero. 1998. "'The Department Is Very Male, Very White, Very Old, and Very Conservative': The Functioning of the Hidden Curriculum in Graduate Sociology Departments." *Harvard Educational Review* 68(1): 1–33.

Maurrasse, David. 2002. "Higher Education-Community Partnership: Assessing Progress in the Field." *Nonprofit and Voluntary Sector Quarterly* 31: 131–139.

May, Vivian M. 2007. *Anna Julia Cooper, A Visionary Black Feminist: A Critical Introduction*. New York: Routledge.

Mazumdar, Sucheta. 1991. "Asian American Studies and Asian Studies: Rethinking Roots." In *Asian Americans: Comparative and Global Perspectives*, ed. S. Hune, H. Kim, S. Fugita, and A. Ling, 29–44. Pullman: Washington State University Press.

McNaron, Toni. 1996. *Poisoned Ivy: Lesbian and Gay Academics Confronting Homophobia*. Philadelphia: Temple University Press.

Mihesuah, Devon Abbott, and Angela Cavender Wilson, eds. 2004. *Indigenizing the Academy: Transforming Scholarship and Empowering Communities.* Lincoln, Neb.: Bison Books.

Mills, C. Wright. 1959. *The Sociological Imagination.* New York: Oxford University Press.

Minami, Dale. 1995. "Guerilla War at UCLA: Political and Legal Dimensions of the Tenure Battle." In *The Asian American Educational Experience: A Source Book for Teachers and Students,* ed. D. Nakanishi and T. Nishida, 358–372. New York: Routledge.

Mintz, Beth, and Esther D. Rothblum. 1997. *Lesbians in Academia: Degrees of Freedom,* 1st ed. New York: Routledge.

Mirandé, Alfredo. 1989. *The Chicano Experience: An Alternative Perspective.* Notre Dame, Ind.: University of Notre Dame Press.

Miyamoto, Frank S. 1989. "Is Asian American Studies a Discipline?" In *Frontiers of Asian American Studies: Writing, Research, and Commentary,* ed. G. Nomura, R. Endo, S. Sumida, and R. Leong, 284–290. Pullman: Washington State University Press.

Monaghan, Peter. 1999. "A New Momentum in Asian-American Studies." *The Chronicle of Higher Education* XLV(30): A16–A18.

Montoya, Margaret E. 1995. "*Máscaras, Trenzas, y Greñas:* Un/Masking the Self While Un/Braiding Latina Stories and Legal Discourse." In *Critical Race Theory: The Cutting Edge,* ed. R. Delgado, 529–539. Philadelphia: Temple University Press.

Moody, JoAnn. 2004. *Faculty Diversity: Problems and Solutions.* New York: Routledge.

Munn-Giddings, Carol. 1998. "Mixing Motherhood and Academia—A Lethal Cocktail." In *Surviving the Academy: Feminist Perspectives,* ed. D. Malina and S. Maslin-Prothero, 56–68. London, England: Falmer Press.

Muñoz, Carlos. 2007. *Youth, Identity, Power: The Chicano Movement.* London: Verso.

Myers, Lean Wright. 2007. *A Broken Silence: Voices of African American Women in the Academy.* Charlotte, N.C.: Information Age Publishing.

National Science Foundation, Division of Science Resources Statistics. 2009. *Doctorate Recipients from U.S. Universities: Summary Report 2007–08.* Special Report NSF 10–309. Arlington, Va. http://www.nsf.gov/statistics/nsf10309/.

Ng, Roxana. 1993. "'A Woman Out of Control': Deconstructing Sexism and Racism in the University." *Canadian Journal of Education* 18(3): 189–205.

Ngai, Mae M. 2004. *Impossible Subjects: Illegal Aliens and the Making of Modern America.* Princeton, N.J.: Princeton University Press.

Niemann, Yolanda F. 1999. "The Making of a Token: A Case Study of Stereotype Threat, Stigma, Racism, and Tokenism in Academe." *Frontiers: A Journal of Women Studies* XX(1): 111–134.

Nieto, Sonia. 1999. *The Light in their Eyes: Creating Multicultural Learning Communities*. New York: Teachers College Press.

Nyden, Philip, Anne Figert, Mark Shibley, and Darryl Burrows. 1997. *Building Community: Social Science in Action*. Thousand Oaks, Calif.: Pine Forge Press.

O'Brien, Eileen, and Michael P. Armato. 2001. "Building Connections between Antiracism and Feminism: Antiracist Women and Profeminist Men." In *Feminism & Antiracism: International Struggles for Justice*, ed. F. Twine and K. Blee. New York: New York University Press.

Okamura, Jonathan. 2003. "Asian American Studies in the Age of Transnationalism: Diaspora, Race, Community." *Amerasia Journal* 29(2): 171–193.

Okihiro, Gary Y., Shirley Hune, Arthur A. Hansen, and John M. Liu, eds. 1988. *Reflections on Shattered Windows: Promises and Prospects for Asian American Studies*. Pullman: Washington State University Press.

Omi, Michael. 1988. "It Just Ain't the Sixties No More: The Contemporary Dilemmas of Asian American Studies." In *Reflections on Shattered Windows: Promises and Prospects for Asian American Studies*, ed. G. Okihiro et al. Pullman: Washington State University Press.

Omi, Michael, and Dana Takagi, guest eds. 1995. "Thinking Theory in Asian American Studies." *Amerasia Journal* 2(1): 181–206.

Orfield, Gary, Patricia Marin, and Catherine L. Horn, eds. 2005. *Higher Education and the Color Line: College Access, Racial Equity, and Social Change*. Cambridge, Mass.: Harvard Education Press.

Osajima, Keith. 1998. "Pedagogical Considerations in Asian American Studies." *Journal of Asian American Studies* 1(1): 269–292.

Padilla, Amado M. 1994. "Ethnic Minority Scholars, Research, and Mentoring: Current and Future Issues." *Educational Researcher* 23(4): 24–27.

Palumbo-Liu, David. 2003. "Re-Imagining Asian American Studies." *Amerasia Journal* 29(2): 211–219.

Pardo, Mary. 1998. *Mexican American Women Activists: Identity and Resistance in Two Los Angeles Communities*. Philadelphia: Temple University Press.

Park, Lisa S., and David N. Pellow. 1996. "Washing Dirty Laundry: Organic-Activist-Research Inside Two Social Movement Organizations." *Sociological Imagination* 33: 138–153.

Pekar, Harvey, Paul Buhle, and Gary Dumm. 2009. *Students for a Democratic Society: A Graphic History*. New York: Hill and Wang.

Pellow, David N. 2007. *Resisting Global Toxics: Transnational Movements for Environmental Justice*. Cambridge, Mass.: The MIT Press.

Pellow, David N., and Robert J. Brulle, eds. 2005. *Power, Justice and the Environment: A Critical Appraisal of the Environmental Justice Movement.* Cambridge, Mass: The MIT Press.

Pellow, David N., and Lisa S. Park. 2002. *The Silicon Valley of Dreams: Environmental Injustice, Immigrant Workers, and the High-Tech Global Economy.* New York: New York University Press.

Pharr, Suzanne. 2008. "Andrea Smith—the Mind Will Not Be Contained." http://suzannepharr.org/2008/02/28/andrea-smith%E2%80%94the-mind-will-not-be-contained/.

Pitzer College Faculty Personnel Policies and Procedures. 2001. Affirmative Action Program, Section V-N.

———. Criteria for Contract Renewal, Promotion, and Tenure, Section V-A.

Pizarro, Marcos. 2005. *Chicanas and Chicanos in School: Racial Profiling, Identity Battles, and Empowerment.* Austin: University of Texas Press.

Plaut, Victoria C., Kecia M. Thomas, and Matt J. Goren. 2009. "Is Multiculturalism or Color Blindness Better for Minorities?" *Psychological Sciences* 20(4): 444–446.

Portes, Alejandro, and Robert D. Manning. 1986. "The Immigrant Enclave: Theory and Empirical Examples." In *Competitive Ethnic Relations*, ed. S. and J. Nagel, 47–68. New York: Academic Press.

Revilla, Linda A., Gail M. Nomura, Shawn Wong, and Shirley Hune, eds. 1993. *Bearing Dreams, Shaping Visions: Asian Pacific American Perspectives.* Pullman: Washington State University Press.

Rich, Adrienne. 1976. *Of Woman Born: Motherhood as Experience and Institution.* New York: W. W. Norton and Co.

———. 1986. "Compulsory Heterosexuality and Lesbian Existence (1980)." In *Blood, Bread and Poetry: Selected Prose, 1979–1985.* New York: W. W. Norton and Co.

Ritchie, Andrea J. 2006. "Law Enforcement Violence Against Women of Color." In *Color of Violence: The Incite! Anthology.* Cambridge, Mass.: South End Press.

Rockquemore, Kerry Ann, and Tracey Laszloffy. 2008. *The Black Academic's Guide to Winning Tenure—Without Losing Your Soul.* Boulder, Colo.: Lynne Rienner Publishers.

Rodriguez, Dylan. 2006. *Forced Passages: Imprisoned Radical Intellectuals and the U.S. Prison Regime.* Minneapolis: University of Minnesota Press.

Rodriguez, Melanie D., Angela Stewart, Ana M. Cauce, Phyllis Sanchez, and James Antony. Forthcoming. "Minority Academic Achievement and Retention in a Selective Public University: The Role of the Campus Environment." In *College Students of Color: Making the Grade*, ed. R. Taylor and M. Wang. Mahwah, N.J.: Lawrence Erlbaum.

Roebuck, Julian B., and Komanduri S. Murty. 1993. *Historically Black Colleges and Universities: Their Place in American Higher Education*. Santa Barbara, Calif.: Praeger Publishers.

Rosaldo, Renato. 1984. "Ilongot Naming: The Play of Associations." In *Naming Systems: The 1980 Proceedings of the American Ethnological Society*, ed. E. Tooker, 11–24. Washington, D.C.: American Ethnological Society.

Rose, Margaret. 1990. "Traditional and Nontraditional Patterns of Female Activism in the United Farm Workers of America, 1962 to 1980." *Frontiers* 11(1): 25–32.

Ross, Fred. 1989. *Conquering Goliath: Cesar Chavez at the Beginning*. Keene, Calif.: Taller Grafico.

Russett, Cynthia E. 1989. *Sexual Science: The Victorian Construction of Womanhood*. Cambridge, Mass.: Harvard University Press.

Ryan, Jake, and Charles Sackrey. 1984. *Strangers in Paradise: Academics from the Working Class*. Boston: South End Press.

Sacks, Peter. 2007. "How Colleges Perpetuate Inequality." *The Chronicle of Higher Education*.

Saito, Leland. 1998. *Race and Politics: Asian Americans, Latinos, and Whites in a Los Angeles Suburb*. Urbana, Ill., and Chicago: University of Illinois Press.

Sanchez, George J. 2008. "Challenging the Borders of Civic Engagement: Ethnic Studies and the Meaning of Community Democracy." Speech delivered at Connecting Communities: The University and Multi-Ethnic Civic Engagement: A Southern California Regional Symposium. February 7, 2008, University of California, Irvine.

Sanders, Mavis G. 2000. *Schooling Students Placed at Risk: Research, Policy, and Practice in the Education of Poor and Minority Adolescents*. Mahweh, N.J.: L. Erlbaum Associates.

Scharlin, Craig, and Lilia V. Villanueva. 2006. *Philip Vera Cruz: A Personal History of Filipino Immigrants and the Farmworkers Movement*. Seattle: University of Washington Press.

Seidman, Steven. 1995. "Deconstructing Queer Theory or the Under-Theorization of the Social and the Ethical." In *Social Postmodernism: Beyond Identity Politics*, ed. L. Nicholson and S. Seidman, 116–141. Cambridge: Cambridge University Press.

Shaw, Randy. 2008. *Beyond the Fields*. Berkeley: University of California Press.

Shefner, Jon, and Denise Cobb. 2002. "Hierarchy and Partnership in New Orleans." *Qualitative Sociology* 25: 273–297.

Shor, Ira. 1992. *Empowering Education: Critical Teaching for Social Change*. Chicago: University of Chicago Press.

Sill, Geoffrey M., ed. 1993. *Opening the American Mind: Race, Ethnicity, and Gender in Higher Education*. Newark: University of Delaware Press.

Simon, Laura A. 1997. *Fear and Learning at Hoover Elementary* (film).

Simpson, Jennifer S. 2003. *"I Have Been Waiting": Race and U.S. Higher Education*. Toronto, Ont.: University of Toronto Press.

Smith, Andrea. 2006. "Heteropatriarchy and the Three Pillars of White Supremacy: Rethinking Women of Color Organizing." In *Color of Violence: The Incite! Anthology*. Cambridge, Mass.: South End Press.

Smith, Barbara, ed. 1983. *Home Girls: A Black Feminist Anthology*. New York: Women of Color Press.

Smith, Dorothy. 1990. *The Conceptual Practices of Power: A Feminist Sociology of Knowledge*. Boston: Northeastern University Press.

Smith, William A., Philip G. Altbach, and Kofi Lomotey, eds. 1992. *The Racial Crisis in American Higher Education: Continuing Challenges for the Twenty-First Century*. Albany: State University of New York Press.

Solomon, Barbara M. 1986. *In the Company of Educated Women: A History of Women and Higher Education in America*. New Haven, Conn.: Yale University Press.

Spender, Dale. 1980. *Man Made Language*. New York: Routledge.

Stanley, Christine A., ed. 2006. *Faculty of Color: Teaching in Predominantly White Colleges and Universities*. Bolton, Mass.: Anker.

Sternberg, David. 1981. *How to Complete and Survive a Doctoral Dissertation*. New York: St. Martin's Press.

Stockdill, Brett. 1995. "(Mis)Treating Prisoners with AIDS: Analyzing Health Care Behind Bars." In *The Sociology of Health Care*, ed. J. Kronenfeld. Greenwich, Conn.: JAI Press.

———. 2003. *Activism Against AIDS: At the Intersections of Sexuality, Race, Gender and Class*. Boulder, Colo.: Lynne Rienner Press.

Stoecker, Randy. 2005. *Research Methods for Community Change: A Project-Based Approach*, Thousand Oaks, Calif.: Sage Publications.

Strand, Kerry, Sam Marullo, Nick Cutforth, Randy Stoecker, and Patrick Donahue. 2003. *Community-Based Research and Higher Education*. San Francisco: Jossey Bass.

Sumida, Stephen H. 1998. "East of California: Points of Origin in Asian American Studies." *Journal of Asian American Studies* 1(1): 83–100.

Tachiki, Amy, Eddie Wong, Franklin Odo, and Buck Wong, eds. 1971. *Roots: An American Reader*. Los Angeles: UCLA Asian American Studies Center.

Takagi, Dana Y. 1992. *The Retreat from Race: Asian-American Admissions and Racial Politics*. New Brunswick, N.J.: Rutgers University Press.

Takaki, Ronald. 1998. *Strangers from a Different Shore: A History of Asian Americans*. Boston: Back Bay Books.

Task Force on Institutionalizing Public Sociologies. 2005. *Public Sociology and the Roots of American Sociology: Re-Establishing our Connections to the Public*. Washington, D.C.: American Sociological Association.

Taylor, Keeanga-Yamahtta. 2005. "Rediscovering Race and Class in America." *International Socialist Review* 44: 22–26.

Tchen, John K. 1999. *New York Before Chinatown: Orientalism and the Shaping of American Culture 1776–1882*. Baltimore: Johns Hopkins University Press.

Texeira, Erin. 2001. "The Subtle Clues to Racism." *Los Angeles Times,* January 11, 2001. http://articles.latimes.com/2001/jan/11/news/mn-11039.

Thelin, John R. 2004. *A History of American Higher Education*. Baltimore: John Hopkins University Press.

Thomas, Gloria D., and Carol Hollenshead. 2001. "Resisting from the Margins: The Coping Strategies of Black Women and Other Women of Color Faculty Members at a Research University." *The Journal of Negro Education* 70(3): 166–175.

Thompson, Martha E. 2008. "Passionate Analysis in Class Discussion: It's Not Sink or Swim." Unpublished manuscript. Northeastern Illinois University, Chicago.

Tierney, William G., and Estela M. Bensimon. 1996. *Promotion and Tenure: Community and Socialization in Academe*. Albany: State University of New York Press.

Tiongson, Antonio T. Jr., Edgardo V. Gutierrez, and Ricardo V. Gutierrez, eds. 2006. *Positively No Filipinos Allowed: Building Communities and Discourse*. Philadelphia: Temple University Press.

Toutkoushian, Robert K. 1998. "Racial and Marital Status Differences in Faculty Pay." *The Journal of Higher Education* 69: 513–541.

Turner, Caroline S. 2002. "Women of Color in Academe: Living with Multiple Marginality." *The Journal of Higher Education* 73(1): 74–93.

Turner, Caroline S., and Samuel L. Myers. 2000. *Faculty of Color in Academe: Bittersweet Success*. Boston: Allyn and Bacon.

Turner, Caroline S., and Judith Rann Thompson. 1993. "Socializing Women Doctoral Students: Minority and Majority Experiences." *Review of Higher Education* 16(3): 355–370.

TuSmith, Bonnie, and Maureen Reddy, eds. 2002. *Race in the College Classroom: Pedagogy and Politics*. New Brunswick, N.J.: Rutgers University Press.

U.S. Department of Education. 2010. *Digest of Education Statistics: 2009*. Institute of Education Sciences. National Center for Education Statistics. http://nces.ed.gov/programs/digest/d09/.

Valenzuela, Angela. 1999. *Subtractive Schooling: U.S.-Mexican Youth and the Politics of Caring*. New York: State University of New York Press.

Valian, Virginia. 1998. *Why So Slow? The Advancement of Women*. Cambridge, Mass.: The MIT Press.

Vargas, Lucila, ed. 2002. *Women Faculty of Color in the White Classroom (Higher Ed, Vol. 7)*. New York: Peter Lang Publishing.

Vaughan, Ted R., Gideon Sjoberg, and Larry T. Reynolds. 1993. *A Critique of Contemporary American Sociology*. Dix Hills, N.Y.: General Hall, Inc.

Võ, Linda T. 2000. "Performing Ethnography in Asian American Communities: Beyond the Insider-versus-Outsider Perspective." In *Cultural Compass: Ethnographic Explorations of Asian America*, ed. M. Manalansan, 17–37. Philadelphia: Temple University Press.

———. 2004. *Mobilizing an Asian American Community*. Philadelphia: Temple University Press.

———. 2010. "Beyond Colorblind Universalism: Asians in a 'Post-Racial America.'" *Journal of Asian American Studies* 13(3): 327–342.

Wallace, John. 2000. "A Popular Education Model for College in Community." *American Behavioral Scientist* 43(5): 756–766.

Wallenstein, Peter, ed. 2009. *Higher Education and the Civil Rights Movement: White Supremacy, Black Southerners, and College Campuses*. Gainesville: University Press of Florida.

Watson, Lemuel W., Melvin C. Terrell, Doris J. Wright, Fred Bonner, Michael Cuyjet, James Gold, Donna Rudy, and Dawn R. Person. 2002. *How Minority Students Experience College: Implications for Planning and Policy*. Sterling, Va.: Stylus.

Weber, Devra. 1994. *Dark Sweat, White Gold: California Farm Workers, Cotton, and The New Deal*. Berkeley: University of California Press.

Weglyn, Michi. 1976. *Years of Infamy: The Untold Story of America's Concentration Camps*. New York: Morrow.

Wei, William. 1993. *The Asian American Movement*. Philadelphia: Temple University Press.

Wells, Miriam J. 1996. *Strawberry Fields*. Ithaca, N.Y.: Cornell University Press.

Welton, Neva, and Linda Wolf. 2001. *Global Uprising: Confronting the Tyrannies of the 21st Century*. Gabriola Island, B.C.: New Society Publishers.

Williams, Robert A. Jr. 1997. "Vampires Anonymous and Critical Race Practice." *Michigan Law Review* 95(4): 741–765.

Wilson, Reginald. 1995. *Affirmative Action: Yesterday, Today, and Beyond*. Washington, D.C.: American Council on Education.

Wright, Sheila. 2006. "Teacher as Public Art." *Journal of Aesthetic Education* 40(2): 83–104.

Wu, Frank H. 2002. *Yellow: Race in America Beyond Black and White*. New York: Basic Books.

Yamane, David. 2001. *Student Movements for Multiculturalism: Challenging the Color Line in Higher Education*. Baltimore: Johns Hopkins University Press.

Yu, Henry. 2001. *Thinking Orientals: Migration, Contact, and Exoticism in Modern America*. New York: Oxford University Press.

Zavella, Patricia. 1987. *Women's Work & Chicano Families: Cannery Workers in the Santa Clarita Valley*. Ithaca, N.Y.: Cornell University Press.

Zinn, Howard. 2003. *A People's History of the United States*. New York: Harper Collins.

CONTRIBUTORS

Michael Armato is an assistant professor of Sociology and Women's Studies at Northeastern Illinois University. His scholarly interests include the intersections of gender and politics. His attention is increasingly drawn to how privilege is reproduced and challenged in the academy, especially how academic practices produce *academic masculinity*—a class-, race-, and sexuality-based notion of masculinity that stands in contradistinction to women inside the academy and men and women outside of the academy. He is currently coauthoring an introductory textbook for courses in the Sociology of Gender. He teaches courses in Men & Masculinities, Social Inequalities, Sociological Theory, Urban Sociology, and Introduction to Sociology. Armato's recent campus activism has involved free-speech issues, antimilitarism, and a research project exploring the relationship between violence in students' lives and implications for their time to graduation.

Rick Bonus is an associate professor of American Ethnic Studies at the University of Washington, Seattle. He is the author of *Locating Filipino Americans: Ethnicity and the Cultural Politics of Space*, is the co-editor of the anthology *Intersections and Divergences: Contemporary Asian American Communities*, and has written essays on the cultural politics of difference, media representations, and multicultural education. His forthcoming book is based on an ethnography of underrepresented students whose college experiences become generative sites for critiquing and transforming university schooling. Bonus teaches courses pertaining to U.S. multiracial society, Filipino American history and culture, ethnographies of Southeast Asia and Southeast Asian America, and education in relationship to race. He has been involved in the creation and sustenance of several UW mentorship programs that specifically target the retention and eventual graduation of students of color. He also works on advocacy for underrepresented faculty, curriculum transformation, and nurturing community linkages with many groups. He was a former president of the Association for Asian American Studies.

Jose Zapata Calderon is a professor in Sociology and Chicano Studies at Pitzer College. For his work in building partnerships between communities and higher education, the California Campus Compact has honored him with the Richard E. Cone Award for Excellence and Leadership in Cultivating Community Partnerships in Higher Education. Between 2004 and 2006, he was the inaugural holder of the Michi and Walter Weglyn Chair in Multicultural Studies at Cal Poly University, Pomona. As a community-based participant ethnographer, he has published numerous articles and studies based on his community experiences and observations. Calderon's publications include: an edited book, *Race, Poverty, and Social Justice: Multidisciplinary Perspectives through Service Learning*; an article in the edited book "Linking Critical Democratic Pedagogy, Multiculturalism, and Service Learning to a Project-Based Approach"; "Organizing Immigrant Workers: Action Research and Strategies in the Pomona Day Labor Center," in *Latino Los Angeles* (edited by Enrique C. Ochoa and Gilda Laura Ochoa, 2006); "Lessons from an Activist Intellectual: Participatory Research, Teaching, and Learning for Social Change," in *Ethnic Studies Research: Approaches and Perspectives* (edited by Timothy P. Fong, 2008); "Inclusion or Exclusion: One Immigrant's Experience and Perspective of a Multicultural Society," in *Minority Voices* (edited by John Myers, 2004).

Mary Yu Danico is a professor and vice-chair of the Psychology and Sociology Department at California State Polytechnic University, Pomona. She is the author of *The 1.5 Generation: Becoming Korean American in Hawai'i* and *Asian American Issues*, coauthored with Franklin Ng. She is the co-editor of the special issue titled "Challenging Inequalities: Nations, Race, and Communities" in the *Journal of Asian American Studies* (JAAS) with Jonathan Okamura (forthcoming). She has written several articles on immigrant families, Asian/Korean American communities and identities, and youth culture. Her current book project, "Korean American Diaspora: Gyopos Reverse Migration to Korea," is based on her research as a Fulbright Scholar. She developed and runs the peer mentoring program in her department, and has organized panels and conferences on addressing inequalities in higher education. She was a chair of the Asia/Asia America section for the American Sociological Association, and is the president elect of the Association for Asian American Studies (2010–2012).

Christina Gómez is an associate professor of Sociology and Latino and Latin American Studies at Northeastern Illinois University in Chicago. Her research focuses on race relations, discrimination, and immigration. Her book, Mi Vida, Mi Voz: *Latino College Students Tell Their Stories*, is an edited anthology of fifteen essays written by students about growing up Latino in the United States that blend personal, anecdotal, political, and cultural viewpoints. She has published numerous articles on Latino identity, skin color and discrimination, and Latino education. She has received many prizes and fellowships, including a Henry Luce Foundation Scholars Fellowship, a National Science Foundation fellowship, and a Social Science Research Council grant. Her current research examines undocumented university students in the Chicagoland area.

David N. Pellow is the Don A. Martindale Professor of Sociology at the University of Minnesota. His teaching and research focus on environmental justice issues in communities of color in the United States and globally. His books include *Resisting Global Toxics: Transnational Movements for Environmental Justice*; *The Silicon Valley of Dreams: Environmental Injustice, Immigrant Workers, and the High-Tech Global Economy* (with Lisa Sun-Hee Park); and *Garbage Wars: The Struggle for Environmental Justice in Chicago*. He has served on the boards of directors for the Center for Urban Transformation, Greenpeace USA, and International Rivers. He is currently the facilitator of the Minnesota Global Justice Project.

Brett C. Stockdill is an associate professor in Sociology, Women's Studies, and Latino and Latin American Studies at Northeastern Illinois University. He has authored publications on racist violence, HIV/AIDS in prison, AIDS activism, and other topics related to oppression and resistance. His book *Activism Against AIDS: At the Intersections* *of Sexuality, Race, Gender, and Class* analyzes AIDS activism in New York City, Chicago, and Los Angeles. He is currently doing research on anti–domestic violence work in Quetzaltenango, Guatemala; the experiences of undocumented gay Latino immigrants living with HIV in the United States; and the impact of homophobia on the death penalty. Stockdill teaches Introduction to Sociology, Social Inequalities, Sociology of HIV/AIDS, Introduction to Latino and Latin American Studies, Senior Seminar in Sociology, Social Movements, Sociology of Health and Illness, Sociological Research Methods, and Senior Seminar in Sociology. He has been active in campus activism around LGBTQ rights, antimilitarism, and free speech. He is the faculty advisor for Students Against War (SAW) and the Movimiento Cultural Latinoamericano (MCLA/Latin American Cultural Movement).

Linda Trinh Võ is an associate professor and former chair of the Department of Asian American Studies at the University of California, Irvine. She is the author of *Mobilizing an Asian American Community* and the co-editor of three books: *Contemporary Asian American Communities: Intersections and Divergences; Asian American Women: The "Frontiers" Reader;* and *Labor Versus Empire: Race, Gender, and Migration.*

INDEX